W9-AEK-632

WITHDRAWN

LONG LIVE COLUMBUS
(Leben Zul Columbus)

Other books by Harry Golden

ONLY IN AMERICA

FOR 2¢ PLAIN

ENJOY, ENJOY

CARL SANDBURG

YOU'RE ENTITLE'

FORGOTTEN PIONEER

MR. KENNEDY AND THE NEGROES

SO WHAT ELSE IS NEW?

THE SPIRIT OF THE GHETTO
(with Hutchins Hapgood and Jacob Epstein)

A LITTLE GIRL IS DEAD

ESS, ESS, MEIN KINDT

THE BEST OF HARRY GOLDEN

THE RIGHT TIME:
The Autobiography of Harry Golden

SO LONG AS YOU'RE HEALTHY

THE ISRAELIS

THE GOLDEN BOOK OF JEWISH HUMOR

THE GREATEST JEWISH CITY IN THE WORLD

TRAVELS THROUGH JEWISH AMERICA

OUR SOUTHERN LANDSMAN

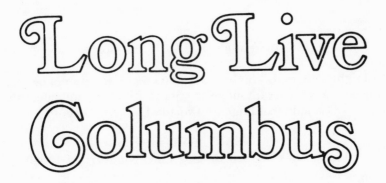

Long Live Columbus

(Leben Zul Columbus)

by

Harry Golden

LIBRARY
BRYAN COLLEGE
DAYTON, TENN. 37321

FOUNDED 1830

GPPS

G. P. Putnam's Sons
New York

97155

Copyright © 1975 by Harry Golden

All rights reserved. This book, or parts thereof, must not be repro-
duced in any form without permission. Published simultaneously in
Canada by Longman Canada Limited, Toronto.

SBN: 399-11440-8
Library of Congress Catalog Card Number: 74-16599

PRINTED IN THE UNITED STATES OF AMERICA

Acknowledgment

I acknowledge with thanks the help of my second son, Harry Golden, Jr., of the Chicago *Sun-Times*, who made the selection of the essays that went into this book.

This book is dedicated to the memory of my father, Reb Lebche, who had the courage to leave an Eastern European Jewish village, travel through Europe and across the Atlantic to bring us all to the United States in 1905.

Contents

Introduction

A *klug zu Columbus'n* was a familiar expression among immigrants of the Lower East Side of New York City. Freely translated, it meant Columbus should have broken his head before he discovered America. It was, however, an expression used with good humor and with sincere fondness. It was an expression denoting familiarity of the millions of strangers somehow finding themselves at home in a new land.

Jewish immigrants associated America with Columbus, which even now seems logical enough. It was a mass inspiration, perhaps, to right an injustice. Columbus had discovered America but it was named after an interloper, Amerigo Vespucci. Yet the words "America" and "Columbus" were interchangeable, at least to the Jews. The Italians, who staged a big parade on Columbus Day, thought of Columbus as a national hero of Italy.

To the Jews, Columbus, like Moses, led the way to the Promised Land. He was also a contemporary. At Ellis Island the Jews disembarked with the mystical notion that only Columbus had preceded them. They knew that America was independent, but if they thought about the derivation of that independence, they would have guessed it came from God. They were not knowledgeable about Jefferson or Washington or Franklin or Kosciusko or Lafayette; they did not know about Ulysses S. Grant or Dwight Moody.

A *klug zu Columbus'n* bemoaned a kid's bloody nose in a fight and the lukewarm water of the Turkish bath. My mother used to tell me of the promises made by Jehovah to her and to all living under his vine and fig tree in the land of Canaan. We struggled through the crowded streets with the bags of piecework she finished to eke out our meager living. When we reached our tenement at Eldridge Street opposite Waller's

Horse Stable, she lay aside reminiscences about God to look up to our fifth-floor apartment and say, "*A klug zu Columbus'n.*"

But Columbus was more than a whipping boy. He was also the template. The immigrant mother always referred to the first American-born child as "*mein Columbus'l*" (my little Columbus). This was the special child. Interestingly enough, the older brothers and sisters felt no resentment. The youngest child was their *Columbus'l* too.

Columbus was omnipresent when times were good. When the immigrant father received his first papers, he looked heavenward and said, "*Leben zul Columbus*" (long live Columbus). "*Leben zul Columbus*" was the benediction bestowed upon the youngster just graduated from high school. *Leben zul Columbus* was the new job, the pretty girl, the public library, and the election of "Tudder" Roosevelt.

The tie between Christopher Columbus and the Jews was no accident. When Columbus left Spain in three caravels to man a new route to the Indies, five Jews sailed with him. Columbus names them in his *Journals*. They were Alonzo de la Calle, an able seaman; Señores Marco and Blanco, fleet surgeon and fleet physician; Roderigo Sanchez, a nephew of Gabiel Sanches, one of Columbus' benefactors, who shipped as Queen Isabella's personal inspector; and Luis Vaer de Torres, the interpreter. These Jews were Marranos, Jews who had accepted baptism. *Marrano* in Spanish means "swine" and these Jews had converted to Christianity to save themselves from the Inquisitorial pyre or burning at the stake.

In his opening entry Columbus wrote, "After the Spanish monarchs had expelled the Jews from their kingdoms and lands, in that same month they commissioned me to take a voyage to India with a properly equipped fleet." Ferdinand and Isabella helped finance Columbus with money they confiscated from Spanish Jews. On August 2, 1492, the last of the Jews fled Spain. On August 3 Columbus weighed anchor from Palos.

Columbus, by the way, had a sympathy for the Jews, and an occasional historian has now and then suggested he, too, was a Marrano. Was Columbus a Jew? His origin and birthplace are shrouded in mystery. It is said he was born Cristobal Colón in Genoa in 1451. His mother's maiden name was Fonterosa. Celso G. de la Riega, in a paper to the Geographical Society of Madrid in 1898, wrote that Cristobal Colón was born in Pontevedra in 1437 and that his mother was Sizanna Fonterosa, daughter of Jacob, granddaughter of Abraham, and a Jewess. His father, Domingo Colón, was a Marrano and a map seller. Did not Columbus write the King of Spain that his ancestors were interested in maps? If he was born in Genoa, why didn't he know Italian? Wasn't San Salvador named after a place near Pontevedra?

Henry Vignaud in the *American Historical Review* maintains Columbus was both a Spaniard and a Jew because Jews by the name of Colón were burned in Tarangone in 1489.

Is that why it was advantageous for Columbus to mislead posterity? In Pinkerton's *Voyages and Travels* Ferdinand, Columbus' son, writes that his father's progenitors were of the blood royal of Jerusalem, and it pleased him that his "parents shall not be much known." Christopher Columbus wrote, "I am not the first admiral of my family, let them give me what name they please; for when all is done, David, that most prudent king, was first a shepherd and afterwards chosen King of Jerusalem, and I am a servant of that same Lord who raised him to such a dignity."

In 1500 Columbus wrote to Juana de Torres, probably of the same Marrano family of Luis de Torres, his interpreter, and Antonio de Torres, saying that he was troubled by "wicked Christians" and said, "Our Lord, who rescued Daniel and the three children, is present with the same wisdom and power as He had then."

It is more likely, however, that Columbus liked Jews because he was a seaman and many of the Jews of his time were pilots, navigators, and mapmakers. The quadrant Columbus used was called Jacob's staff, an invention of the Jew Jacob ben Makhir, and the maps he studied were drawn by Abraham Cresques, nicknamed the Map Jew.

Columbus sighted the island of San Salvador on October 12. He did not enter the name of the first man to set foot in the New World because he thought he had reached India. But he did name the first Jew to set foot on the American continent. It was Luis de Torres, who went over the side in the longboat and proceeded from the beach inland to find the palace of the Great Khan of Tartary. De Torres spoke Spanish, Arabic, Hebrew, Chaldean, and French, one of which, everyone presumed, the Great Khan would speak. In addition, De Torres carried a letter written in Latin and signed by King Ferdinand.

There was no great palace, and De Torres had to converse with the natives he met in sign language. He returned to the flagship with a leaf of a curious plant. "The natives fold it," he said, "set fire to it, and smoke comes out of their mouths and nostrils." He also saw strange birds, which he called "*tukki*," the Hebrew word for "peacock." The word "*tukki*" was later corrupted and became our modern word "turkey."

De Torres was one of the Spaniards who stayed behind to forge the first settlement in Cuba, the second island Columbus sighted. He spent the rest of his life there, receiving a grant of land from the King in return for his services.

His plantation was a far cry from the neighborhood populated by the immigrant Jews from the Russian *shtetl*. The pushcarts were jamming the streets and the children were jamming the tenements. The old men, discussing Talmudic law or anarchy, were jamming the tea shops, and the able bodies were jamming the factory lofts.

But that neighborhood disappeared forever lo, thirty or forty years ago.

Leben zul Columbus has not disappeared, although I haven't heard *A klug zu Columbus'n* for as many years as I have been away from the Lower East Side. *Leben zul Columbus* still survives in the pages of the *Jewish Daily Forward*, still printed in Yiddish. On the occasion of the *Forward's* seventieth birthday in 1967, *Life* magazine asked me to celebrate the event with an editorial. It is hard to believe that a Yiddish-language newspaper has outlived *Life*, but indeed that is the fact. There are, to be exact, still thirteen weekly and monthly Yiddish-language periodicals in New York City. The publishers assure me all these journals and magazines are published at a loss and when I ask them why, then, do they persevere, they answer, "A man has got to make a living somehow."

PART 1

The Land and the
Naked Lady

Turning down the polo franchise

OVER THIS desk have passed some of the most hare-brained schemes ever hatched in the mind of twentieth-century man. I have been privy to hear these for the simple reason that if a lunatic gets on my front porch, he is in my office. To see a big businessman, the promoter has to pass muster with the receptionists and then a steely-eyed secretary. Businessmen are notorious for making decisions at luncheon and there are only five possibilities during a given week. The harebrained have to wait their turn. But I am always available.

One fellow, thwarted in his urgent desire to see the president of the North Carolina Bank, the board chairman of Cannon Mills, and the owner of a radio-TV station, pounced on me instead. He had the panacea for the world's troubles. He was carrying it in his hand. It was a large sheet of rolled-up paper—the blueprints for an interdenominational chapel to be built in the Andes. He chose the Andes because building costs are exceptionally modest in Peru and, besides, the convicts who mine guano in the Andes would be therefore nearer redemption. He was pretty sure he could bring it in for less than one million dollars. I reminded him that the Peruvian building permits were complicated. Additionally, the president of the bank, the board chairman, the owner of the radio and TV stations, and I, as a publisher, would feel much more comfortable if the interdenominational representative spoke Spanish. I bade him repair to night school—there to master this difficult tongue.

I have to admit he was sincere; he phoned for college catalogues in my presence before dashing off to register.

But I have never received my thanks from the banker, the mill owner, or the broadcaster.

Not too long ago I saw a man suffused with the prospect of

3

money in such amounts that we would have to hire armored cars to cart the stuff away. He was doing me a great favor. He was going to let me in early. I could have the Charlotte franchise in his professional polo league.

Polo?

He cited all the statistics—how many millions attended baseball games; the TV revenues for professional football teams; how hockey filled every rink in America; how the folks were so goofy about basketball the teams had to play double-headers. Polo was the only thing left, the untouched base.

For polo, I reminded him, we needed not only fields but horses and stables as well as mallets and white helmets. He explained why these were extraneous considerations, and I remembered the famous remark made by a millionaire polo player to a sportswriter. The sportswriter noted that in football, baseball, and boxing the legs went first. He asked the millionaire what went first in polo. The millionaire replied, "The money goes first."

The hollow domination

LETTERS ARRIVE by the hundreds each week.

What do they say?

Very often my correspondent says he or she is lonely. Despite the tremendous technical advances of the past few years, there is a longing and hunger in Americans, a longing for something that is missing, that is urgently needed. The new cars, the new homes, the powerboats, the push buttons cannot anchor us. We seem internally adrift. We are not careening as much as we are drifting, looking for a mooring, an identity of sorts to make us happy. The mothers and the housewives write and say, "You remind me of my father, who used to read the paper to us after supper every night."

The boys and girls, the students who write me ask about

4

writing and about books, but underneath their questions I sense the tone of dismay. They live in a society that is at one and the same time worshipful and jealous of youth. But one gets the idea the young aren't sure they have as much going for them as everyone keeps saying.

While there is no question that we are on our way to the moon and to Venus, the question still haunts us: *Quo Vadis*?

Has the progress of science brought benevolence to the hearts of men? We have not only segregated the black and the poor but we seem well on the way to segregating the elderly.

No one ever describes a home for the aged or homes for the "retired" without adding that the "surroundings are beautiful" and that their parents are always "so happy."

The folks write me about the new countries that change hands as soon as the ink on the new constitution is dry. Will these countries make a real effort for peace and justice? All over the world we make material progress but no moral progress at all. Man dominates everything on the planet but himself.

Gold, land, and women

THROUGHOUT THE occasionally glorious but more usually dim history of man three things have not only kept their value but, because of it, have provoked much of history. These three are: gold, arable land, and women.

Cortez laid waste an entire people and their culture for gold. He ravaged the Aztecs and in the process taught them the meaning of Christianity when he plundered the halls of Montezuma. Cortez knew there was gold in Mexico, knew it with such fever that, when he disembarked his conquistadors, he burned the ships before their eyes to let them know there was no retreat without riches.

In 1869 Jim Fisk, who was said to be first in war, first in

peace, and first in the pockets of his countrymen, and Jay Gould, simply described as the meanest man born since the beginning of the Christian era, tried to corner the gold market. Gold in those days sold at $135, which is to say 135 greenbacks bought $100 worth of bullion, of which there was $15,000,000 in circulation. If they bought up all the gold, Fisk and Gould could set their own price. But the country operated on the gold standard, so the higher the price of gold, the less the net assets of a corporation. On Black Friday these two men dual-handedly produced a catastrophe as weak firms folded in bankruptcy and other men were ruined by the minute. President Ulysses S. Grant finally released government gold reserves and defeated the corner.

The Revolutionary War started as a farmers' revolt, although John Adams and Ben Franklin turned it into a mercantile revolution, and the Russian Revolution had land reform as its prime mover, although later Lenin, Stalin, and Trotsky turned it into a political revolution. The twenty-five-year-old war between the Israelis and the Arabs started over who owned the arable land, and whether the Israelis own Israel or not is still at the root of the fighting.

In our own society the people who live in the valleys, the bottom land, have churches, schools, and stores and the people who live in the mountains are hillbillies and own rifles, Bibles, and stills.

Agamemnon, Menelaus, Achilles, Odysseus, and an army sailed off to Troy to recapture the beautiful Helen, who had fled with Paris, the son of King Priam. They fought a lifelong war in which many brave men died. And when the Greeks spilled from the Trojan horse and put to death the Trojan survivors, Menelaus walked through the castle with a drawn sword looking for Helen so he could cut her head off. He found her. She bared her bosom and Menelaus sheathed his sword and said, "All right, let's go home and remember, no more fooling around."

Mark Anthony cut off the battle of Actium to follow the

trireme that bore Cleopatra and left a world to Augustus Caesar. Nurse Edith Cavell, executed by the Germans, inspired a generation of British Tommies. King Edward gave up a throne for the twice-divorced Wally. The list is endless and I do not think women's liberation will depreciate the value of a woman.

Millions of immigrants

FIRST THERE was the land in America. And then the people came. Everyone in America belongs to a family that came here from somewhere else, even the Indians. We are all immigrants.

There were all kinds of people from many countries. Some came three hundred years ago, some two hundred, some a century ago, and some just yesterday. "America is God's crucible," wrote Israel Zangwill. "He is making the American."

They got off the boat and they had no money, only the faith and hope that had brought them to the New World. But as soon as they had recovered their shore legs, they managed to get along. As early as 1838 we read of Irishmen driving the Whigs from the polls in New York and putting the mayor and sheriff's posse on the run with "Irish confetti"—brickbats. Many a man who began by peddling old clothes from a pushcart ended by sending his son to medical school.

First there was the land. Then the people came. The country grew; and the people grew, too.

The American idea

IT IS a land of fifty states, of Maine and Michigan, Alaska and Alabama, North Carolina and North Dakota, Iowa and Arizona, Coney Island, the Great Plains, wheat fields and skyscrapers, seashores and mountains.

It is a dream of everyone voting, everyone reading, everyone having a chance for decent work and a time to pray and space to live.

It is an idea of being able to say "no" even if everyone else says "yes" and not having to be afraid.

Girl makes good

HOMETOWN BOY MAKES GOOD is virtually an American tradition. In fact, the hometown boy has a formal speech to deliver on the occasion of his triumph.

The heavyweight would say, "Hi ya, Ma. I'm okay." Sometimes he would offer, "I trew him a left in the eighth and caught 'im widda right in the ninth."

Babe Ruth one season signed a contract with a New York newspaper to describe his feats. A reporter sat at the ready to transcribe. On the day he hit his sixtieth home run the Babe phoned the reporter and said, "Low and inside."

A reporter asked Lindbergh, "What did you think when you landed, Lindy?"

"I wondered if this was Le Bourget Field," he answered.

The times have enlarged upon the tradition. Now we have Hometown Girl Makes Good. I heard one of the first of them intervieaetelevision news program in New York.

Her name was Marilyn Briggs Chambers and she had returned to the East, where she had been born and learned her good manners. She was now the star of a hard-core pornographic movie entitled *Behind the Green Door*. Millions of other consumers had seen her as the mother with babe in arms on the Ivory Snow box.

When asked why she made the movie, Marilyn replied, "It

was a challenge." She also revealed the producers had promised her a piece of the action. Her words.

"What does your husband think of your work?"

"He's behind me all the way."

"Would you rather make porno movies or pose with babies?"

"It's hard relating to a baby," replied the Hometown Girl.

I had every intention of betaking myself to *Behind the Green Door*, but a movie critic of long acquaintance told me Marilyn doesn't have one line in the film. Maybe the producers knew what they were doing.

However, the young are always refreshing. Marilyn discoursed summarily on her career.

Times have changed. *Behind the Green Door* costs five dollars admission. I remember when the movie owners used to give away dinner plates to draw a crowd. Women's lib also has changed us. And certainly film techniques have changed us.

The last word I had from the Hometown Girl was better summed up by Carl Sandburg in his poem "Harrison Street Court":

> Some man got it all,
> Every night's hustlin' I ever did.

The price of desertion

IN THE pages of the recently reprinted Mexican *Chronicle*, which was the only paper published in Mexico during the Mexican War, I came across the story of the San Patricio Battalion. This battalion was composed of Americans who had deserted the United States Army to join with the Mexicans. Most of these deserters were recent Irish immigrants. Historians surmise they deserted perhaps because there were no Catholic chaplains at the time and that priests traveling with the Mexican Army subverted them.

With Santa Anna's defeat, eighty of these men were captured and sentenced to be hanged. Sitting on their own coffins, the men rode to their execution in horse-drawn carts. They were hanged in groups of five. As each group was led up the scaffold, the remaining men were forced to watch at attention.

A memorial marks the spot where these hangings took place. On the memorial are a gamecock, a deck of cards, and a set of dice showing snake eyes. These were fighters who gambled and lost.

General Winfield Scott showed mercy to thirty of the deserters. They were not hanged because they had deserted before the official declaration of war. Each of these men suffered fifty lashes and was branded on the forehead with the letter D. They served six months at hard labor all the while wearing a collar surrounded by spikes to interfere with sleep.

Americans have always been ingenious at this sort of thing. Seven of the conspirators who helped John Wilkes Booth had their faces and heads covered by heavy canvas masks all the while they awaited trial.

History loses track of these surviving thirty members of the San Patricio Battalion at the expiration of their sentences. They must have made for Mexico because they could not have survived long with the branded D, even on the frontier.

The Mexican War ended with the acquisition of California and New Mexico by the United States in exchange for fifteen million dollars.

The final commitment

WHEN THE railroads were first invented and the ties were laid across Europe, the French government used to hire actors and singers to ease the minds of the nervous passengers who were rocketed along at twenty-one miles an hour. The railroad officials hoped that music and jokes would keep the passengers preoccupied and reduce their anxiety. It must have worked, for the railroads were not only successful but ubiquitous within a generation.

No airline provides singers and actors on airplanes. Not even for the fastest jet. Yet flying is the absolute commitment. Marriage you can get out of; from a jail you can escape or get a parole; you can leave your job, move from one city to another; even in a landing craft under heavy fire there's a chance; but once a plane takes off, you have made the absolute commitment, probably the only absolute choice in all our lives. It's an either-or proposition. Flying admits no shades of gray. You either land or you are gone—forever.

It is interesting to note that at twenty-one miles an hour in 1875 people needed entertainment to distract their attention from the risk involved, but at five hundred miles an hour we are quite casual about the whole thing. I believe we take this "final commitment" in stride because of our faith in the technological advances of the past half century and our reliance on the training and efficiency of the wonderful fellows who usually bring us down safely.

Advice to the lovelorn

I ONCE printed a letter from a girl who asked me what to do because her boyfriend disappeared, leaving all his shirts, socks, and two pairs of pants at her apartment. I wrote her, "Honey, don't do anything about *him*. Just find another man who can wear the same size."

Symbolic time

THERE ARE no doubt several Americas but one America I know is pulling in two directions at once. That is the America that goes to work. There are businessmen who say, "I wish there were sixty hours in a day and sixty weeks in a year and sixty years in a half century and then maybe I could get something done" (i.e., make more money).

Then there is the other American who constantly threatens he will not sign a union contract unless it contains a clause guaranteeing him a thirty-two-hour week or a twenty-five-hour week or some kind of temporal week less than forty hours.

We could resolve this paradox, I suppose, by putting the laboring man in the businessman's world, where the days are too short, and the businessman in the workingman's place, where the weeks are too long.

It is curious that time is such a central fact in American existence. The American businessman is proud that he has no time. The harder it is to get to see him, the more successful you know he is. If you never see him at all, you know he's at the very top; he is always busy. In Italy, however, exactly the contrary is true. If you can't see a businessman, it means he is in the dumps, struggling hard. Once he becomes successful, he becomes more accessible. When he tells his most menial employee, "Come in, spend an hour, tell me everything on your mind," he has reached the pinnacle.

Similarly, there are workmen, let's say in India, who have never put in a forty-hour week for the simple reason that there has never been enough work to justify this time. But they long for the full week and long for it not necessarily because it will bring more money but because it will give them a security they have never known.

Thus I wonder how real these demands on time, or denials, if you will, really are. No one works a shorter day on the average than the professional athlete but the baseball and

12

football players now complain that the schedules are too long, and they are supposed to like what they're doing.

Is it possible that the housewife who tells her friends she simply is too busy, she simply doesn't have time, is using time to confer status upon herself? We are, said Thorstein Veblen, a nation of conspicuous consumers. Have we incorporated time as one of our regular symbols of affluence?

Perhaps. My daughter-in-law works for a national women's magazine. Some years ago, before air conditioning was so widespread, the staff of this magazine decided they would work twelve hours a day, four days a week, during the summer, which would give them three days to cool off. The system worked fine. They even were able to reduce the twelve hours a day to eight and the magazine came out on time as good as it ever was. They even thought of trying a three-day week until the corporation manager put all these impracticable, revolutionary women back on a five-day week with a grouchy directive.

When Jack Dempsey fought Firpo

I DID not see Babe Ruth hit his sixtieth home run or his 714th. Nor did I see the World Series where the Babe called his shot to center field. I did not see Ty Cobb assault a fan behind home plate. There are many notable events I never saw. When Henry Aaron tied the Babe's record, many asked me if I remembered the Babe setting his. It is another way of telling me I am old.

I did not see MacArthur come home or Eisenhower, nor did I wave at any of the parading astronauts. I did see the parade for Lucky Lindy. Four to five million people lined the streets of New York and tossed ticker tape from offices. If you saw Lindbergh come home, you are nearing fifty at the minimum and if you remember his welcome, the chances are you are nearing if not past seventy. That in itself is a distinction of sorts.

I did not see Jack Dempsey tame Luis Firpo, the wild bull of the Pampas, nor did I see Tunney take the long count. I did go to see the second Louis-Schmeling bout; or rather I went but did not see it. I lit my cigar at the bell for the first round and by the time I exhaled there was Schmeling on his hands and knees trying to crawl away from Louis and I understand they are still looking for the mouthpiece in center field.

Now, of course, television makes it possible to see everything.

Everyone has seen Hank Aaron's 714th home run, even housewives and concert pianists who would never, in the normal course of events, have thought about home runs. If one cannot remember all the names of the original astronauts, it certainly is not the fault of television.

In fact, everyone has seen Hank Aaron's 715th home run, even Al Downing, the Dodger pitcher who wishes he hadn't seen it.

The fact that we are privileged to see everything that is important will no doubt maximize the trivial. If everyone can see Aaron's record-tying and -breaking home runs, the important event is to have witnessed his first home run, which was hit off Vic Raschi, the old Yankee turned Red Bird, in April, 1954. Do you know, not one of my grandsons was born in 1954? Richard Nixon was a forty-year-old Vice President of the United States and Lowell Weicker wasn't out of Yale University. The heavyweight champion of the world was Rocky Marciano, whose last fight I cannot remember.

Bonanza in the street

A NEWS story from the wire services told of thieves who stole several sample cases of jewels from a salesman in

14

Wytheville, Virginia. The jewels were valued at $150,000 but the thieves made a clumsy getaway and the police gave chase. The two cars were careening along the highway at 115 miles an hour and the jewel thieves were getting apprehensive about the police car, which they could not quite outdistance.

They began to throw the cases of jewels out so that if they were caught, they wouldn't have the incriminating evidence. As the cases of jewels hit the highway, they spewed the precious stones right and left and the fields for several miles looked like miniature green skies with twinkling stars.

The folks were out there in no time with gallon pails picking up sapphires, rubies, pearls, and whatnot.

There are two things that get the folks away from the television sets and out in the fresh air these days. One is a nearby fire and the other is free things in the street.

My wife's father owned a candy factory in Scranton, Pennsylvania, many, many years ago. She remembers that when she was a little girl, the factory caught fire and burned to the ground.

The strong smell of roasted chocolate permeated Scranton for a couple of days and then someone discovered that all the candy hadn't been burned. The gumdrops had charred and the charring was an effective insulation against the fire. For the next several years, she told me, the kids all went up to the old factory and scoured the ground for the black gumdrops. For years they scraped them off and spoiled their dinners. No other gumdrops are as good as free gumdrops.

A kind word for the bottle

NEW YORK STATE's Liquor Authority has decided to let distillers and winemakers offer their hooch in fancy bottles. Imported cognac from France and blackberry wine from Japan were offered in crystal flacons and hand-painted por-

15

celain. The American distillers were getting restless about this competition.

The reason for the ban goes back to the repeal of Prohibition. Those who framed the law suspected that anything that lent class or prestige or interest to ordinary whiskey would do a disservice to temperance.

Most state-controlled stores in the South stock a quantity of rolls of paper towels. When a lady purchases two or three bottles, the clerks stuff the paper towels on top so her neighbors will think she's been shopping at the supermarket. This happens to be a very good deal for the manufacturers of paper towels. It is the despair of temperance workers.

Some years ago a clever distiller in Georgia decided to bottle "white lightning" legally. White lightning is the bootleg corn liquor that is poured liberally throughout the South. At first he had relatively little success marketing it. He could not believe the bootleg lightning was better than his. Then he hit upon the happy idea of bottling the lightning in regular mason jars, just like the bootlegger. Lo and behold! It was another American success story.

A variety of disguises were adopted to cloak liquor during Prohibition. Bootleggers used to set up as florists to deliver the stuff inside wreaths and gladioli arrangements. When I worked in Wall Street, the bootlegger looked just like a client coming into the brokerage to go over his portfolio except that he was carrying his portfolio and it was unusually heavy.

All I hope is that the distillers do not take away the ordinary bottle that many of us have dearly come to love. The unadorned fifth of bourbon is a symbol of comfort and help in a world too often rent by distress and tention.

The suburban bum

SINCE THE beginning of the country, boys have been

taking off; they used to take off for the West, acquiring a wife, family, land, and a Bible before old age or hard winters did them in.

They were after something. They did not undertake the Herculean tasks of clearing the land of mammoth trees, chinking the log cabins, breaking the sod, and wresting a living from the stubborn earth for the edification of future generations. From the wealth of the land they wanted cash in hand.

About the turn of the century and for a few decades after, the boys took their chances in the big city. Horatio Alger heroes and Hemingway's Nick Adams are the same man. The Alger hero wants to succeed, to make something of himself, while Nick Adams has heard that money isn't everything and that there is a great war going on in Europe.

Even the cities and the foreign lands became chancier than the frontier and less rewarding and there were two generations of boys who stayed on in college instead of venturing to the horizon. They were the academic deadbeats. They majored in French and then went after a degree in fine arts and finally settled for a training program as a claim adjuster.

Now there is a new breed, the boys who are bumming in the suburbs. They finish high school, and because the Vietnam War has ended, college has no meaning: They are not eligible for military service. They are loath to accept the values by which their fathers live and even more loath to find their own.

They work in the malls or in the gigantic drugstores or in the hamburger palaces for the money with which they buy cigarettes, record albums, and pot, and they bum a place to sleep from accommodating adults or in tool sheds or they even chip for a place of their own until their landlord's rage gets the better of his greed.

The suburban bum may sound like an odd avocation but we have had bums in the city for as long as there has been a city and we are all of the opinion that the suburbs are an infinitely nicer paradise so there is no reason why that paradise shouldn't be populated by even nicer bums.

It is impossible to convince them that, while the Horatio Alger hero may have been a square and Nick Adams a nihilist, neither of them leaned on anybody.

Losing the job

WHEN I was a young boy, I unionized myself out of my first job. I worked as a hat sizer for the firm of Arnold Rosenbaum and Company. A union organizer got a good foothold in the plant and soon we were on the street parading with picket signs that read, "Arnold Rosenbaum Unfair to Labor." While we paraded, Mr. Rosenbaum stood on the sidewalk, real tears cascading down his cheeks. He cried, "What are you men doing to me? Didn't I put bread into your mouths?"

The union man said, "Be strong," and two days later Mr. Rosenbaum gave in to our demands and I think we got ten cents an hour more.

I was in my early teens and Mr. Rosenbaum figured for the twelve dollars a week he might as well have a responsible family man as a kid who had no more sense of duty than to go out on a strike. So he fired me. Had the union been stronger, I suppose, I would have become one of the ace hat sizers in *chapeau* history.

Being out of work is never a pleasant prospect but it is not terrifying when you're young. There's another job soon and another job is another adventure. I remember the despair of the men I saw lined up at the soup kitchens in the 1930's. One of them, I remember, offered a bowl of soup for a nickel and a man could take all the stale bread he could eat. The pieces of bread were stacked like books in a library. Many a young man in that line had a briefcase under his arm. I saw them stuff bread into those cases. Whether the men carried their brief-cases to bolster their morale or simply to smuggle bread I don't know.

With the Depression passed, still I myself have been out of work, sometimes stranded in Southern towns, hoping for an opening as a telephone space salesman on a local paper. Those problems worked out, too. Sometimes the paper was preparing a centennial edition and needed more salesmen. Sometimes I met a friend who lent me the money to get to the next town.

What is more despairing, however, than to lose a job when you're into or past your forties or even older? Nothing is so painful as running short of tomorrows.

Those of my friends who fall upon these days tell me the experience has the same components. Other pals rally round for a week or two, counseling not to worry. But once the man has to start operating from a telephone booth, friends are mysteriously busy or engaged in endless conferences. Prospective employers talk about the "age differential" and the openings in the training program.

I remember a captain of industry asserting at a press conference that we are all ball bearings turning the same giant wheel. What he did not mention is that ball bearings do not have hearts and minds and feelings.

Streaking and long hair

SOME YEARS ago I got an assignment from a magazine to write an article about the Beatles, of whom I knew nothing at the time. But my pencil is for hire, so I set about finding out what the Beatles were. I didn't have to search far until I learned that their arrival in America was to provide the biggest news ever at Kennedy Airport. I did not even have to go. I let the other reporters go and then I cleverly summarized what they wrote. I watched the Beatles on Ed Sullivan and an original comment I inserted haphazardly into this now-forgotten analysis was that what made the Beatles a phenomenon was the long hair. Had I followed this insight with some rigorous study, I might well have prophesied what would become of the shrieking, giggling generation that applauded Ringo *et alii*.

Now let's examine the phenomenon of streaking. One of the bad dreams all of us have is running through the streets naked. The college kids have turned dream into reality.

I now predict that sooner or later boys will wear their hair short.

I predict this because the kids are not going to stop with one dream.

If they like running nekkid they will also play Samson and Delilah, for the shearing of long hair is the actual nightmare of the younger generation. I predict the country will be better off for this because short hair will give the hat manufacturers a new lease on life.

The population explosion

A FAMOUS firm of stockbrokers has published a handsome pamphlet about the population explosion. The pamphlet is called *The Population Explosion: It's Impact on Investors*. It proffers no remedial steps for today. But it does analyze how investors can make a dollar or two figuring out what the growing population will need in, say, 1990.

The problem in the Far East is there is not enough food, and in America there are not enough jobs. Nevertheless, the pamphlet points out, a whole army of companies stands to prosper. Among them, the pamphlet reports, are ATT, Anheusher-Busch; Holt, Rinehart and Winston, and Sears Roebuck.

The funny thing about the stockbrokers' concern is that it is in a way so remote. Most of these fellows fight against public housing, and Medicare sent them into apoplexies of despair. Yet they are so terribly worried about the world in 1980 and 1990 and the year 2000.

How to win over the machine

I KNOW a decent fellow who has a lovely wife and six children. The kids are always spic and span, and they look like illustrations in a first-grade primer. Only thing, though, whenever the washing machine breaks down, which is often, the wife retires with a migraine headache. The husband is talking about psychiatric or at least therapeutic treatment but I am able to propose an even simpler method for restoring this lady's health: Get rid of the washing machine. Admittedly, the kids won't be clean, but since when did kids have to be clean except when they go to bed? I understand that all the health surveys indicate that the dirtier the kid is, the more resistance he has.

The modern kitchen appliance has begun to tyrannize woman and, as we have seen, has not only run down her health, but the health of her kids. If you buy the little woman an automatic cake mixer she begins to feel remiss until she starts baking cakes even though she may bake bad cakes.

Two cars are supposed to be the world's greatest convenience but for all the walking they save, they are two steel animals that run out of gasoline, out of oil, whose batteries go dead, and they represent eight wheels that can go flat. And there is the inevitable morning when neither of them will start and if you think that lady has a migraine headache, you should see the man with six thousand dollars in the garage which is not functioning.

21

Neon kosher-style

IN NEW YORK CITY the owner of a delicatessen was fined for selling ham in his publicly advertised kosher store. When confronted with the majesty of the law, which frowns upon misleading the public, he explained, somewhat lamely, that he thought selling the ham was all right because he only included the ham slices on Jewish rye. The Jewish rye sort of sanctified the ham.

Why didn't this dope save himself the fine and the embarrassment by advertising his store as "kosher-style"? Most of the Greek delicatessens that brighten the South advertise themselves as "kosher-style" and, though many of my landsmen object to this as blasphemy, nothing warms my heart more than to see a neon "kosher-style" blinking on and off. There ought to be thousands more, for those hundreds of thousands of Gentiles who ask for Jewish rye and kosher dill pickles. In recent years they've been buying frozen knishes like mad.

I miss the lobby

THE OLD hotels had wide and spacious lobbies. Some of them even had promenades. All were equipped with comfortable chairs where a guest and a wayfarer could relax and enjoy a newspaper while keeping one eye on the pretty girls who came to and from like decorative birds of passage.

Now the lobby is narrow, sometimes nothing more than a hall leading to the registration desk, and the chairs are gone. If it has any space at all, that space is usurped by a pool with dripping water that makes concentration difficult. All the seats in the bar. It is advisable to go along with the times and take a room because any perch in the bar sooner or later wobbles out from under you.

Investments of celebrities

ONE OF the startling financial phenomena of the past decades is the amount of money movie stars, recording artists, and athletes can make by diversifying themselves and going into business. Never more, apparently, will we be treated to those human-interest stories around Christmastime and whenever there is a news lull about old actors spooning potato soup at the indigent gentlemen's home. Never more will we read about the athlete gone to seed through booze. Eighteen-year-old crooners are set for life.

Perry Como owns his own TV production company and is a partner with the golfer Jack Nicklaus in Mississippi oil ventures.

Bob Hope is one of the owners of the Cleveland Indians.

Frank Sinatra owns movies, recording companies, a metal forming company, a plane charter company, and goodness knows what other diversification.

In the years gone by a celebrity put out to pasture, as it were, usually opened a bar. In fact, most of our larger cities are dotted with the neon spelling of the great and near-great of yore. My own idea is that if I ever accumulated the money, I would open a kosher delicatessen and poolroom in some small Southern town. At minimum I would have enough to eat, plus all the Dr. Brown's Cel-Ray I could drink, and could cut the take at the pinochle games in the back room.

The off-hours risk

WHEN I was young, and I mean a young stockbroker, not a young kid, I worried about Babe Ruth. Babe Ruth liked to play golf and the sportswriters convinced me golf would ruin the Babe's batting eye and without the Babe the Yankees would never win the pennant. During my Wall Street years, however, golf never did the Babe in. High living did.

Later, I read that Jim Lonborg, the great Red Sox pitcher, tore his knee apart skiing. It is very sad. But every profession has the risks its practitioners must take to prove themselves truly part of their times.

Not all of us choose risky avocations. Doctors are musical in great numbers. There is a symphony orchestra in New York staffed wholly by doctors and dentists. Why they should have this additional ability I don't know.

It seems to me newspapermen and printers take to John Barleycorn as their off-hours risk. At least I never knew a reporter to turn down a bourbon. Nor a printer. It has been suggested that perhaps the ink in the newsprint drives them to drink. My own opinion is that it takes a lot less than newsprint. It takes five minutes with nothing to do. Even if they have something to do.

Politicians apparently prefer the fair sex. One remembers Warren Harding and Nan Britton and a paternity conceived in a White House closet. Aaron Burr nearly lost a leg at the age of ninety jumping out of a married lady's bedroom window. John Profumo of England went into social work when his dalliance with Christine Keeler came to the attention of the Parliament, Scotland Yard, and the newspapers. Franklin D. Roosevelt entertained a mistress of long standing.

The only risk, I, a more-than-middle-aged writer, think of taking is to put my hands in hot water. Somehow this stimulates my brain cells. I once washed the dishes and I found once, when Margaret was washing the windows, that I like hot water and ammonia.

I do zip Jet Spray with Ammorphaline on the television screen once a night.

What is a celebrity?

A CELEBRITY is a man who eats celery with celerity.

Working around the house

I HAVE never been much of a hand at doing repairs around the house. I have been characterized sometimes as absolutely negligent. I once pushed a lawn mower around in Shrewsbury, New Jersey, but I could never remember whether the roller was supposed to lie flat on the grass or spin uselessly toward heaven.

Tinkering seems to me the most dangerous of the avocations they follow. One chap is always fooling with his car. He fools with it and fools with it and invariably a day or two after he has tuned it up I see the repair truck outside his home. Another chap has a sailboat that he stores in his garage. He is always scraping and painting that sailboat, which is a positive hazard to the neighborhood. Every now and then the boat forgets it is not on the Catawba River and moves out into Independence Boulevard. One day it moved straight toward the corner garage of the tinkerer, who fainted dead away.

Raking leaves seems to go on interminably. The rakers are always scraping all the leaves into the gutter, where they light them, and the smoke permeates the neighborhood all afternoon.

Nor can I say I would like painting. There are too many scaffolds to rig and ladders to climb and a gallon of paint these days costs as much as a television repair bill. Gardening is beyond me. My dear neighbors tender me the very produce with which my refrigerator is stocked, all of it in nice little packages quick-frozen.

Now chopping wood seems to me a manly activity. I understand that's how they cleared the Northwest and while I would not like to fell redwoods, nature's oldest living organism, I can see how repressed hostility can be relieved by splitting firewood with a five-pound sledge and wedge.

And were I consigned to any work around the house at all, I would choose to wash windows. Washing windows must be a lot like writing a novel, every window standing for a symbolic chapter while the washer mounts ever higher and higher around the house.

Everybody in my home and office, however, smokes cigarettes and cigars and I cannot see the percentage of cleaning my interior windows.

Soap wrappers and trading stamps

THE WOMAN walked into the Stamp Redemption Center in Dallas, Texas, and paid no attention at all to the displays of toasters, electric rotisseries, collapsible bridge tables, and vacuum cleaners.

"How many stamps do I need to get a school bus?" she asked.

John Ditzel, zone 'manager for Top Value (trading stamps) Enterprises, without batting an eye, replied, "Bring in eight hundred and seventy books and we will give you a Ford Econoliner school bus."

But the answer seemed simple enough to Mrs. John A. Witmer, a vivacious brunette and the wife of a professor at the Dallas Theological Seminary. She was asking the question because she was the projects chairwoman of the Dallas Christian Grade School Parent-Teacher Association and the school desperately needed another bus.

The Dallas Christian Grade School is a nondenominational private school, supported by tuition and charitable donations. Its student body comes from all over Dallas and the car pools were becoming a model of meticulous logistical planning.

Model though this schedule was, its daily execution was getting the parents down. One morning Mrs. Witmer stood in her kitchen, pasting up trading stamps, and wondered, "Why not?"

After all, everyone saves trading stamps. What gives them such wide popularity, I suspect, is that the mothers and the children and often the husbands get to paste them in a book. Fifty years ago my mother simply laid her Octagon Soap wrappers aside.

(From my own observation, I believe the early vitality of the labor movement was in part derived from pasting a coupon that represented union dues into a book. The modern check-off system—necessary of course—lacks this excitement.)

Thousands of things sold my mother on America. What kept her sold longest was that Octagon Soap wrapper. When she had saved enough of them, she got cut glass—free. Religiously, she saved her soap wrappers, storing them on the shelf above the iron stove along with the Vulcan Stove Polish and the tin container of pennies she saved for the Singer Sewing Machine fellow every week.

During the depths of the Depression, somewhere around 1933, the movies also started to pass out premiums to the folks who went to the Wednesday-night show. You used to buy a ticket and turn in your stub in the lobby and spend the evening watching such artworks as *The Invisible Man* followed by *Five Little Peppers Grow Up*, nursing a dinner plate or a soup tureen in your lap.

The modern trading-stamp industry, however, has abolished the simple premiums my mother collected in the early 1900's. Trading stamps are not only a multimillion-dollar industry, but they have probably revealed the intricate complications of the American character as no other industry has.

What led me to these reflections was that small dispatch that indeed this Dallas housewife had collected enough stamps for the school bus.

The next time I visited Dallas, I called on Mr. David C.

Higgins, the principal of Dallas Christian Grade School. I asked him who thought up this plan and he introduced me to Mrs. Witmer.

In the beginning, Mrs. Witmer told me, she thought all she had to do was tell the PTA to save stamps and collect the stamps their friends and neighbors saved. But she soon discovered that saving the stamps and pasting them in a book is a habit the folks do not willingly give up. The fellow who would think nothing of transporting a whole busload of friends out to the Cotton Bowl on New Year's Day, supplying all of them with tickets, has no intention of sacrificing the two books he wants to trade in on a tin of tennis balls.

Mrs. Witmer concluded it was up to the parents directly involved to save the stamps they needed. I learned that a family of five will collect on the average one and three-fifths books a month. No doubt the PTA could get its bus, but it would serve generations yet unborn.

But Mrs. Witmer found out that Dallas housewives would be willing to give her the stamps they didn't save. The woman who saved S&H stamps, for example, would donate the Plaid stamps she had been issued and the lady with Frontier stamps could be persuaded to give away her Top Value stamps. So Mrs. Witmer posted a plea for these in every Dallas washateria. The stamp collectors had to fan out throughout Dallas for the next eighteen months, collecting Plaid stamps here, S&H stamps there, Frontier stamps someplace else.

But this was only the beginning. The stamps had to be pasted in their respective books and then Mrs. Witmer had to trade these books off for Top Value stamp books. In turn, this process was complicated by the fact that it took 1,500 stamps to fill a Top Value book and only 1,200 to fill some of the others. The Top Value people figure a book buys between $3.75 and $4 worth of merchandise while a book with 1,200 stamps will buy, say, $3 worth of merchandise. In many instances Mrs. Witmer couldn't trade book for book, except to her own disadvantage. She had to trade stamp for stamp —1,305,000 stamps in all.

Of course, there were many people who did indeed donate their stamps, and donate them over and over again, especially after they too got caught up in the excitement. But most of it was plain, ordinary horse trading.

You can see how far we have come from my mother's soap wrappers on the Lower East Side of New York in the year 1910. Now Mrs. Witmer and her PTA are embarking on a project to collect five thousand books of stamps for a new kindergarten in a specially built schoolhouse. John Ditzel, the trading-stamp manager, says he will count them up and hire a contractor to break ground.

"You're not discouraged by the prospect?" I asked Mrs. Witmer.

"God will provide," she said. "God and Top Value."

A farewell to landmarks

ONE BY one the American landmarks disappear. They are the victims of neglect, of ignorance, and the profit motive.

On Cranberry Street in Brooklyn Walt Whitman's place was boarded up, waiting for the demolition crew. The city planned in its place one of those huge rabbit-warren housing projects that are the despair of urban sociologists and the delight of a few favored big-time real estate operators.

Are there any who care today about the place where Whitman set his own type for the first edition of *Leaves of Grass*?

New Yorkers also dismantled Mark Twain's house in the Village area and the Pennsylvania Station, one of the great architectural masterpieces of modern Western building.

A dozen other cultural and historical landmarks have gone the way of all American progress. The Gettysburg battlefield (not the cemetery) may become part of a building development although Gettysburg itself is now so desecrated by neon lights and shill booths it probably won't make much difference.

Ripping up landmarks is as American as apple pie. Back in 1901 President McKinley's Congress and the President himself deeded over to the Pennsylvania Railroad fourteen acres of the Washington Mall simply because that stretch of green between the Washington Monument and the Capitol was beautiful. The Washington Park Commission fought the transfer of land and, surprisingly, won.

Anyone who has ever enjoyed a trip to Washington's home at Mt. Vernon can breathe in relief that it is owned and administered by a private organization called the Mt. Vernon Ladies Association.

No Italian, no matter how "progressive," would tear down Dante's home in Florence (if indeed Dante's home is known); no Frenchman would tear down Francois Villon's home for any reason; and an Englishman would take pains to preserve Marlowe's home, though he might charge a few bob to tour it. But Americans are always on the lookout for some significant place to tear down.

One can wonder how we can pour such millions into our schools and yet have an educational system that leaves so much to be desired that neither constituents nor legislatures nor chief officers can appreciate the American past about which they endlessly declaim on any given holiday.

It took a superhuman effort on the part of Mrs. Adda George to save Carl Sandburg's birthplace in Galesburg, Illinois, and I remember when the ladies of Shrewsbury, New Jersey, ringed themselves around the thirteen sycamores planted at the end of the Revolutionary War to save them from axmen intent on building a post office.

But these are isolated victories. Only the American Chinese have been able to preserve some of the cultural traditions in their various Chinatowns.

As of this moment, there are easily fifteen thousand commissions dedicated to saving the downtown areas of our American cities. In fourteen thousand of these instances, downtown will go.

We Americans are so fast and so progressive, we can't even keep up with ourselves. Lewis Mumford has predicted that one day we Americans will have to sit down and reinvent the railroad train.

PART 2

My Mother,
the Exorcist

The untold Jewish story

WHEN THE real story of the American Jewish commun-
ity is told, it will not be in terms of who was a biologist or which
Jew was a prizefight champion, however necessary such facts
in an encyclopedia. But American Jewish history will be in
terms of the fabric of communal living and social philosophy
that the Jews brought to America and that have now become
part of the American way of life, just as the Jews for their part
breathed deeply of the American air and sounded the very
depths of the American milieu. Basically the story has not yet
been told because we are the only ones who could tell it, and
we have hesitated to do so.

We have hesitated because the basic history of the American
Jewish community revolves around the vast immigration
from Russia and Eastern Europe. The ghettos of Eastern
Europe between 1890 and 1912 poured into America the
most influential and important immigrants since the Pilgrims
landed on Plymouth Rock.

Thus I maintain that "The History of the American Jewish
Community" has not yet been told in depth. And it is understandable. All peoples like to link themselves with the "earliest
beginnings" of the country, and we are no different. I like to
read about Asser Levy and Hayam Salomon and the Jewish
pioneers and patriots of the eighteenth century and the first
half of the nineteenth century. But the fact remains that the
American Jewish community, with its tremendous institutions
and its vitality, was molded into substance by the third wave of
immigration from Eastern Europe between the years 1890
and 1912. It is timidity concerning the idea of being a
"latecomer" that has kept us from telling one of the most
wonderful immigration stories in all the history of mankind.

From the ghettos of Eastern Europe came an intellectuality

and a vitality that in fact helped shape the American way of life. Another reason for our timidity is the fact that its impact upon America was in the nature of the social sciences, which on the surface lack the glamour of wars and early pioneering.

The Jews from Russia, Austria, Galicia, Ukrania, Poland, Lithuania, Rumania, and Hungary brought an understanding of life that is as much a part of our country today as the accomplishments of the early Dutch and English settlers. It is the story of workman's compensation, the trade union, medical insurance, death benefits, and organized visits to the sick. It was this immigration that gave to both the Hebrew and Yiddish literature in this country their poets, journalists, critics, novelists, song writers, and stage directors. This generation of immigrants gave America the fabric of its social service, welfare workers, settlement houses, boys' camps, and communal leaders. Their influence spread to the American stage and to the entire American world of entertainment. They wrote many of the songs that all Americans sing and the vaudeville house and the recreation park were their inventions.

Who has told that story of the Third Wave from 1890 to 1912?

These Jews established the community-chest idea of organized philanthropy because they had brought with them a basic tenet of Judaism, which even those who did not go to the synagogue believed in with pious instinct. It is the introductory section of the daily morning prayer: "There are things for which the Torah has fixed no limit; leaving grains at the corners of the field for the poor; first fruits; offerings brought to the temple on the Three Festivals; the practice of charity; and the study of the Law."

No more skating in the tenement

MANY OF US, of course, lived on the top floor because it was the apartment with the cheapest rent. There was a front apartment and an apartment "in the back." The advantages of the front was that the family could have a piano hoisted up through the window via block and tackle. If you lived "in the back," you overlooked a yard filled with the outside privies.

All of us figured out ways and means of avoiding those five flights. We would call up to the apartment, where our mothers invariably answered. Your mother would lower money or whatever it was to you below. If your father wrapped it and lowered, all complications possible ensued. First, the rope got tangled on the downstairs window and your father had to race down two flights to untangle it. Next you couldn't untangle the note with which he had secured the object.

The tenements of the Lower East Side of New York were originally outfitted with gas jets to provide illumination. Later on the folks used a white shield, called a mantel, to cover the jets and make it look like one of the new electric lights coming into vogue uptown. The mantel cost ten cents and it was a status symbol.

But it was oh so delicate. It never lasted long. Its perch was precarious and it often fell. Sometimes the gas jet burned and it cracked.

Ten cents was a lot in those days but still we craved status. The mantel introduced us kids to a new frustration. Until it came on the mass market kids could do as they wanted in the tenements. We played hide and seek, cowboys and Indians. We even roller-skated from the front room to the back.

With the mantel installed on the gas jet, this play came to an end. The reverberations of skipping feet shattered the mantel as did the shudder of the walls, quaking under roller skates. Downstairs the folks soon learned to grab a broom and pound on the ceiling and yell for the kids to quiet down.

The sad thing was that after electric lights came into use, the people downstairs did not give up their broom or their shouting. Pounding on the ceiling became a habit, never to be broken.

Another reason we had to give up roller-skating was the piano. The piano in the tenement was the status symbol supreme. It took roughly thirty years of weekly quarters plus interest to pay for it but it was all worth it, even if no one in the place could bang out "Chopsticks."

A piano in the apartment meant the landlord called once a month for his rent, not once a week. It meant credit at the grocer's. It meant proud moments displaying the instrument to envious friends. But it also blocked up a good portion of the living room that served as the roller skater's runway. With the advent of the piano, it was hard to get any kind of good skating start.

The mantel and the piano were our passports into the middle class.

Public School 20

PUBLIC SCHOOL 20 Alumni Association held its annual dinner at the Statler Hilton the other night in honor of one of its graduates, Irving Caesar. Irving Caesar did as much for tea as Sir Thomas Lipton. Irving wrote the lyrics for "Tea For Two," which, along with his other song, "Swanee," became a popular classic.

Other graduates of this school on the Lower East Side include George Gershwin, Edward G. Robinson, and Senator Jacob Javits. But P.S. 20 is more than a repository for the names of successful sons sprung from the Lower East Side. Public School 20 represents one of the most visionary experiments in the history of human relationships, the making of an immigrant population into a citizen body politic. The teachers in Public School 20 not only taught American history but shared it. The first students were German immigrants, then the Irish, the Jews, the Italians, and the Poles.

In my era lunchtime came when we kids in the classroom heard the cry of the hot-chick-pea vendor calling, *"Haysa arbus!"* We'd spend our penny on chick-peas that were heated over a galvanized stove that resembled a dresser drawer. Sometimes we'd go across the street to the candy store we called "Cheap Haber's." A penny would buy two sticks of licorice or eight squares of butterscotch or ten marbles.

My mother, the exorcist

THE CONSTANT fear on the Lower East Side among the immigrant Jews was the fear of the Evil Eye, *kein ahora* (representing the devil and other evil spirits), and the Jews were always on the alert against it.

The major impulse was to keep evil spirits safely misinformed and so deeply engraved was this that it became a constant reflex of the entire community. One avoided mentioning the date of a birthday or the exact age of a person. When the census taker came around and asked about the age of the young son, the answer would be something like this: "He was born two days after Passover and a month after Tittel got married and a week before Uncle Shmul came to America," and let the census taker figure it out. And you mustn't count because the Evil Eye would be listening. So when the maitre d' came up to the banquet chairman and asked how many diners you had, the chairman began to count, "not, two, three," all to confuse the Evil Eye.

If a person must tell his age, he would be likely to say, "forty to one hundred and twenty," meaning, "I am forty years old and may I live to one hundred and twenty like Moses."

During the period before the baby is named it is in special danger from Lilith, Adam's first wife, who wants to snatch all babies to make up for her own demon children.

If the child laughs during the night, the mother must slap it quickly, for Lilith may be playing with it.

Nobody was supposed to look at the child except the mother, father, and granny, or, if they do, they must spit three times and say, *"Kein ahora"* (no Evil Eye).

The Evil Eye could be gotten through too much staring at the baby, at its beauty or its health, or from jealousy. So if the neighbor praises the child too much, he is warned by the parents, "Do not praise him too much, he may get the Evil Eye."

If a neighbor complimented Mother on little Harry winning a prize in school, Mother would immediately change the subject, "Look at the lamp, there is something wrong with it today."

If, in spite of precautions, the boy seemed to have incurred the Evil Eye, more drastic measures were taken. The professional exorcist would be called to talk away the "badness."

And a good way to trick the angel of death was to change the name of the sick child so when the angel of death came to claim little Moysheleh, he was not found. A child named Vigdor would be in his crib, and, since the child is all-important, death will not take the little one and the search will continue and Vigdor will recover.

My mother was a sort of exorcist. If a neighbor unthinkingly said of me, "What a handsome little boy you have," I could feel my mother's hand tighten as she quickened her steps to get home. Once home, she spit three times, repeated, *"Kein ahora,"* put a glass upside down, and made a fig (the thumb between two fingers).

If I ran out of the house saying "I'm going to the movies," my mother always followed me and repeated, "God willing."

So strongly embedded is this experience that, to this day, I,

40

an old socialist agnostic, will always repeat, "God willing," when discussing a contemplated project of any kind.

Mr. Washburn, the Presbyterian

ON SUNDAY evenings the Young Judeans Debating Club met at the University Settlement on Rivington and Eldridge Streets. Mr. Washburn was a teacher at the East Side Evening High School. During the day he taught at DeWitt Clinton High School, and on Sunday nights he advised the Young Judeans Debating Club, on his own time, I am sure. He was a fine-looking man. When you are fourteen years old, you have a distorted idea of the ages of adults, but thinking about Mr. Washburn now, I would say he was between forty and forty-five years old at the time.

We all chipped in a few cents and Mr. Washburn and one of the boys went to Marcus' delicatessen store on Rivington Street and bought salami, pastrami, bread, pickles, mustard, for an enjoyable hour of fellowship after the session of debating. The subjects in those days were "Closed Shop Versus Open Shop" and, so help me, "Should Immigration Be Stopped?" and many other issues.

On one occasion Mr. Washburn happened to mention that he was a Presbyterian. We understood only two general terms—"Christian" and "Catholic"—and the word "Presbyterian" sounded both strange and mysterious. But the world turns. I had no idea then that some day I would be living in the very citadel of the Presbyterian faith of America and that the great Presbyterian Queens College of Charlotte would one day ask me to write a story for the local press, "What Calvinism Has Meant to America."

One Sunday evening I went with Mr. Washburn to buy the food from Mr. Shapiro, the elderly counterman in Marcus' delicatessen. After Mr. Washburn paid the bill, he said, "Let's walk around the block before going in [to the settlement house]." It was apparent that Mr. Washburn was in deep thought. Finally he said, "You know, I just heard something wonderful." I thought he had reference to the music coming out of one of the tenements, but he said, "No, not that. It was Mr. Shapiro back there in the delicatessen store."

I wondered to myself what Mr. Shapiro could have said that was impressive, but Mr. Washburn was already relating, "It was when Mr. Shap-pyro told me how much we owed him that he made a lasting impression on me. A Gentile would have rung the cash register and told me it was 'a dollar and twenty-four cents,' and that would have been the end of that, but ah, what did Mr. Shap-pyro tell me? He told me a great deal, a great deal of history and quite a bit of philosophy, too. It is true that Mr. Shap-pyro also said, 'One dollar and twenty-four cents,' but how did he say it, that's the whole point of this wonderful lesson, how did he say it? First, you will remember, he started low, but his voice kept rising steadily with each syllable of those few words until it came to a magnificent crescendo, ending in both a question mark and an exclamation point; while at the same time his head was slowly sinking between his shoulders, his eyes were widened in an expression of wonderful optimism, as his arms came up almost in supplication, palms up; all at the same time and all within a few seconds: What Mr. Shap-pyro was indeed telling me was that my purchase was a very small matter to me; that I was getting my money's worth; that I should come back again, soon; and that I hadn't bought enough in the first place."

I said nothing. There was nothing to add to Mr. Washburn's wonderful observation of a fleeting moment of life on the East Side. But I never forgot it. A few years later I was asked to make my first speech, by actual invitation, before a fancy club "uptown" and I told them the story of Mr. Washburn, the Presbyterian, and Mr. Shap-pyro.

42

Shakespeare, Kwartin, and Koufax

SAMUEL BUTLER, the English novelist who gave us the imperishable *The Way of All Flesh*, confided in his notebook that his father was one of the few men he knew who confessed to not liking Shakespeare. Butler the elder used to complain that Shakespeare was so very coarse.

The argument about taste goes on forever. It never wanes. Men who loved Carl Sandburg and his work have been arguing lo these many years with the New Critics, who have been arguing with the Sandburg people—and people still read Sandburg and the others still follow the dictates of the New Criticism.

I remember my father conducting arguments long into the night about who was the better cantor, Rosenblatt or Cantor Kwartin.

My father would be sitting around with his closest friends, men who loved each other from back in the old country. But before they were through, they were like wild tigers when they championed their favorite cantors. (For those who may not know, a cantor chants the liturgy and prayers in the synagogue.)

My father was a Kwartin man. Very deliberately he would say to his colleague, "I heard the divine Kwartin on the holidays. What a voice! What skill! What an inspiration!"

One of his colleagues was a great Rosenblatt man, who would just as deliberately say, "Kwartin! Kwartin should be a peddler. A good peddler he might make. You should only be so lucky as to hear Rosenblatt without your unreasonable prejudice."

"I could listen to Rosenblatt," my father would say, "if he was a part-time cantor who worked every day in a butcher store. To listen to Rosenblatt before a congregation, better you should stuff the ears."

I think we will find this sort of thing in most of the argu-

43

ments concerning personal heroes. If you champion an athlete or an artist, you do not concede that your friend's champion is at least second. You insist that he doesn't belong in the league at all.

Were my father alive today, I think he would have relished the opportunity to argue that Sandy Koufax was the greatest pitcher in baseball.

My father, incidentally, wrote the first sports story to appear in a foreign-language paper. He analyzed the Jeffries-Johnson fight and what it meant in terms of the American civilization.

Charity on the East Side

THE *meshullech* (agent, deputy) was an accredited official sent out by various Jewish organizations and institutions (often schools and seminaries) to solicit and collect funds.

No one, of course, can estimate accurately the monies collected this way, and there is no doubt that there was much overlapping and much waste. The emergence of the federation idea in Jewish philanthropy has eliminated the *meshullech*.

Now and then, of course, a stray *meshullech* will come into town and explain why his organization is not on an accredited list of worthy charities, but he cannot collect any money. The *meshullech* is gone, but strange as it may seem, I miss him sometimes. I miss his long black coat, his beard, and mostly I miss his humor. The *meshullech* added a certain spice to life that the businesslike UJA agent can never supply.

Speaking of charity, my father was a leader in his several organizations of landsmen, and he went to the cemetery every second Sunday to officiate and to manage the burial of one of his friends and associates. My father once asked one of us for a ten-dollar bill on this trip to the cemetery. And this was an unusual request because my father had no concern at all about money and I doubt seriously whether he ever handled as much as twenty dollars for himself at any time in his life. But we eventually discovered the secret. I was with him on this occasion and after he had finished the "management" of the burial of a society brother, he said, "Now we'll take a little walk." We walked for five to ten minutes through the lanes and pathways of the cemetery and through the great crowds that were always at the Jewish cemetery on Sundays. Finally my father spotted his man. He was an elderly fellow with a long white beard whom I recognized immediately as a professional mourner, one of the old gents who went to the cemetery regularly to utter prayers for the deceased for funeral groups. My father chatted with him a few minutes and as they shook hands, I noticed that my father pressed this ten-dollar bill into the old man's hand.

On the way home I asked about it and my father explained it. My father had come to America two years before the rest of the family. This was the usual pattern. A man came here to work and save up enough money for a *shiff's carte* for the rest of his family. It seems that during those days when he was alone my father had visited a friend from the old country who had come over a year or two earlier. When my father left his friend to return to the room where he slept with two other immigrants, the friend had pressed a five-dollar bill into my father's hand. And now when my father's sons and daughters were doing well, he made certain that he remembered an old man who was now all alone in the world earning a few dollars reciting the prayers for the dead.

Dragons of old

OUR MOTHERS on the Lower East Side never told us stories about dragons. They told us stories about "lendlers."

The "lendler" was the landlord and he was more frightening than any monster.

I suspect this attitude was a hangover from the feudal ages when the landlord was the baron who owned the castle and the serfs tilled his lands.

The "lendlers" of the Lower East Side collected the rent personally on the same day of every month and, sometimes, if they didn't trust you, on the same day of every week. Today's landlord sends you a bill and very often not even that. This is a country that runs itself on trust and credit and probably most landlords expect their rent by mail and presume no tenant is ever going to forget something so important.

Fire on the *General Slocum*

In the Triangle factory fire of March 25, 1911, one hundred and forty-six girls died.

They were buried in a mass grave provided by the Arbeiter Ring (Workmens Circle). In the funeral procession for these Jewish girls marched groups of Christian working people —Italians, Poles, Ukranian, and Irish.

Only a few years before, the Jews of the East Side had contributed to the relief fund for the surviving members of the Christian families who died on the excursion steamboat *General Slocum*.

Sorrow and tragedy unite people more than anything else. It dramatizes our helplessness in the face of accident, illness, or tragedy. And it makes us more tolerant. Few people are unkind to those who are in mourning.

The *General Slocum* was an excursion steamboat usually hired for outings by German, Irish, Italian, and Jewish societies. It happened on June 5, 1904, one of those beautiful late spring days—perfect for an outing and excursion. The *General Slocum* had been engaged by the St. Mark's Lutheran

Evangelical Church on New Year's Lower East Side. The membership of the church included Protestants among the Hungarian, German, and Czech peoples, who at that time lived east of Third Avenue, fron Fifth Street up to and including Yorkville.

The boat started on its trip with 1,358 passengers, mostly women and children. About one hour later, just as it was entering Hell Gate, fire broke out. It started in a room filled with straw. Right then the captain did a very strange thing. He was Captain Van Schaik, who had been skipper of this General Slocum for many years. No one could understand it, but this old captain put on speed and kept on going as the fire and the panic spread.

Hundreds of women threw their children into the sea and followed them, only to be torn apart by the huge propellers of the steamboat. The flaming ship kept going at full steam until it neared a place called North Brother Island. Meanwhile frantic passengers grabbed for the life preservers, which came down in a shower of dust and rust. Not a single one was found to be in serviceable condition. The only water hose on the boat disintegrated into dust. Later it was found that it was the first attempt to use the hose in fourteen years. The women and children who weren't burned to death were cut up by the huge paddle wheels. You couldn't see these from the boatside—it all looked clear below; but they worked like grim reapers that June day.

The General Slocum finally came to rest at North Brother Island, and by this time a Health Department boat was standing by for the rescue of those who were still alive. Of the 1,358 passengers, 1,021 had died. Entire families were wiped out. Some surviving members of families, bewildered by the loss of all their loved ones, committed suicide. The Charities Department of New York supplied more than 1,000 coffins for the bodies recovered. The skipper, Captain Van Schaik, survived and was sent to Sing Sing for a term of three years for criminal negligence. The officers of the steamboat line were indicted but the authorities found that they could not hold

47

them because there were no laws on the statute books under which they could be prosecuted.

All the safety and inspection laws came after the *General Slocum* disaster. Down on East Sixth Street on New York's Lower East Side they erected a little stone marker in memory of practically the entire membership of the St. Mark's parish, and many a tear, by Christian and Jew, was shed over that little stone marker for many years afterward.

Confusion in the Bronx

WELL OVER fifty years ago the Irish families living in Hell's Kitchen began moving up to West Farms, an area that later became famous as the Bronx. At first the Bronx was a veritable paradise for Irish boys. They could go swimming in the Bronx River a quarter of a mile below the old dye works and there were no cops to chase them.

But then the Bronx began to spawn apartment buildings and into these moved the Jews and then the Irish boys couldn't go swimming unless they wore bathing suits.

An old subscriber and a Bronx Irishman named Leroy Day informs me that the arrival of the Jews ruined the cigarette-scalping business. The Irish boys used to scan the sidewalks picking up discarded cigarette butts, three of which would be rolled together in another piece of tissue to produce a two-inch cigarette. Then the electrifying news came—the Jews over on One Hundred and Seventy-fourth Street were discarding at least an inch and a half of cigarettes. The Irishers converged on the One Hundred and Seventy-fourth Street subway station. Sure enough, there were cigarettes an inch and a half long. But the Irish boys found out soon enough these weren't cigarettes, but the old cardboard mouthpieces that came in Jewish cigarettes. The Irish boys were picking up cardboard. It created confusion all over the Bronx. Boys never knew whether they were about to pluck an inch and a half of tobacco from the sidewalk or an inch and a half of cardboard.

The Jewish mothers got to the Irish mothers, which also began to have an effect on the Irish boy. The Irish boys were told they'd have to dress up a little more often and the mothers wouldn't let them drink up their pay.

Mr. Day tells me that among his Jewish neighbors was a family with a boy just his age named Jake. Jake spent all his time in his uncle's factory gluing boxes. "Jake, the glue brush," the Irish boys used to call him. But Mrs. Day soon began to ask her son why he couldn't get something to do like Jake instead of spending all his time toasting mickies (potatoes) in the vacant lots. In fact, Mr. Day recalls his mother even picked up the Yiddish argot and used expressions like, "Why don't you get something to do like Jake? Do you want to be a corner bum all your life?"

Music and pretensions

NOWADAYS WHEN an American traveler meets Jews in Hamburg, Bonn, Berlin, or Vienna, the chances are these Jews will say they are Israelis who emigrated originally from Poland. This may or may not be true. I smile because I remember when many of the Eastern European Jews said they were from Vienna. "*Aus Wien*," they all claimed.

The first evening I spent at the City College of New York on Twenty-third and Lexington Avenue each of the new students rose in his place and told the professor some of the salient facts about himself and his family. We described what our fathers did for a living and what we hoped to do and I distinctly remember three fellows preceding me whose fathers all belonged to my *shul*, fellow Galitzianers from Lemberg, Stanislau, and Mikulincz telling the professor with a straight face they were *aus Wien*.

Once in a while a more daring soul told people his father and mother were from Germany. This was stretching things a little too far. It was reaching for the clouds because there was no prestige or status that could compare with that enjoyed by the German Jews.

But ah! How the world has turned upside down. A rabbi who was born in Germany and educated at Hamburg tells me, "I am an Israeli."

Dr. Ludwig Erhard, a humorless German minister of finance, told me, "Without Jews, Germany is not a nation—only an economy."

Along came my subscriber, Mr. Alfred Reed, who some summers ago was a guest composer, lecturer, and conductor at the Summer Instrumental Workshop at the Appalachian State Teachers College in Boone, who legitimately did come *aus Wien*. Mr. Reed's father was a singing waiter in the famous Little Hungary Restaurant on East Houston Street, a place I've written of many times.

I identify the Little Hungary with a great event because I stood outside the restaurant shouting the headline, "Austrian heir to the throne assassinated by Serbians."

Many of the Viennese Jews were frequently miffed because all the Galitizianers kept claiming Vienna as their birthplace. But the Galitizianers weren't from Vienna for long. Pretty soon they were from America, then from New York, and finally from the Lower East Side.

Alfred Reed will confirm this and also confirm what a deep concern the Lower East Side had for music. Music was a terribly important event and it never mattered to orthodox Jewish boys whether they brought home to practice the church music of the Middle Ages or the chants of the Jewish *shul*.

There were concerts in the park during the summer that

invariably featured the trumpet solo *Inflammatus* from Rossini's *Stabat Mater* (See the Weeping Virgin Mary). Rossini also wrote an opera less well known than his others called *Moses in Egypt* and the Great Prayer chorus was always a favorite for trumpet and cornet players of the time. It is still to be found in the standard Arban method, as is the encore piece, *Carnival of Venice*.

In my books I have often mentioned the interesting fact that the sextet from *Lucia di Lammermoor* and the intermezzo from *Cavalleria Rusticana* were far and away the most popular operatic selections on the Lower East Side.

Very few homes with a phonograph, however, were without a recording of Alma Gluck singing, "Lo, Hear the Gentle Lark." This selection was particularly beloved because Alma Gluck was a Jewish girl from Rumania; her name was Reba Firestone. She was the wife of Efrem Zimbalist, who was one of the world's great violinists.

Caruso, of course, was the most popular and revered singer and most beloved non-Jew in the history of the entire immigrant era. There was, however, another tenor who had great popularity on the Lower East Side named Paul Althouse, a Metropolitan Opera star. I haven't heard an Althouse recording nor have I seen his name in print anywhere for the last forty years.

There was plenty to eat

LET'S BE realistic about the Lower East Side, that district of teeming humanity at the height of free immigration thirty-five and forty years ago. We were a big family and we never starved, and that goes for every other home I ever entered. The tables fairly creaked under the weight of the food—white fish, cream cheese, butter, bagel, lox, and dozens of delightful culinary concoctions. When novelist Burke Davis was on the

Baltimore *Sun*, he became a devotee of *tsimmes*, which he had tasted at the home of a friend. To the best of my recollections, *tsimmes*, like my mother used to make, was a sweet-sour preparation that included squares or slices of beef cooked with potatoes and prunes to which raisins were added. With a large hunk of bread in one hand to keep sopping up the wonderful juice, *tsimmes* can be a real treat.

In legal combat

THE JEWISH CONCILIATION BOARD OF AMERICA is well known to legal officials throughout New York. The board has saved the state and city millions of dollars in court expenses. The board litigates between Jews who sign a binding agreement to abide by its decisions. It is composed entirely of volunteer judges.

Most of the plaintiffs and defendants who come before the court are in domestic difficulties. A minority charge breach of contract or business misunderstandings between employer and employee.

One of the cases recorded by the late Samuel Buckler, who served the board in its earlier days, concerned a *shadkhan*, or marriage broker.

The *shadkhan*'s advertisement had attracted Miriam, a young widow with two small children. As a plaintiff, Miriam testified, "I decided to try my luck when I read Esther's advertisement that she guaranteed 'everlasting' marriages. But I am convinced Esther is a fraud. This marriage didn't last four full months. And when my second husband left, he took all the money. I want my fifty dollars back."

The judges asked Esther how much she would willingly return.

"Not one cent," answered the marriage broker. "Would she return the man I gave her?"

The two women were ready to start hair pulling when the board handed down its ruling.

"Today," said the arbiter, "marriage brokerage is commercialized. People are patched to one another instead of matched. The *shadkhan*'s consideration is to earn a dollar. Yet the board does not reject the custom. The marriage brokers have achieved some marked successes. The plaintiff is not entitled to a refund."

At which point Miriam turned to Esther and asked, "Can't you earn the money, at least, by getting me another husband?"

The mechanical *shadkhan*

JEWISH HUMOR is filled with references to the *shadkhan*, the marriage broker, who, for a fee, matches up a lonely bachelor and a willing spinster. The *shadkhan*, of course, is not a Jewish invention but a European institution.

By and large, the marriage broker never got too firm a foot in America. When I was a boy along the Lower East Side of New York, the marriage broker was already vanishing as fast as the Indian. But nowadays the *shadkhan* has come back with a bang, or should I say a whirring click. A couple of enterprising outfits have installed computers and have distributed questionnaires to the teenagers so they can match up the proper boy and girl. One of these outfits has even adopted the slogan "Pick-'em-cuter-by-computer," which is so effective as to lead to a grand jury investigation.

But then you have to remember that any innovation in America eventually leads to a grand jury investigation. In New York a Kings County grand jury is scrutinizing the motives and profits of the mechanized *shadkhan*.

What ought to bring a glow to the collective red neck of the grand jury are such possible self-descriptions of the customers in questionnaires as, "Sexy, in favor of petting, liberal in moral values, and of the opinion that the current American attitude toward sex is too conservative. Check yes or no."

I am not clear whether the grand jury is investigating just why such questions should be asked or whether it is investigating what the computer does if lies are submitted to it for processing. I know that Americans have always been enamored of machines and that sooner or later they would find a mechanical gauge for sex.

Evolution of the dowry

In the old days a poor family worked hard to build up a dowry for a daughter. And if there were two or even three daughters (it shouldn't happen), this actually became the whole drive behind the life of the entire family—to get those daughters married.

But the dowry wasn't all. First there was the *kuk* (kook), the supposedly accidental meeting where the prospective bride was looked over by the mother of the prospective groom. A full-dress inspection too. The girl, too, geared herself and made ample preparations for this accidental meeting. The girl would maybe carry a book to show that she's an intellectual, or she would be busy working on a piece of lace to show that she can do fine needlework. But you know the story already. If she was pretty, she needed no props, nothing, and she knew it. This is the same story all over the world and in every culture of man.

In many of the orthodox homes there was little variation, as yet, from the traditions observed so rigidly in Europe. A written contract was drawn up between the two families that stated the precise conditions of the relationship, the arrangements for the engagement party, the date of the wedding, and, of course, the amount of the dowry and how it was to be paid and also the official agreement for the payment of the fee to the *shadkhan* (matchmaker).

In the Jewish villages of eastern Europe the contract often included a provision for the years of *kest*, literally, "room and board." If the groom were still a student at the yeshiva, this *kest* was usually for four years, until the fellow became a rabbi; but in the meantime there was a baby every year, too. And the contract called for other grants-in-aid to the groom; a silk *talith* (prayer cloth), a long black caftan, a hat, and sometimes even a fur coat for the guy. And all of this made it quite a problem for a Jew with daughters, and it still is quite a problem.

It is true that today it is all Americanized and there is no contract or even a dowry, as such, and certainly few of the prospective grooms ever heard the word *kest*, but they get it under different names and in different ways. The groom does not get *kest* today, so the father-in-law buys the couple a home or furnishes the home for them. So this is fancy *kest*, but the principle remains the same. The folks will pride themselves about how modern they are.

The bride's father may not give his new son-in-law a dowry based on the old system of a contract, but he fits him up in a dentist's office or takes him into the business or buys him a car. There are a million ways in which this is being done exactly as it was done in the European pale of settlement in Europe and on the Lower East Side of New York. Nothing has really changed much. Whether it's Miami or Los Angeles, or Dallas or Boston, he's still getting *kest*.

The Yiddish press

WHEN IT was at its zenith, the Yiddish press flourished simultaneously with a great era of cosmopolitanism in

America. Young men like T. S. Eliot and Carl Van Vechten had emigrated to England or the Continent to write. Stuart Merrill, the American poet, wrote all his sonnets in French. Every graduate planned for at least a year of study in Heidelberg. Clark University, up in Massachusetts, brought Sigmund Freud here long before his name became a byword.

Those were the days when Abe Cahan was the editor of the *Daily Forward* and Sholom Aleichem and Sholom Ashe were writers on it. The *Daily Forward* was a socialist paper, like most of the Yiddish press, and it supported William Jennings Bryan in his fight for the eight-hour working day. The *Daily Forward* was also interested in literature and theater. Some of the first plays of Ibsen, Shaw, and Sudermann in America were produced at the Neighborhood Playhouse on Eighth Street on the East Side, and drama critics from the Yiddish press reviewed all of them.

The Yiddish press was also interested in sports because that was an integral part of American life. My father, Reb Lebche, was a part-time essayist for the Yiddish press and he wrote what may have been the first essay on a sports event to appear in Yiddish in America. He wrote about the Jeffries-Johnson fight in Reno.

There is a famous story about the time Abe Cahan was taken to a ball game by one of his assistant editors. McGraw was manager of the Giants. Cahan was a good socialist, so he decided to root for the underdog, Pittsburgh. The editor explained about first base and second base and home runs and strikeouts and Cahan settled right into the spirit. Midway in the first inning, Cahan decided that Honus Wagner was Jewish. Honus Wagner, of course, was the great Pittsburgh shortstop. He had hands as big as your grandmother's dining-room table. Seven times he led the National League in batting, once with .355. Jewish, however, he was not.

That made no difference to Cahan. He was for Pittsburgh and Pittsburgh was losing and it would be a nice thing if that Jewish shortstop could save the day. But Pittsburgh was having a very bad day. The top of the ninth rolled around and it was Pittsburgh's last chance. With two out, it was Wagner's turn at bat. By this time Cahan had invested Wagner with messianic proportions. On the first pitch, Wagner popped up. Cahan leaped from his seat, his hand on his skull cap, and shouted at the Giant second baseman, "Drop it! Drop it! Drop it!" From behind, a Giant fan reached out and pulled Cahan back to his seat and said, "Sit down, Pop. There's no drop here but rain."

The bar mitzvah *shikker*

HOW MANY of my readers have attended a bar mitzvah lately, I do not know. For those who have never seen a young man made a member of a temple, let me say it is an inspiring ceremony. A young man becomes a bar mitzvah by virtue of his ability to conduct the service, interpret the Talmud, and make a promise to the elders to keep the Law. It is inspiring because it celebrates the injunction, "Thou shalt tell it to thy son," it reinforces the union of father and son, and it makes a thirteen-year-old boy responsible now for manly acts. Afterward, of course, the guests share bread and wine with the new member of the congregation.

I had an uncle who was a *shikker*, meaning he liked to drink. He went to a bar mitzvah every Saturday. Anyone unwary enough to set down a glass of wine found it gone. My uncle was known as a "bar mitzvah *shikker*." He wished every young boy, however, success and luck. In addition, he became a leading expert on variations of the bar mitzvah ceremony. He was forever haranguing rabbis about this or that slight shading. When the caterers moved in, with the innovation of the guest list, my uncle sobered up and the rabbis in the neighborhood were able to conduct a bar mitzvah as they saw fit. Only the title, "the bar mitzvah," is what cousin Leon left behind him when he departed this vale of tears and Saturday wine.

At the last bar mitzvah I attended, I saw a lot of *shikkers*, but all of them had been invited. All of them were having such a good time they weren't interested in the bar mitzvah boy, who was off in the corner opening up his war bonds and his chess sets.

The *Morro Castle*

THE FIRST warning of what our dedication to comfort and high living portended came to us on a rainy fall day in 1934. The worst of the Depression was over and people were once more trying to find some fun. Off Barnegat Point in New Jersey a luxury liner was steaming back to New York on the return trip from Havana. It was a vacation cruise. That night, while the rain fell heavily, there was the traditional ship party. People were intent on enjoying themselves, intent on drinking and eating, on making love and on planning next year's trip. They were so intent on these activities they did not even notice when the captain withdrew from his table quite ill and went to his cabin. An hour later the captain of the *Morro Castle*, R. Willmott, was dead.

Chief Officer William F. Harms became captain and within hours his command was over. For late that Saturday night flames raced through the ship and the new captain, faced with this sudden crisis, kept his ship at nineteen knots into gale winds. The *Morro Castle* hadn't a chance.

The crewmen deserted in panic.

Passengers trapped below in their flaming cabins could see the lights twinkling on the Jersey shore. They could see other ships standing off from the *Morro Castle*. They could see the panic-stricken crew in lifeboats rowing away. On deck others threw themselves into the sea to escape the intense heat. Those of the crew who stayed did not know how to manage the fire-fighting equipment. Lifeboats hung uselessly in their stays.

What made the *Morro Castle* so startling a symbol was that as she was towed still flaming and smoking toward New York by a Coast Guard cutter, she ran aground on a sandbar off Asbury Park, right in front of Convention Hall. All day Sunday tourists who had hurried toward the beach paid twenty-five cents to enter the pier and get a closer look at the still-smoldering wreck.

Yeshiva University

IN 1886 a large group of Jewish immigrants living on the Lower East Side of New York chipped in their nickels, dimes, and quarters to help found a small religious school called the Yeshiva Eitz Chaim at the Mariampol Synagogue at 44 East Broadway. The Yeshiva Eitz Chaim is today Yeshiva University. This little religious school spawned seventeen institutions of higher learning, including liberal arts colleges, teaching institutes, and the Albert Einstein College of Medicine. Yeshiva University was the first school in America established under Jewish auspices.

Thus, in its founding and growth, it bears a remarkable similarity to schools like Yale, Harvard, and Princeton, which were also founded by immigrants and devoted to religious instruction.

Around the turn of the century the Yeshiva Eitz Chaim had an annual budget of $5,000. Today its annual budget is in many millions.

In the beginning, tuition was twenty-five cents a week and the faculty consisted of the late Abe Cahan, editor and novelist; Rabbis Elyah and Adelman; and a fourth whose name survives only through the nickname bestowed on him by the students—"Butternose."

One of the gauges by which to measure the success of the immigrants to America is to count up the schools they have established. Certainly the Protestants lead, but the Catholics run them a close second and have a wider elementary and high school base. If we base it on percentage of adherents, no religious group can compare with the Quakers, who established ten great schools of higher learning and dozens of secondary schools.

The Jews have founded two institutions of higher learning, Yeshiva and Brandeis universities. There is no more significant tribute to America than the history of all these schools, which were founded, supported, and nursed along by immigrants.

Hot dogs

WHEN I was a boy, a hot dog cost three cents—and that included mustard and relish. Now they cost fifty cents, but they taste no better.

Ode to the country club

WHEN THE ladies arrive at the Jewish country club, they go immediately to the swimming pool, and when no one is looking, they enter the pool with the same delicacy and in the same posture that their grandmothers used to enter the *mikvah* (ritual baths). And the country-club ladies are so happy; and of course I am so very happy, too, because I am the only one who shares their secret. And so we do not need any fifteen-volume history of the Jews in America. I can do it in four words: from *shul* to pool.

The survivors

Visiting a fashionable Miami Hotel on my last lecture swing, I met at the swimming pool a woman I remembered having evicted from the Hotel Markwell twenty-five years before. She had failed in her rent at the time and bore no grudge to our heaving her out on the street. In those days she worked in a big brothel on West Seventy-ninth Street.

Now she was past middle age and very sentimental. She told me all the old-time panderers are either waiters, bartenders, or hotel handyman. They are reduced to this since they never acquired any skills nor did they ever work enough to collect Social Security.

Wistful, these old-timers still hope to find some woman stupid enough to support them in their dotage and talk nostalgically of the days when they had a stable of four, seven, ten, and even thirty girls working for them.

The prostitutes who saved their money are now all diet addicts and are conversant with the latest of middle-age fashions. This woman said all her friends from the old days take an active interest in the stock market.

The family in the Jewish city

I am not at all sure that Jewish family living and family life in the 1970's differs appreciably from what we may conveniently call American family life and family living. I am quite sure that if it did, Jews themselves would see to it that it did not for long. By nature, the Jew is the eternal postscript, a

61

wanderer through history, a member of a race that has known all time and all places. If nothing else, he is adaptable. It is not surprising that he is adept at reflecting and assimilating the values of the majority around him.

In Charleston, South Carolina, for example, many of the Jews are ardent segregationists and vocal defenders of the doctrine of states' rights.

But once upon a time there was a difference between Jews and the rest of the Americans. There was a completely homogeneous Jewish society.

The philosopher Eric Hoffer put his finger on it: "The ghetto was a fortress as much as it was a prison." I remember women (including my mother) coming home from the ritual baths (required at the end of the menstrual period) with the towels around their necks and a neighbor warning good-naturedly, "I hope you make a boy tonight."

My mother undoubtedly enjoyed this homogeneous society and it is interesting to note that she had some correct ideas about the future of Jewish family living in America. "America will assimilate our religion," she said, and she even eyed the kosher butcher with suspicion.

When the Jew came to America in the closing years of the nineteenth century and the opening decades of the twentieth, he was the first immigrant since the Englishman at Plymouth Rock and Roanoke Island to bring his whole society with him.

The medical student in Milan did not come to America, nor did the music major in Poland. The Italian doctor remained in Milan and reaped the benefits of his practice and the concert master stayed in Poland and enjoyed the conversation of pianists and cellists and basked in his prestige. But the Italian peasant did come here and so did the Polish peasant. They had compelling reasons for emigration—poverty, unemployment, and actual starvation.

True, Jewish tailors and laborers came here, but their migration involved something more than mere poverty; it involved the hopelessness of third-class citizenship. And so with them came the Jewish medical student, actor, journalist, and intellectual, and America welcomed them. The Jews came to America with all the "paraphernalia" of a society. They had their doctors and lawyers, conservatives and anarchists, tailors and peddlers, printers and poets, rabbis and atheists.

They settled on the Lower East Side of New York City, where the tenements rose immediately to house them. The Jews read their news in a Yiddish newspaper, argued in their union halls with men who came from the same pale of settlement, and patronized the countless coffee houses. I remember my mother remarking once that she and the man who collected her weekly payments for the Singer Sewing Machine Company grew old together. They saw each other twice a week: once when he climbed up five flights of stairs to collect her weekly twenty-five cents and then when they nodded to each other in the *shul*.

An advantage to life in this homogeneous society was that these recent immigrants did have time to develop a family life. There were bad hours and bad conditions in the sweatshops and in the lofts, there were many evils, but withal these immigrants lived in a cohesive, organized community. The family unit was not left to shift for itself in a strange land, groping to understand strange customs, victimized by occasional cruelty.

The Lower East Side, with the exception of the free public schools, was virtually a Jewish city. Because it was a city, the local Tammany politicians, who at this time were mostly Irishmen, did everything to encourage active political participation. This active participation meant voting the Tammany ticket, of course. It is also true that many of these Jews would not have earned a livelihood without the help of Tammany. Tammany put more coal in the cellars of the poor than all of Scranton, Pennsylvania, ever mined.

But it was religion that played the important role in unifying the Jewish family. Fifty and sixty years ago no Jewish family sat at the table without a religious service. My father

63

wouldn't offer the evening prayer until every one of the family was present, and if everyone wasn't present, we had to devote ourselves to a search. We weren't worried about the little rascal, we were just hungry, and we couldn't eat till we found him.

But there are no longer any "Jewish cities" in America and home is no longer the sole focus for the religious and social life. Long since, the public school has supplanted the American home as the thesaurus from which we derive most of our opinions and attitudes.

In the old days my mother never left the home except to go to the *shul* once a week and during the High Holy Days. She went shopping, of course, but it was never casual shopping. She went at a specified hour every day.

On the Lower East Side there were no bridge clubs or cultural committees. There were no benefits of any kind save those arranged by the fraternities and the vereins and the lodges and these were strictly the province of the men.

There were many marriage brokers but we never heard of a marriage counselor. The big hurdle was to get the people married. After that the only problem was how many people were to be invited to the first bar mitzvah thirteen years later.

All the problems had to be solved within the home or not solved at all. The happiest memory of life on the Lower East Side was that Papa was the boss. In the Jewish household he was the last word. He was authority, pure and simple, never to be contradicted. Despite the propaganda circulated by the television serial, the newspaper comics, the radio and the movie, Papa is still the boss in the majority of American homes.

The Jewish father was not a tyrant. But no one would ever say the family ought to have a certain something if he decided *no*. And it should be noted, too, that we didn't speak until we were spoken to or until he asked us a question. Jews call this *derekh eretz*, literally translated as "the custom of the land." In actual usage, it means respect for elders, particularly parents.

We know that sons are often as right as fathers. *Derekh eretz* was not submission to authority but rather a *respect* for your father, nothing else.

Close family ties extended from the home into the whole neighborhood and pervaded all of the Lower East Side. When a neighbor fell sick, every woman in the tenement collected at her bedside and took her children under wing. Some women brought the patient white rolls and butter, others milk, and still others the universal remedy—hot chicken soup.

Some distance away from where I grew up on Eldridge Street was a dairy-grocery store run by a blind man. It was under the Williamsburg Bridge and not at all convenient. But there were many times my mother sent me there for a last-minute purchase. She would say, "Run down to the blind one. . . ." She considered the "blind one" part of the community, despite the exactitude of her language. She made some spare purchases there to tell him so, as did many of her neighbors.

Nor was there ever shame in the household about the afflicted. The blind were called blind and the lame, lame. They were accepted as many accidents in life are accepted and it seems to me, looking back over the years, it was a much healthier attitude.

None of us who lived along the Lower East Side then was faceless. We were not anonymous in the sense that those of us who walk the modern city's blocks or tend the suburban ranch house are anonymous and rootless.

From what I have heard, the American small town was never this way, and from what I know, neither was the Lower East Side. Both were much more uninhibited.

Parades always wound through the Lower East Side. Every Saturday a bar mitzvah boy would lead a phalanx of fathers, uncles, aunts, cousins, brothers, sisters, and well-wishers through the streets. They sang. They sang and marched with a full heart and passed out pieces of honeycake to the cheering children who lined the curb. And the cop who halted traffic so the parade could pass got a piece of honeycake, too. The street was joyous because a bar mitzvah represented the advent of a new male adult to the family circle, to the congregation, and to the community.

Through these streets too wound the Italian funerals, no joyous occasion certainly, but a splendid one. The horses pulling the hearse had their manes bedecked with vivid plumes and pranced in perfect time to the Garibaldi hymn or Chopin's Funeral March.

But the most important of all events on the Lower East Side was the wedding. The entire neighborhood was invited or as many as could crowd into the hall to lift their glasses in a toast. A wedding represents no less today, but everything has gone out of it. Weddings are so dignified today they are almost restful. Once the people danced all night and only the dawn of a working day put an end to the gaiety. I have attended recent weddings where the guests were allowed to take a nap be-tween the service and the reception. I would like to recom-mend to modern caterers the old Jewish expression that says, if half the neighborhood doesn't dance till dawn, the marriage doesn't have much of a chance.

No society, however, is built strictly on its ability to express unrestrained joy. The Jewish society of the Lower East Side had another ingredient. It was early adulthood. By early adulthood I mean that boys and girls as soon as they were able became responsible members of the family.

One of the first words the immigrant learned was "working papers." You had to have working papers before you could get a job and if you weren't the proper age, you went to a notary public, who, for a quarter, swore you were. I shall not romanticize about this. Child labor was an evil, fortunately abolished by the law, and we can thank God for the dedicated social workers and public-spirited citizens who brought about the reforms.

Yet I speak here of a different time and a different way. A young boy went to work not because he needed the money but because his family needed the money. My older brother,

Jacob, was the first of us to venture into the working world and I can remember the evening he brought home his first pay envelope. Not only Jacob, but the rest of us were suffused with a great pride. One of us was finally able to help. Jacob handed over his unopened pay envelope. The unopened pay envelope was a tradition. Wives and mothers boasted, "He doesn't open the pay envelope."

At the age of nine the Jewish girl became a junior mother. There was always a baby to take care of, and in thousands of homes when the baby cried at night, the little sister arose and saw that he was fed and changed. Hundreds of men who grew up on the East Side will recall the little girls playing potsy (a sidewalk game), with one eye peeled on "the bundle"—the baby brother—on a nearby stoop.

PART 3

From Marcus Aurelius

to Solzhenitsyn

The Marcus Aurelius health plan

THE HISTORIAN Gibbon teaches that the moment in world history when mankind's condition was at its happiest and most prosperous was during the consecutive reigns of the Roman emperors Antoninus Pius and Marcus Aurelius, a period that lasted a short eighty years.

Marcus Aurelius was a "conservative." Few radicals come out of palaces but it was this same Marcus Aurelius who reminded us that good men can indeed come out of palaces. Marcus Aurelius was born to the purple, as the Romans put it, and did not subscribe to the belief that men could suddenly become good and loving if pure democracy were universally established. He was a pragmatist, believing the best a man could do was to try to make things just a little bit better.

For the underlings of the Roman Empire he lightened the tax burden; for the oppressed he provided relief and kindness. When his ambassadors in foreign provinces reported crop failure or drought or flood, Marcus Aurelius dispatched a fleet of ships carrying grain and supplies along with technicians to see if Rome could somehow lighten the burden. Marcus Aurelius was interested in succor, not in remaking the world, for he had long since resigned himself to a world where corruption and wickedness flourished.

What he set out to do, he brought to pass, which is better than par for the course. Liberals have long argued that Prince Otto von Bismarck of Germany initiated the first "Medicare" system in 1881. But they are wrong. Marcus Aurelius had a health plan in A.D. 165. His Rome also had a limited program of social security. To the shocked amazement of politicians, Marcus Aurelius insisted on speaking to the slaves as though they were equals.

Some of the tribes in the German forests mistook this

emperor's mode of government as a sign of Rome's weakness. In his old age Aurelius was burdened by wars, but he showed himself as great in warding off and defeating military aggression as he was effective in warding off the sense of hopelessness of the poor.

He remains for us, of course, a preeminent philosopher. His great gift to mankind was his *Meditations*. It was a book he never published yet it has endured through all the centuries since his death. He wrote:

> One good corrective to vainglory is to remember that you cannot claim to have lived your entire life, nor even from youth up, as a philosopher. To many another it is no secret, and no secret to yourself, how far you fall short of philosophy.
>
> Where is there happiness? In doing that which man's nature craves. How do it? By holding principles by which come endeavors and actions. What principles? Principles touching good and bad—to wit, that nothing is good for man which does not make him just, temperate, big, free; nothing evil that does not produce the opposite results.
>
> Of every action ask yourself: "What does it mean for me? Shall I repent of it? A little while and I am dead, and there is an end of all. Why crave for more if only the work I am about is worthy of a being intellectual, social-minded, and on a par with God?"
>
> Protest—till you burst. Men will go on all the same.

Several bastards succeeded Marcus Aurelius as emperor. Those who say a nation dies from within are right to consider Rome. These emperors encouraged corruption and decay by their avarice and their lust for power. The delator—the vigilante—set neighbor to spying on neighbor and son to spying on father, who promised to accusers one-third of all the property of the accused "subversive." One hundred and fifty years after Marcus Aurelius, Rome had lost all confidence in itself. She was afraid. No one really cared anymore and so when the men from the northern forests came down again there was no Marcus Aurelius to hold them off with wisdom and self-confidence.

Among ironies

THE IRONY of history reminds me of a story out of the *Arabian Nights* (the Burton translation).

There was a traveler who stopped at a great mansion. In accordance with custom, he was given a hearty welcome and the master of the household gave him the finest guest room.

After a day the traveler took a shine to his host's young daughter, a girl of fourteen. Pretty soon she was in the traveler's well-appointed bedroom. The traveler knew that he was risking his life and he told the young girl, "Now be sure you don't tell your father."

Then the young girl kept coming back to the traveler's room night after night, and each time the traveler would say, "Now be sure you don't ever tell your father."

Finally the kid kept coming back so much that the traveler, a middle-aged man, in terrible distress and exasperation, shouted to the young girl, "If you don't get out of here, I'll tell your father."

Washington's birthday

HE HAD big hands and a big appetite, which in later years caused him considerable distress because his teeth hurt him so. He enjoyed a good story and he had an eye for a pretty woman. He was a highly successful farmer, who also distilled

73

whiskey and played cards for moderate stakes. They called him, first, Colonel Washington, then Mr. Washington, then General Washington, and later on, Your Excellency. No one called him George.

Washington allowed familiarity from only two of his contemporaries. General Henry Knox, the artilleryman, called him General, without adding the last name, and so did General Nathanael Greene, whom Washington called Brother Nat. Of course there was no nickname for this aristocrat. Has there ever been a nickname for King Arthur or for Sir Lancelot?

At the time of the French and Indian Wars, Washington was twenty-two but already a lieutenant colonel in the Virginia Militia. His abilities were known not only throughout the Colonies but in the mother country as well. He was a Virginia gentleman, a fact that played him false when he had to surrender Fort Necessity to the French. He signed the surrender, never dreaming that another professional soldier would attempt trickery. In the surrender, unwittingly Washington admitted to the "assassination" of a Frenchman named Jumonville, a scout killed in combat. During the Revolution the Tory journalist James Rivington printed a poem recalling this "cruel assassination."

When the Continental Congress fled from Philadelphia and thousands of American neutrals and Tories came out of hiding to help the British, things looked black indeed. But by the end of the Revolutionary War it was clear there would have been no United States of America if there had been no Washington. The old Prussian Frederick studied the American campaigns and was so impressed by Washington's retreats into victory that he sent the American general a sword inscribed, "From the oldest General in the world to the best."

At 2 P.M. on Friday, October 19, 1781, His Majesty's army marched out of Yorktown to surrender, their band playing, "The World Turned Upside Down." Cornwallis, ill, was restricted to his bed and he passed the burden of surrender to

74

General O'Hara. O'Hara started toward the lines of America's allies, the French, but the French general redirected him. "You deceive yourself, sir, the Commander-in-Chief of our armies is to your right." General O'Hara was turned around toward Washington and offered his sword, which Washington declined with the comment, "Never from so good a hand." February 22 is his birthday. No man in the English-speaking world deserves an annual holiday more.

Benedict Arnold

BENEDICT ARNOLD was a valiant soldier and a brilliant general. Because of his wound at the Battle of Saratoga, Washington took him out of the field and placed him in command at Philadelphia. Here Peggy Shippen was the belle of the ball and a good time was had by all. Peggy was the head of the Cliveden set—the "Better Hitler than Blum" folks. She and her circle of friends had contempt for the ragged rebels. When the British held Philadelphia, Peggy and Major Andre were very good friends. The major was much more than a messenger-spy. He was quite a fellow, Major Andre—urbane, sophisticated, a brilliant conversationalist, and an actor of considerable talent. When the Americans and Arnold came back, Peggy switched from Andre to the general himself. A widower, Arnold immediately fell in love with Peggy and asked her to be his wife. They were married but Peggy did not settle down. Gaiety was the big thing. Eat, drink, and be merry, for tomorrow we die stuff. Wine, entertaining, gambling, full steam ahead. First thing you know, Arnold was head over heels in debt. This forty-year-old widower should have known better. We may well imagine the extent to which this social fling went when the serious men of the American army saw fit to bring Benedict Arnold before a court-martial on charges of "extravagances" and conduct unbecoming an officer. Arnold expected an acquittal, but the court ordered a reprimand. There was one old gent on that court—what a brain that fellow had—General Van Cortlandt, the presiding officer, who seems to have seen through Benedict Arnold —right through him—over and above this comparatively minor charge. General Van Cortlandt voted for outright dismissal from the service, but he was outvoted.

General Washington was on his way from a meeting with the French generals at Peekskill, New York, when Arnold caught up with him to get the reprimand. Washington, who could get so tough that he could make a man's hair curl, was unusually gentle with Arnold. Who knows what is in a man's heart? Washington may have thought of Saratoga. Washington got the technical business of the "reprimand" over with and told Arnold he would like to have him around in command of one of the armies under him. Arnold said he did not believe his wound was well enough for a field command. How about West Point? Washington gave him the commission right then and there. Arnold already knew what he was going to do. Peggy, of course, knew it from the beginning. Whether Peggy had remained the mistress of Andre after her marriage to Arnold will never be known, but it is a possibility.

Luck, sheer luck, or was it Providence that saved the day and saved America and the stature of General Washington? Major Andre was to carry the plans and the instructions for the surrender of West Point to the British, and his route was comparatively simple. He had only some four miles to go to board the British *Vulture*. One of the *Vulture*'s small boats was coming toward the shore to pick up Andre when two farmers spotted it and opened fire. One of the two British sailors was killed and the other fellow began to row back toward the warship. A quarter of a mile away at a place called Verplancks Point was an American patrol under the command of Colonel Livingston. When Livingston heard that shot, he made immediate inquiry and it was then that he saw the *Vulture*. Livingston placed a gun on a hilltop known as Tellers Point and opened fire on the *Vulture*. There was some amazing artillery work done that morning because the *Vulture* suffered a direct hit and started down the Hudson as fast as possible. Andre was well on the way toward Verplancks Point to meet the sailors when he saw what happened. No ship. Nothing to do but reach the British lines on foot. Everything went right for the Americans and Washington that day. If these two farmers hadn't shot at the British sailors, if Livingston hadn't hit the *Vulture*, Andre would have made his escape with the papers, plans, description of West Point and the plan of the disposition to be made by Arnold of the American troops. And think of this for luck. Neither General Arnold nor Andre had the presence of mind to get a pass with Arnold's name on it in case something did go wrong. A pass from the American commandant of West Point would have been all that Andre needed. Coincidence piled on coincidence. Major Andre was proceeding carefully on his way to New York with what was probably the hopes of defeating the Revolution hidden in his boots. Along came a young boy—John Paulding—who only two days before had escaped from a British prison. With Paulding were two other Americans, Williams and Van Wirt. When Paulding escaped from the British, he had taken a British uniform and this is what he was wearing when he came upon the aristocrat Major Andre. Andre saw Paulding's uniform and he assumed that the three men were a British patrol and the first thing Andre said to Paulding was that he was carrying some important papers to General Clinton in New York. By this time it was nightfall and Paulding, Williams, and Van Wirt held their man a prisoner and then took him to Colonel Livingston, the same fellow who had hit the *Vulture*. Word went to Arnold that Major Andre had been captured and he fled at once. Young Alexander Hamilton, Washington's aide, was notified at once by Major Varick and Captain Franks that "Arnold had apparently abandoned his command." Hamilton rushed to West Point from Peekskill and there found the papers that had been found on Andre and the whole story was brought into the open. Andre, of course, died like a gentleman, smiling and chatting nonchalantly with the American soldiers. The only thing that did not go exactly right was the fact that Arnold got away, but maybe Providence had a hand in that, too. He lived a long time after that, but he was an outcast among the British, to whom he had sold out. Once the war was over, a certain pride began to creep into the English consciousness about America. After all, they were blood brothers, and the British had no truck at all with Arnold. One incident was written by Talleyrand, one of the most famous statesmen in Europe. Talleyrand, himself a refugee, had fled to England in 1794 and prepared to sail for America. While waiting for his ship to sail, he heard that "an American" was visiting in a nearby country home. Talleyrand had two days before his ship sailed and naturally he thought it wise to speak to an American to be briefed about the country. Talleyrand sought out this "American" and began to state his mission. The officer rose and said, "Sir, I am Benedict Arnold." Talleyrand, without further word, fastened his cloak around him and walked away.

John Stuart Mill

The "spirit of the age" is in some measure a novel expression. I do not believe that it is to be met with in any work exceeding fifty years in antiquity. The idea of comparing one's own age with former ages, or with our notion of those which are yet to come, had occurred to philosophers; but it never before was itself the dominant idea of any age. It is an idea essentially belonging to an age of change.

JOHN STUART MILL ventured these insights more than 135 years ago, which is one of the reasons philosophy professors keep his books on the reading list. Mill was inspired by the constant change induced by the Industrial Revolution. Change constantly afflicts us too, and we try to understand ourselves either by analyzing what preceded or what will succeed us. The newspaper reader can find an editor comparing America to decadent Rome or a college president talking about a new Athens.

I am myself devoted to another age, that of the orthodox Jewish immigrant who settled on the Lower East Side of New York between eighty and sixty years ago. It is only by recreating the tensions, habits, despair, and joy of the 1900's that I can sometimes make sense of the 1970's.

One of the reasons for the popularity and excellence of writers like Mary McCarthy and Norman Mailer is that they are able to see and understand today without the paraphernalia of the past.

Sensing the constant flux of Western society, John Stuart Mill hoped to define the kind of world that could emerge. He thought there were two possibilities. One was a society in which those who held power were purposely selected for their fitness; the other was a society in which power itself conferred upon its holders special gifts.

It is not hard to pin labels on these two possibilities.

Henry Ward Beecher and the brothel

HENRY WARD BEECHER was the pastor of a fashionable church in Brooklyn. From 1865 to 1885 he headed the Plymouth Congregational Church, during which time he impressed all with his oratory and became a powerful voice in the Republican Party. Recently I thumbed through one of Henry Ward Beecher's books, *Twelve Lectures to Young Men*, published by Appleton in 1902.

Mr. Beecher was an amazing man. He not only survived a

devastating scandal but kept his church and his reputation, too. One of his best friends accused him of adultery. Theodore Tilton brought the suit and he had the goods on Beecher. Mrs. Tilton, Beecher's lover, was a gabby sort of gal, and in the fall of 1868 she told her best friend, Susan B. Anthony, that she and Henry Ward were enjoying some of the slap and tickle of an afternoon every now and then. Then Mrs. Tilton told her mother and after running out of close confidants, she told her husband, the Beecher-worshiping schnook, Theodore Tilton. Needless to say, this information terribly disappointed Mr. Tilton, and, also, Mr. Beecher didn't seem of the same heroic proportions anymore. What to do?

Mr. Tilton confided in one of the pillars of the congregation, a certain Mr. Molton, a personal friend of both Beecher and Tilton. Mr. Molton cautioned discretion, which meant —silence.

Not too long after this, Tilton was all shook up when a scandal sheet operated by Victoria Woodhull, the first woman ever to run for President of the United States, published the whole steamy story of Beecher's dalliance with Mrs. Tilton. Molton hadn't advised Susan B. Anthony and Susie was spreading the word. The sordid details made Mr. Tilton mad. And they made Mr. Molton mad. And maddest of all was Henry Ward Beecher. Tilton did the manly thing—he took Henry Ward to court and sued him. Beecher did everything he could to save his neck. He said he hadn't wanted relations with Mrs. Tilton, she had forced herself on him and what was a fellow to do?

Meanwhile, back at the fashionable Plymouth Congregational, the thin plot thickened when Henry C. Bowen stood up and declared that Beecher had had his evil way with Mrs. Bowen, too. Mrs. Bowen had confessed all to her husband on her death bed.

The trial ended in disagreement, a Mexican standoff. Neither Tilton nor Beecher had satisfaction. Beecher recovered from the blow, however. He was a genius at gauging public opinion and getting in step. Coming from a family of famous abolitionists, he did not speak out against slavery until others made it safe to do so. After the war he urged immediate reconciliation with the South on honorable terms, but switched this argument when he saw the pack racing after President Andrew Johnson.

I remembered all this reading Henry Ward Beecher's warnings to young men to avoid the brothel.

Wrote Henry:

> The flowers grow richer, their odors exhilarate, the very fruit breathes perfume, the birds themselves seem intoxicated with delight . . . soft and silvery music steals along the air. Are they angels? You say, O fool that I was to Fear this place. Ridiculous priest to tell me that death lurks here where all is beauty and fragrance. This is all the heaven I need. Now he comes closer, closer, ever closer. Into his ear the beautiful herald pours the sweetest sounds of love. Hail and welcome. Now it is too late. He has gone in who shall never return. He goeth after her straightway as an ox goeth to slaughter. For this moment of revelry you are selling heaven . . . and all night you will sigh and weep, "Mother, mother."

Henry Ward Beecher, unctuous as only an adulterous preacher can be, gave hypocritical advice that was pure junk. The brothel was much more representative of morality than this old goat imagined. It was the brothel that helped guarantee the purity of wives, daughters, and sisters. Young men who thought of sex outside of marriage always conceived of it in terms of the brothel, and the brothels only.

Though indeed the brothel has just about disappeared from the scene, prostitution has never abated one whit. The Henry Ward Beechers and the Mrs. Tiltons of their day went

81

after the legalized brothel and helped its demise. They would not have been successful except that after World War I there was a new attitude about sex outside of marriage. The growing "amateur competition" put most of the decent prostitutes out of business and eventually closed down the red-light districts. The brothel has been one of mankind's most valuable institutions. The "fallen woman"—it was she who established the "decency" of her sister in respectable society.

William Randolph Hearst

I WAS reading of the brutal kidnapping of Patricia Campbell Hearst and of the torment of her father, San Francisco *Examiner* publisher Randolph A. Hearst, and Mrs. Hearst.

And this made me think back to my days on the Lower East Side of New York.

The immigrants loved young Patricia's grandfather, the late William Randolph Hearst, especially during his "socialist" days. You will recall that the late publisher had run for mayor of New York on a platform pledging "municipal ownership" of all public utilities—gas, electricity, etc.

But Hearst did much more to endear himself to the immigrant groups. On St. Patrick's Day the outside pages of the *Evening Journal* were printed on green newsprint. On Easter Sunday there was a full-page drawing of the Resurrection. On Columbus Day the New York *American* put the Italian flag beside the Stars and Stripes on the masthead; and on Yom Kippur the *American* devoted two inside pages to photographs of the blowing of the *shofar* and other scenes from the synagogues and temples of New York.

And in those days there would be a two-column photograph of William Randolph Hearst below a headline—GOING TO EUROPE—and upon his return from abroad there would be fifty newspaper reporters at quarantine writing down the great man's opinions on "the state of the world and its future."

But then came the labor unions and government expanded its facilities into the realm of welfare, health, and human relations, and the kindly Mr. Hearst felt that he was being robbed of his prerogative of "doing good."

But it was just that the whole thing became too big for any of us, including even a W. R. Hearst.

But this was a fabulous man, the late William Randolph Hearst, and make no mistake. It was good to have lived in at least part of his generation, and as time goes on, you realize more and more that you somehow miss him; you miss his individualism and you miss getting mad at him. Somehow none of the mediocrities rattling around the country arouse your ire as did this Mr. Hearst.

Mr. Hearst spared no expense when it came to hiring the best men in the profession and following up a good story. My close friend the late Jimmy Street (*Nothing Sacred, The Biscuit Eater, Goodbye, My Lady*, etc.) worked for Mr. Hearst on and off for many years. Once Jimmy was in a saloon somewhere between Cairo and Addis Ababa and running short of money. He wired Mr. Hearst that he needed another six hundred dollars in expenses to find the Magic Carpet and Mr. Hearst cabled him the money.

His great driving ambition, of course, was to be elected to the Presidency of the United States. He made no secret of this ambition. And why not? Much lesser men than William Randolph Hearst became Presidents. He had wealth, brains, energy, and a tremendous personality. If he had won the prize, it is extremely likely that he would have implemented the famous Socialist Party platform long before Roosevelt, Truman, and Eisenhower adopted it as their own. Hearst soured on "socialism" only when he realized that he would never be called upon to serve.

Charlie Murphy, the boss of Tammany Hall, had more to do with frustrating Mr. Hearst's ambition than any other man in the life of that great publisher. They made political deals; they consulted each other often, but there was something about the Irish Tammany chieftain that drove him, too, and one of his great ambitions was to prevent William Randolph Hearst from becoming President of the United States. Why? We'll never really know.

If Mr. Hearst had beaten Charles Evans Hughes for the New York governorship, it would have been difficult to stop him at the Democratic Convention in 1912, which resulted in Wilson's election.

Just imagine to what lengths Mr. Murphy was willing to go in order to stop William Randolph Hearst. To beat Hearst meant the loss to Tammany and the Democratic Party of the entire state government; the election of Hughes; no politician could do "business" with the high-minded and completely incorruptible Judge Charles Evans Hughes.

The story around New York was that Mr. Murphy had said to Hearst, "You want to be governor, it will cost one million dollars." And Mr. Hearst was supposed to have brought the million. Then Murphy nominated the publisher, but a week before election sent word down to all his henchmen and workers, "Cut this fellow's heart out." And of course the precinct workers followed instructions to the letter. Around midnight of Election Day a Tammany chieftain of the borough of Brooklyn was heard to say, "I have just done the dirtiest day's work of my entire life."

The beloved Gaynor

IT IS interesting how many people throughout the country remember the great Mayor William J. Gaynor of New York (in office 1910-1913) with such kindness and respect. I wrote a story about him and received hundreds of letters, most of them from elderly New Yorkers.

84

I'd like to add a few things about Gaynor.

Here is a story that two well-known biographers have attributed to Woodrow Wilson, and a third biographer has attributed to Fiorello La Guardia, but that is one hundred percent pure GAYNOR. It was a letter dated August 1, 1911, and addressed to a Mr. Reiss. A city magistrate had just died and this Mr. Reiss wrote to Mayor Gaynor offering himself as a candidate "to take the deceased judge's place."

Mayor Gaynor replied, "I have no objection to your taking the deceased judge's place, but you'll have to arrange it with the undertaker."

There was a letter Mayor Gaynor wrote a Mr. O'Gilby of Staten Island on May 23, 1912. Mr. O'Gilby had complained about the lack of police protection and that his chickens were being stolen. Gaynor replied, "I sympathize with you in the loss of your chickens. You have sixty-five policemen in your precinct and a few more won't solve your problem. The thing for you to do is to train your chickens to roost higher."

Another Gaynor letter touched me deeply. I'd like you to think of the two good men involved and then reconstruct in your mind the circumstances of the moment, and you'll shed a tear, too:

April 18, 1912
Dr. John H. Finley, President
College of the City of New York

MY DEAR DOCTOR FINLEY:
I cannot spend the evening with you as I had hoped. I am sitting here considering the death of those who went down on the steamship "Titanic," and I am preparing to take care of the survivors of that awful catastrophe upon their arrival here tonight.

WILLIAM J. GAYNOR

The old-time waiters

THE OLD-TIME waiters were the finest gentlemen in the world. When I sold newspapers outside Captain Churchill's Restaurant at Forty-ninth Street and Broadway I remember the respect and dignity these waiters had and the respect and dignity they accorded everyone, even the newsboys.

The headwaiter let me sell my papers in Churchill's because he wanted to give the newsboy a chance—the true mark of the gentleman.

One of the finest gentlemen I ever knew was a Mr. Newman, who had a hatchecking concession in one of the night-clubs. I met Mr. Newman sometime in the 1930's and he was eighty then. In his hatchecking booth he had a framed picture of himself and a friend, both young waiters in their white jackets, their towels draped over their arms. The friend in the picture with Mr. Newman was Mr. Munchenheim, who rose from waiter to owner of the Astor Hotel.

I wish these old waiters all the luck in the world and a long life. Next to newspaperman, I love best the men and women who wait on the tables in our restaurants, cafés, and hotels. And I regret that the chrome-lined cafeteria and the pine-paneled, dimly lit cocktail lounge have conspired to foist upon us their inhospitable impersonality and indigestion. I pity the diners who never knew the civilization of an eight-course meal well served.

The waiters and "toting"

THE HISTORY of the waiters and their ever-continuing fight with the Internal Revenue Service will one day make good reading for future sociologists, for nothing will tell us more about life in the American middle class than this fight.

Do tips count as income? How do you estimate your tips? Do meals count as income? How do you estimate these?

The tax man says yes, meals are income because otherwise the waiter would have to pay for them. The waiters say they'd bring their sandwiches to work.

I am with the waiters in this struggle. Not only logic but tradition is on their side. The Internal Revenue is trying to drag us back to the days of "toting."

"Toting" is a form of payment first introduced to the United States through slavery. It was an established custom among the blacks of the South even after the Emancipation Proclamation. Thousands upon thousands of Southerners paid a black, say, five dollars a month for his services with "toting." "Toting" was a special privilege. Not every black received it, some worked with "toting," some without.

If he had this privilege, a black toted home what food he needed for his family either from his master's storehouse or from his master's table.

The late novelist Sam Ornitz introduced this conception to the New York law courts. In his earlier years he had been a probation officer.

A black man was brought before the court charged with stealing food from his employer, one of the university clubs in New York. The indictment charged he had stolen over a thousand dollars' worth of food during his eighteen months as a waiter.

Sam Ornitz prevailed upon this fellow to change his plea to not guilty and helped him get a lawyer to base his plea on the old custom of "toting."

The waiter came from South Carolina, where "toting" was the custom of the land.

In the university club this fellow had been receiving twenty-five dollars a month, which was not at all sufficient to feed his family, and since he came from "toting" country, he naturally readopted the system. A South Carolina college professor was a corroborating witness and the man was acquitted. He proved that the food he took every evening was enough to feed his family, no more and no less.

Now the waiters are being told their "toting" should be recorded on their income-tax returns. "Toting" was never much more than the leftovers. We haven't progressed so far after all.

Wilshire Boulevard

I HAVE often wondered whether the big planters of the Sacramento Valley, the rich Knowland family, the Pacific Gas and Electric Company, the Chandlers of Los Angeles, and all the other great Republicans of the California empire are aware of the fact that Wilshire Boulevard was named after a rip-roaring socialist.

When the American socialist movement was at its height in the days of Eugene V. Debs, Victor Berger, Morris Hillquit, and J. A. Wayland, Mr. Gaylord Wilshire was making quite a stir with his radical paper, *Wilshire's Magazine*, and one of his writers was Upton Sinclair. Of course, some of the most dedicated socialists did not like Wilshire. They claimed that he used his radical paper to sell gold-mining stock. Wilshire was of British extraction. He had a Vandyke beard and wore pince-nez glasses attached to a black ribbon. He looked like a successful obstetrician, although no one could really attack his sincerity about the need for economic reform. However, it is also true that Mr. Wilshire was torn between two great causes: (a) his devotion to the cause of socialism and (b) his devotion to making money. He dabbled in Los Angeles real estate successfully and that's how Wilshire Boulevard got its name.

Eventually he gave up his money-making schemes because he said the capitalist press was after him, and in his last years he settled down to selling a contraption that was called "the magic horse collar" by the American Medical Association. Wilshire claimed therapeutic values for this gadget. You attached it to an electric outlet and put it on your neck and the vibrations were supposed to cure you of rheumatism, fatigue, loss of appetite, cancer, tuberculosis, and most of the other ailments. The horse collar sold for fifty-six dollars and was advertised all over the country, often in full-page ads. Wilshire died in 1928, a rich man for the third or fourth time in his life.

The mysterious Mr. Andrews

He was a short man with a dark complexion in an old coat and dirty hat who introduced himself as John Andrews and said he was a Portuguese. It was during July of 1917 and after a long wait he had come to the Secretary of the Navy with a startling proposal.

"I can furnish a substitute for gasoline that will cost only two cents a gallon," he said. "My invention is yours exclusively, but you must pay me two million dollars spot cash."

The Secretary of the Navy was Josephus Daniels. He and his assistant secretary, Franklin D. Roosevelt, had been hard pressed to keep the Navy and Merchant Marine running. Prices were sky high. Oil was scarce.

"Buy it, Chief," said Roosevelt.

The Secretary leaned forward and asked, "What guarantees can you give that this invention of yours is practicable?"

"State any conditions you want," said John Andrews.

"You're on," said Daniels.

Two days later Andrews appeared at the Brooklyn Navy Yard and informed the duty officer that he had an appointment to demonstrate that he could propel gas engines with water as fuel.

An admiral showed the furtive Andrews a launch that rested in dry dock, its fuel tank empty.

Andrews carried nothing with him save a small gallon can, which was empty, and a doctor's satchel. He asked for a gallon of water. When it was brought to him, he took his empty can, his satchel, and the water and disappeared into the back seat of his Packard. He emerged in a few minutes carrying the can now filled with water. He poured it into the launch's gas tank, made a few adjustments in the carburetor, and presto, the motor kicked and the propeller spun. It sputtered once and Andrews poured six drops from a small vial into the tank and the motor surged ahead.

When he had finished, the admiral said, "I believe you have something there, Mr. Andrews, but how do I know you didn't switch cans on me while in the car?"

Andrews offered to repeat the experiment. The officers lead him to a small brick building, a one-room affair where there was no chance of hiding anything or of draining any water.

Once again Andrews was furnished with a bucket of water. In a few minutes he came from the room carrying the gallon can. The launch's gas tank was drained and Andrews poured in his curious mixture. The motor worked this time better than before. Andrews had performed a miracle.

The next time he met the Secretary of the Navy, it was no casual interview.

"We are prepared to buy your formula," said Secretary Daniels. "There are conditions. You must guarantee that there are sufficient chemicals available for us to run the Navy and that their cost is not prohibitive."

Still dressed in the shabby clothing, Andrews answered, "The chemicals are in plentiful supply and it will cost no more than I said it would—two cents a gallon."

"Very well," said the Secretary, "we will place two million dollars in escrow in any bank you name and the money is

90

yours as soon as you have taught ten officers how to mix this stuff in quantity."

"No," said John Andrews, "two million dollars cash first."

"This is public money," explained Daniels. "I've got to know what you're selling."

"You're haggling," accused Andrews.

"We can't buy a 'pig in the poke,' " said Roosevelt. "Just tell us your ingredients and the money is yours."

"I can sell this invention to a government that won't haggle," said Andrews, and he turned and left. Disappeared. Nor was he ever heard of again. He had vanished once and for all.

The fact that nothing was heard of him again and that no one else ever used his invention suggests that there was something of a fraud about his claim. Yet he had carried no special apparatus and there was water in the tank of that Navy launch. What it was, neither the Navy nor the world will ever know, because John Andrews that July day vanished from the face of the earth.

Prohibition judges

AT THE University of North Carolina in Chapel Hill the jurists of North Carolina formed a commission to advise on how to charge the jury in more understandable terms and achieve a consistency in sentencing. Daily in North Carolina one judge will sentence a man to twenty years for the same crime for which another judge sentences a man to two years.

This type of reform is hard to attain because people don't care much what happens to convicted criminals.

During Prohibition, which President Eisenhower called the "noble experiment," Judge A. M. J. Cochrane of Kentucky sentenced a man to five years in the federal penitentiary on the evidence of a mash stain on the man's vest.

Southern boys were terribly disadvantaged by the federal Prohibition law. Before the passage of the Volstead Act, the revenooers used to destroy their stills, fine them a few dollars, and lock them up for three months. Once moonshining became a federal crime, the federal judges of the South, to a man fanatical Prohibitionists, imposed maximum sentences.

Judge John McClintock was as mean as Cochrane. He was a circuit judge traveling the districts in West Virginia. Often his courtroom was a clearing in a backwoods area. He would announce to all the moonshiners, "Those pleading guilty, step over here. Those not guilty, over there."

When the defendants divided, McClintock would say, "I'm being lenient with those who plead guilty. I'm giving each of you only three years." When court reconvened in the morning, a great many defendants changed their pleas.

At the same time, in New York City, Judge Francis J. Coleman, who hated Prohibition, gave Big Bill Dwyer, who owned a fleet of rum-running ships, a year and a day plus a one-thousand-dollar fine.

The Justice Department once assigned McClintock to one of the Manhattan benches when its presiding judge died suddenly. The New York bootleggers, part of the organized crime syndicate, had, as a matter of custom, pleaded guilty to their offenses and paid fines of one hundred dollars.

That first morning McClintock presided, he came near to dealing a deathblow to organized crime. He handed out ten-year sentences with the facility of a cardsharp tossing aces. At noon the Justice Department had to prevail upon the New York City police to disperse the eight waiting sedans that lined the streets, each car containing a hood with a machine gun waiting for McClintock's exit from the court.

The night he died there was sustained cheering in the cellblocks of the federal penitentiaries all over the country.

It is well to remember that there are several hit-and-run drivers out on suspended sentences while the late Martin

Luther King pulled time for trying to integrate a public facility.

Ruth Snyder and Judd Gray

BLONDE RUTH SNYDER provided New Yorkers with one of the most sensational murder cases of the 1920's. It was the case of Ruth and her lover, Henry Judd Gray. If there ever was a man who did not look like a lover, it was this mousy little corset salesman. Ruth was a good-looking blonde who looked for all the world like just another substantial suburban housewife, taking care of her home and rushing to the station to pick up her husband every night. Her husband, Albert Snyder, was a quiet gent, an art editor on a trade paper. Said Alexander Woollcott: "Ruth Snyder is so like the woman across the street that many an American husband will be haunted by an unconfessed realization that she also bears an embarrassing resemblance to the woman across the breakfast table."

It was in March, 1927, when Ruth Snyder and Gray decided to get rid of Ruth's husband, Albert. They decided to commit the perfect murder, collect the twenty-thousand-dollar life insurance, and live happily ever after. Judd rode up to Syracuse with his corset samples, checked into his usual hotel, left his samples, messed up the bed, and sneaked out again. He put a sign on the door, "Do not disturb," and walked down the rear stairs and out the service exit. He then doubled back to New York and to the Snyder home. It was now past midnight. Husband Albert was sound asleep. The conspirators had an added advantage. Husband Albert had defective hearing and did not sleep with his hearing aid. Ruth let Judd into the house and they sat in the kitchen talking over the program for the night. Ruth showed Judd a bottle of chloroform. They were to give Albert a whiff of the stuff first so that it wouldn't hurt too much when they cracked his skull. Around one in the morning ice-water-in-the-veins Ruth and jellyfish Judd went to work. Ruth was willing to do all the planning and to provide the tools, but she did not want to do the actual killing. That was to be Judd's job.

But the little corset salesman did everything wrong. First Judd fumbled with the handkerchief and the chloroform. When he saw husband Albert stirring as though he had been tickled in the nose, Judd got frantic and poured the whole bottle of chloroform on the victim's face. This sent the two perfect murderers running from the room using their handkerchiefs for gas masks. They listened for a while and when they heard nothing, they tiptoed back. Ruth handed Judd a window sash weight. That was to be the second step. Judd crashed the weapon in the direction of Albert's head, but he kept his eyes closed and just barely skinned Albert's forehead. Then Juddy-boy dropped the sash weight on the floor. The thing didn't look decisive to Ruthie. She picked up the sash weight, said, "Look, like this," and with both hands cracked down on Albert's head—dead center.

Step No. 3 was the picture wire. Ruth pulled that out from under her housecoat. She straightened it out as Judd wound it around Albert's neck, winding it three times. Then they both pulled. They watched for a couple of minutes and when Albert didn't move, they turned out his light and tiptoed out to the kitchen again. There Ruth pulled out a bottle of bootleg scotch and they hoisted a few. But back to work. Now for the perfect crime. Ruth and Judd started to make it look like robbery—pulling out drawers and turning over chairs. Finally Judd tied up Ruth, but not too tightly, kissed her good night, and caught the 3:40 train back to Syracuse.

He got to his room without attracting any attention and went to sleep. Ruth struggled out of her bonds and ran for help. It was now 5 A.M. Even our modern television cops would have suspected something. Why would a robber spend

94

four hours pouring chloroform, cracking sash weights, and winding picture wire around a victim's neck, assuming that such a crazy man decided to rob a modest suburban home occupied by a four-thousand-dollar-a-year trade-paper employee? The trail at once led to lover-boy Judd. Judd said he had been in Syracuse all night. So the cops went to his room to see and they found it all in the wastebasket. Judd had thrown a timetable into the basket. The timetable was carefully documented with Judd's check marks. "Arrive Syracuse." "Leaving Syracuse." "Leaving New York." All in the same night. Judd heaved a sigh of relief and told all.

The trial took place in April and May of 1927, and both Judd and Ruth had previously signed full confessions. Judd blamed Ruth for everything. She made me do it, he said. It was her idea. Ruth sat in the courtroom showing no emotion except contempt for Judd. The women spectators loved the guy and cheered him at every turn. They all ah'd at this little corset salesman. No one can understand women. Women show no sympathy for a murderer for profit like the killer of a bank teller, but if sex is involved, they go all out. Warden Lewis E. Lawes has written that every sex murderer receives packages, flowers, candy, Bibles, and proposals of marriage. The newspaper people really went to town during the Ruth Snyder-Judd Gray trial. Miss Watkins, a reporter for the Scripps-Howard *Telegram*, wrote about the courtroom crowd: "They came for gore and they got gore . . . nauseating details of the lacerating blows on Snyder's skull . . . of the blood that squirted from nostrils and ears, of the tongue swollen thick as he strangled." Miss Dixon of the same newspaper gave her opinion: "Ruth Snyder is oversexed . . . in the presence of men her pores open and desire exudes therefrom." Hearst covered the case from every angle. David Belasco, the great man of the stage, was one of his experts and was described as the "supreme diagnostician of the human heart; psychoanalyst who can translate the beats of the heart into flaming, fascinating pictures that live and breathe."

Ruth Snyder and Judd Gray were convicted and sentenced to die in the electric chair. After the formal appeals they both went to execution on January 13, 1928. Gene Fowler wrote the story for the New York *American*:

> "Jesus have mercy," came the pitiful cry. Ruth's blue eyes were red with weeping. Her face was strangely old. The blonde bobbed hair, hanging in stringy bunches over her furrowed brow, seemed almost white with years of toil and suffering as the six dazzling, high-powered lights illuminated every bit of Ruth's agonized lineaments.
>
> Tightly corseted by the black leather bands, Ruth was flabby and futile as the blast struck her. Her body went forward as far as the restraining thongs would permit.
>
> The tired form was taut. The body that once throbbed with the joy of her sordid bacchanals turned brick red as the current struck. Slowly, after half a minute of the death-dealing current, the exposed arms, right leg, throat, and jaws bleached out again.

There was yet another sensation. A photographer of the New York *Daily News* obtained entrance to the execution chamber as a legal witness. Although like all the others he had been put on his honor by Warden Lawes not to attempt to take any pictures, he had a specially devised camera strapped to his ankle. He got a picture of Ruth Snyder at the instant of death. The next morning the portrait was splashed across the whole front page of the *Daily News*. A few years ago a fellow sold a copy of that issue for fifty dollars.

My father's compliment

MY FATHER had no idea whatever of money; to him it was a complete nuisance. Once he was going to Canada and I took him to the railroad station. Suddenly I asked him if he had any money and he said, sure, he had money, and he opened his wallet and there was one of those large, old-fashioned dollar bills. I said, "You are going to a foreign country, you'll need money," but he brushed me aside.

"I have my tickets, the committee meets me at the station, takes me to a home, and in a few days they escort me back to the station," he said. Sure enough, he returned with that big dollar bill intact. He wore a Prince Albert coat and carried a cane and on the Sabbath he wore a high silk hat. His only luxuries were a couple of brandies a day and cigarettes. For years he made his own cigarettes with a small machine. You attached the paper to a roller, put the proper quantity of tobacco into a little well, and then rolled. He turned them out by the dozen.

Years later, when he cut down on smoking, he bought factory-made cigarettes. They were called Afternoons, and they had a long mouthpiece. I do not see them anymore, and I suppose they are off the market. Another similar brand was called Fifth Avenue. But beyond these two luxuries, my father devoted his whole life to talk—good talk—the favorite Jewish pastime. When he was close to eighty, he had a slight stroke; not enough to put him to bed, but a stroke nevertheless. He returned from the doctor with a list of what to do and what not to do. The first thing I did was pour him out a good drink of brandy. He picked up the glass, held it up to the light, rolled it in his fingers, smiled, and said, "I have a smart son; the doctor tells an eighty-year-old man, who has used brandy for sixty years, never to touch another drop, and the first thing you do is pour me a drink—I call that wisdom."

This was the greatest compliment I ever received.

The secret of long life

THE SECRET of long life is—involvement. When my father visited me, he never asked me, "How's business?" or even, "How're the children?" but he pulled clippings out of his pockets and angrily said, "Did you see that editorial in this morning's paper? Let's answer it." My father was involved in mankind and that is why he lived into his eighties.

A man is like a tree; he dies on top first.

The perfect year

I HAVE never had much passion for the New Year. First, I was never that eager to see a year slip away. There was always something I wanted to preserve out of each section of life and New Year's Eve always made me realize it was gone forever. New Year's Eve is like always coming back upon your fortieth birthday. The first time around is enough to make a man shiver.

Looking back, the year 1925 seems to have been for me the year that was absolutely without personal anguish.

Would I want to repeat the year?

No, of course I wouldn't. It would be nice to be young again, in good health, with no cavities, no debts, no vast mistakes. But I already know how a lot of things turned out. I doubt I could enjoy 1925 again realizing Sacco and Vanzetti were languishing in jail, nor could I enjoy the champagne realizing that Prohibition was giving organized crime a tenacious foothold in the American economy, and certainly I would be without restraint in prophesying who would fly the Atlantic ocean alone and when.

What makes age bearable is the expectation we are going to see how some things turn out. My father was quite old when he died, way out there on old age, and one of the last discussions I had with him was about World War II.

He suspected he wouldn't live to see its end and I assured him of course he would. He held up his hand and said he probably wouldn't, but he really wanted to see how the whole thing turned out. Then, after a long pause, he said, "Of course there is always something we want to see turn out. If I were the only man who didn't get to see how some things turned out, I would write the Congressman. But there were events Washington didn't see and still others Jefferson missed."

The Roosevelts

THEODORE ROOSEVELT was our twenty-sixth President, a man with a mustache and a cigar, who loved to hunt wild animals, liked to be where the action was, and enjoyed big families. My father always said slowly, "Rawza-veldt," to make his name last longer, or, in a lighter mood, he would refer to him matter-of-factly as plain Tudder, Yiddish for Theodore.

Eleanor Roosevelt was her husand's legs. She went where he could not manage to go in a wheelchair and thus visited hospitals, miners in the basement of the earth, ladies' teas, and tough, political debates. I remember her as a skinny, long-legged woman in bloomers and black stockings, teaching dancing to the little kids in the settlement house on the Lower East Side of New York. Like Mary Poppins, she looked like an exclamation mark. She was beautiful though homely, noble though humble.

Franklin D. Roosevelt, our thirty-second President, brought hope to America during the dark depression and the Second World War. He led first a hungry nation, then a warring one. He led his people out of the shadow of darkness by assuring them that the only thing they need fear was fear itself.

Justice Michael Musmanno

THE LATE Michael Musmanno, justice of the Supreme Court of Pennsylvania and the author of eleven books, was one of the judges at the Nuremberg Trials. He sat in judgment of the *Einsatzgruppen*, those Nazi murdering squads that machine-gunned Jews.

In the last few years of his life Justice Musmanno did a lot of lecturing before Jewish audiences, particularly Bonds for Israel and United Jewish Appeal gatherings.

When he arrived on the dais, shaking hands with the functionaries, Judge Musmanno carried with him a briefcase. The folks always suspected that in that briefcase rested the notes and pages from which Musmanno would later compose what he had to say. But they were mistaken.

There was no speech within the briefcase. Instead Justice Musmanno carried in it olive oil, butter, and cream, those very staples that he knew would not be served him at a kosher table.

Justice Musmanno, for example, knew that the sight of butter could prove offensive to his hosts. So he did not withdraw a plate of the seventy-cent spread, but rather two buttered rolls that he had the foresight to prepare in the sanctity of his hotel room. The olive oil, of course, was withdrawn and poured over the salad and put back before anyone else would really begin to conjecture what the good judge was doing.

Before he died, Musmanno received the Four Freedoms Award, a prize he more than earned during his lifetime of dedication to justice. As a young attorney, Michael Musmanno read about the Sacco-Vanzetti case and immediately took a train to Boston, where he enlisted in the cause of the defense for the duration. He was in fact an attorney of record, assisting the chief defense counsel, Mr. Thompson.

What Jew would begrudge him his olive oil, his butter, and his cream?

Point of view

"IF I am right the Germans will say I was a German, and the French will say I was a Jew; if I am wrong the Germans will say I was a Jew and the French will say I was a German."—Albert Einstein.

The innovative *schnorrer*

I HAVE found a new *schnorrer* (professional beggar) with a brand-new idea. This fellow, Bennett by name, checks into the best hotel. He stays a few days, then takes to his bed, and on the night table are medicine bottles, tubes, and vials. He calls the clerk and asks him to call the local rabbi. The rabbi arrives and Bennett says he is sick and has no relatives. He was on his way to Miami for a job but came down with this spell. No, a doctor will not do any good, he has a chronic back ailment that has defied diagnosis. All he wants of the rabbi is a promise that if he should die in this strange town, the rabbi will somehow find a way to bury him on consecrated ground.

Two days later the fellow has recovered somewhat and goes to see the rabbi, who is still very sad when he sees the patient. After a while the *schnorrer* says that he is stranded, the sudden spell of illness has taken all his available money; he needs fifty dollars for his hotel bill and laundry and another fifty dollars for gas and oil to get him on his way. The rabbi goes to see some people. In one, two, the hundred dollars was ready for the fellow when a member of the community happened to be talking to a relative in Winston-Salem. He mentioned the plight of this poor fellow and the Winston-Salem man howled, "Why, that's exactly what he did here." This cost Bennett the second fifty dollars. The folks decided to pay his hotel bill as a matter of communal policy and told him to "git."

I admit this is an original idea, but it is far too risky to be consistently effective. I still say that Jacobson is the top *schnorrer* in my book. You will recall I wrote two articles about him last year. I miss him terribly and even welcome those abusive letters he sends me from his winter home in Miami and his summer home in New York.

David Ben-Gurion

THE LAST time I saw Ben-Gurion, the only Israeli of Biblical proportions, I drove from Tel Aviv into the Negev to his kibbutz, Sdeh Boker. The trip took a Friday afternoon and a Saturday morning. I stopped overnight at Beersheba.

It is hot driving into the Negev, a Hebrew word that means simply "south." It is so hot you see the camels running north.

I followed a scraggly desert path at Sdeh Boker to his home, a rude affair, a corrugated tin roof covering a small wooden bungalow. An old lock secured a sun-beaten door.

The sentry told me David Ben-Gurion had been called to Tel Aviv that morning. I could knock all I want. No one was going to answer. Clutching the four-dollar brandy I intended to present the old war horse, I went back to the car and drove to Tel Aviv, which I made at nightfall, having given a lift to a soldier at the gates of the kibbutz.

A day later I saw Ben-Gurion at his Tel Aviv villa. Villa is a word adored by the Israelis although it denotes nothing more than a cement house.

Bookshelves lined the walls of Ben-Gurion's three large rooms. The white tiled floors were covered with Persian rugs and Ben-Gurion sat behind a large desk piled on three fronts with newspapers, clippings, magazines, and manuscripts.

That morning we discussed Israeli politics. He apologized for missing me at the kibbutz. He had come back to Tel Aviv to tell the members of his political party he was resigning from the Knesset (Parliament). He would make his reasons clear later, he said. So for a while we discussed Sdeh Boker. He moved to Sdeh Boker after his prime ministership because it was a kibbutz and because it was in the Negev. Usually he insists that his visitors see him there. The Negev is Israel's future, said Ben-Gurion. It is the most underpopulated area in the country and, with the exceptions of the Sinai and Saudi Arabia, the most underpopulated area in the Middle East. Sdeh Boker was a new kibbutz, the goal of which is to become a self-contained community.

With water the Negev will become industrialized. Then Israel will find its markets in Africa and Asia. The Negev is nearer to both than to Europe. The Negev means independence. A country achieves economic independence only by vast and ever-continuing exports.

Ben-Gurion in his later years and now certainly in death represents both a political and moral force. He helped create Israel in the way King Arthur helped create England or George Washington the United States; and he is part of the land and the people in the way the prophets were part of the land and the people. He was a bantamweight, really, quite small, with white tufts of hair around his ears. He was the one Israeli who always wore a necktie though he affected slippers for comfort. He was a bantamweight with a gigantic vision.

A true short story

ALL THE letters and telegrams had been signed "Mrs. Ida Wasserman, program chairman." Arrangements as to date, hour, arrival, publicity, the reception, "with just a few people," before the speech; the procedure during the speech; and the reception, "with just a few people," after the speech. All these preliminaries were handled by mail, long-distance telephone, and telegrams by "Mrs. Ida Wasserman, program chairman."

Came the day and at the airport were three women to greet the speaker. "Mrs. Wasserman, anyone?" No, Mrs. Wasserman did not come to the airport. But at the reception "before the speech" there was no Mrs. Wasserman and this began to puzzle the speaker. In the large auditorium there were five women seated on the dais, the president, the vice president, the secretary, the treasurer, and the chaplain. The guest speaker went down the line shaking hands: "Mrs. Wasserman?" No, no Mrs. Wasserman. "But where is Mrs. Wasserman?" The answer from each of the five officers was neither yes nor no. A mystery.

Finally the speech was over, the question-and-answer period was over, and the guest speaker had disentangled himself from a few people around the platform and began walking toward the exit when suddenly a lady came toward him. "That was a good speech," she said, "I'm glad I came. I am Mrs. Wasserman."

"Mrs. Wasserman? The Ida Wasserman who arranged all of this?"

The lady smiled and said yes, she was indeed the Ida Wasserman who did all of the arranging, but somewhere along the way something happened that altered her status completely.

What happened? Mrs. Wasserman told me that for many years it has been the custom for the program chairman to introduce the speaker. "But this meeting began to snowball and it became the most important meeting in our history," she related, "and so the president insisted that this time she would introduce the speaker. The officers upheld her, so I resigned from the committee, I resigned from the temple, and I came here as a plain spectator."

A soft answer

A FRIEND of Winston Churchill once remarked, "Winnie, I never told you about my grandchildren, did I?"

"No," said Churchill, "and don't think I don't appreciate it."

Smile, Shorty, smile

THERE IS no doubt that the short fellow is at a tremendous disadvantage, not only in watching a parade but at every other level of our daily lives.

In a recent survey we find that bank presidents are five feet ten and a half inches tall, while the bank clerks are five feet, nine inches (it should happen to me already). They found that the sales managers were five feet ten and a half inches, while the salesmen were five feet, nine inches. I am sure this is true in love, salesmanship, or politics.

Colonel Harvey and the other Republicans in the famous smoke-filled room picked Warren G. Harding because he "looked like a President" more than any of the other compromise candidates. This was actually stated as one of the reasons for the choice of the Ohio Senator, God rest his soul.

When Daniel Webster stood on the platform and shouted, "If you dissolve the Whig Party, where will I go?" the delegates would have said, "What do we care where you go?" if he had been a little guy. But when they saw that magnificent head, those shaggy eyebrows, and that fine figure of a man, they said to one another, "Where indeed will he go?" And they kept the party alive for another few years.

Gemma La Guardia Gluck

GEMMA LA GUARDIA GLUCK died in her apartment in New York at the age of eighty-one. She had been a teacher and a translator and she had married a Hungarian Jew named Herman Gluck and had lived with her husband in Budapest during World War II.

When the mayor of New York City, Fiorello La Guardia, said of the Nazi regime that it was a government composed of gangsters, the Nazis arrested Gemma, his oldest sister, and her husband. She was confined in concentration camps until the end of the war.

The interesting thing about this is that the Germans killed her husband along with the six million Jews of Europe, but they never killed Gemma. In the last days of the war, when the Russians were overrunning Hungary, the Germans made haste to transport Mrs. Gluck to a German concentration camp in the interior. Even as the Nazis faced certain defeat, they sped up the work of the incinerators, to kill as many more as possible.

But they did not kill Gemma La Guardia Gluck, whose survival gives us a key as to why the six million Jews perished.

The reason the Nazis did not kill her is that they knew someone was "interested" in her. The mayor of New York City was their sworn enemy, and though he was powerless to save his sister, the Nazi murderers knew they did not dare kill her.

At the Evian Conference the nations of the world refused to consider the acceptance of Jewish emigration from Nazi Europe. When Eichmann's hostage emissary, Joel Brand, told Lord Moyne, the British high commissioner at Cairo, that it might be possible to ransom one hundred thousand Jews from Hungary, Lord Moyne said, "Where will we put one hundred thousand Jews?"

Such developments were like green lights to the gangsters of Nazidom.

I have steadily maintained that the Jews of Denmark were saved, not because the Danes were able to keep their plans a secret, but rather because the Nazis saw that an entire nation cared. That was the key to the survival of the few Jews of Denmark and of the survival of Gemma La Guardia Gluck. Somebody cared.

Rags to riches

THE LOCAL church and temple are bound to have at least one rummage sale a year. So is every other local church and temple. And what happens to the clothing no one buys? What happens to the secondhand clothing the Salvation Army cannot distribute?

Used-clothing dealers buy it. There are three such firms in New York and Chicago that have made their partners millionaires. Every item of wearing apparel finds its way into these plants—suits, shirts, dresses, overcoats, hats, nylon stockings, underwear, caps, all of them to be sorted, sterilized, and resold all over the world. The market lists such places as the Congo, West Africa, Pakistan, Indonesia, and India. Who knows? That cutaway coat some suburban husband finds too tight now dignifies a college professor in Sierra Leone.

The clothing that cannot be resold is cut into strips and sold as wipers and rags for industry. Workers use them to wipe their hands and to clean printing presses and silk screens. Furniture polishers use tons of the stuff annually. Some of this clothing is used for stuffing dolls and toys and still more is mixed with tar for roofing insulation.

Now one of the great by-products of used clothing are the buttons. Barrels of them line the processing plants. These barrels are sold to still other firms that dump the buttons into acid tanks to burn away the last of the threads. The buttons pass over huge screens that sort them according to size.

Cleaning establishments are good customers for second-hand buttons. They use them to replace buttons lost or broken in the cleaning or laundering of clothes. Secondhand-clothing stores and tailors buy them for similar reasons.

But the retail end of the enterprise—the sale of secondhand clothing in the United States itself—is a dying business. You can buy new garments for only slightly more than the second-hand clothing would have to bring, and you can buy the new clothing on the installment plan.

Part of this big business is in the sale of discarded or obsolete service uniforms. Army and Navy and Marine Corps uniforms are stripped of all identifying insignia and buttons and are shipped overseas where the military establishments of new countries hurriedly buy them. Algerians, Laotians, and Africans get these uniforms, put their own buttons on them, and they are ready to fight.

Clothes make the man—secondhand clothes no less than new ones.

Merger in Israel

I'VE BEEN thinking much about peddlers during the past year.

Today in Israel there are two kinds of peddlers. One is the classic old-clothes man familiar to most of us from the tenement districts of our big cities. The other is the bottle man. He buys only bottles and sells them back to the distilleries and soft-drink distributors. Bottles in Hebrew are called *bakbukim* and the peddler's call is "*Baaak-bu-kim*," and it is heard throughout the city.

Now I understand these peddlers are having a hard time. The Israeli society is growing affluent and they are no longer interested in old shoes. Plastics are killing the bottle trade.

The solution? The peddlers have merged. Nowadays the same peddler cries, *"Alte zahen! Baak-bu-kim!"* (old clothes and bottles).

Salesmen and solidarity

READERS OF my column know my deep interest in the salesman—the traveling man, the drummer, the man with the polished shoes and the latest cut in lapel.

The salesman has had it rough in recent years. The IBM machines take orders now. The buyer has become the anonymous merchandise engineer, and the big stores now have buying offices in big retail centers and thus eliminate the salesman altogether.

While the salesman has no tenure, as such, it is difficult to fire a Willie Loman after he has given most of his productive life to a firm. There are some employers who can fire such a man, but not many. It happens today through the merger. A salesman has been with the firm for thirty-five years; he is now sixty. He has established the trade; the firm knows that all he's actually doing is taking orders. Why continue to pay him thirty thousand dollars a year commission when a younger man can take those orders for ten thousand dollars?

There are mergers going on all over, particularly in "soft goods." The smaller manufacturers become stockholders in a large manufacturing complex.

Suddenly the sixty-year-old salesman receives a notice, his firm has been taken over by Chicago people of whom he never heard, and the Chicago people never heard of him, either. They send him a notice, "Please leave the samples at the home office the first chance you get," and that's that.

These problems have resulted in the salesmen talking of unionizing. What brought it to a head was a ruling that went against the National Association of Women's and Children's

Apparel Salesmen. This organization includes fifteen to sixteen thousand men and a few women who sell most of the ready-to-wear goods to the American stores. In recent years the ready-to-wear show has become important to the salesman, to his employer, to the customers. The show is a vast enterprise. It is set up in a key city in each state for the storekeepers in the entire area. It's a four-day vacation for them, during which they do their buying. The salesmen have regular showings, storerooms, and the considerable expense of these marts has paid off handsomely and made the life of the salesman easier and brought more business to his manufacturer.

This national association of salesmen, known as NAWCAS, is a fraternal society. One of its requirements is that a salesman participating in any show must have a signed contract with his employer. This requirement was for the protection of the salesman. It gave him tenure of a sort. But NAWCAS, being an association of people who are self-employed, was subject to the rules of the Federal Trade Commission. The Federal Trade Commission said the restrictions against a salesman without a contract is restraint of trade, a blow to free enterprise and to open competition.

What does NAWCAS have to offer the salesman if this "protection" is eliminated? Only one thing is left and that is to transfer jurisdiction over NAWCAS from the Federal Trade Commission to the National Labor Relations Board, which means becoming organized as a local of a union, and start singing "Solidarity Forever" instead of "Sweet Adeline."

The health test

Two OLDSTERS were discussing their good health.
Said one: "I eat good, sleep good, and drink good."
Said the other: "How about your wife, do you satisfy her?"

"I sure do, I come home, eat supper, and get into bed naked and my wife's naked. Then I say to my wife: 'Darling, I don't feel like doing anything tonight,' and she says, 'I'm satisfied.' "

Our friend, the undertaker

An UNDERTAKER is an ill-willer to the human race. He is by profession an enemy to his species. He never sees a picture of health but he longs to engrave it. He has a quick ear for a churchyard cough and a relish for music, to wit, the toll of Saint Sepulcher.

As a neighbor he is to be shunned. He watches your going out and your coming in, your rising up and your lying down, and all your domestic imports of drink and victual, so that the veriest she-gossip in the parish is not more familiar with your modes and means of living, nor knows so certainly whether the visitor that calls daily in his chariot is a mere friend or physician. Also he knows your age to a year, and your height to an inch, for he hath measured you with his eye for a coffin, and your ponderosity to a pound, for he hath an interest in the deadweight, and hath so far inquired into your fortune as to guess with what equipage you shall travel on your last journey—to be within sound of his hammering is to hear the knock at death's door. To be a friend with an undertaker is as impossible as to be the crony of a crocodile. He drinks to your good health, but hopes, secretly, it will not endure. He is glad to find you so hearty—as to be apoplectic—and rejoices to see you so stout—with a short neck. He compliments your complexion, when it is blue or yellow, admires your upright carriage, and hopes it will break down. Nevertheless, he hath one merit, and in this our world and in these our times it is a main one—namely, that whatever he "undertakes," he "performs."

111

The golden calf

HENDERSON BELK, one of the leading citizens of Charlotte and North Carolina, one of the owners of the largest retail department-store chain in the South, visited Israel and wrote me a letter of his impressions. Mr. Belk, who is a friend and on occasion a champion, is a religious man. He is a fundamentalist Protestant and he writes that what impressed him most about the Holy Land, what shocked him, was the economy; people were busy in offices and shops and were walking briskly along the streets with briefcases.

In other words, Israelis are "on the move." And this disappointed Mr. Belk.

I have heard this same disappointment expressed by American Jews who visit Israel. They expect to see the girls dancing the *horra*, the children clapping hands, and the men saying their prayers. They want Israel to be their *kappores* (a sacrifice as a means of atonement). Mr. Belk, a young millionaire, is also seeking a *kappores*. I do not blame him. We are all seeking it in many different ways. Mr. Belk was merely expressing a hope, a hope that out of the boredom of unrelieved buying and selling at these three hundred some Belk stores, he would find surcease. And where could he expect to find it but in the Holy Land? But Israel is surrounded by thirty million hostile Arabs, and they, too, are living in the atomic age, and the Israelis have interest to pay on bonds and on loans with which they have built power plants and factories.

People reflect the culture in which they live. Maybe Mr. Belk's dream will come true someday. America is still the dream world for everyone, including the Israelis. Once fellows stop cashing in on the stockpiling racket and the tax evaders start worrying about their own fraud instead of whether boys and girls are mixing together in the swimming pool, and the millions of Americans, Englishmen, French, and Germans stop chasing the golden calf, the Israelis will cease and desist, too, I am sure.

112

Test of character

THE NATION of Israel exists at all, at one level, because it was created by the United Nations twenty-five years ago, made possible by the decent instinct of civilized men and women who thought it important to let there be a Jewish nation in that part of the world inhabited by Jews for thousands of years.

The nation of Israel exists today, as a practical matter, because the United States supports the right of the young nation to survive. This is a blunt truth, one that the fiercely independent Israelis probably don't like. Yet it is a truth. Israeli soldiers have fought with a gallantry admired over the world. But without the continued availability of American weapons, without indeed probably the enormous financial support of the American Jewish community, Israel simply could not and would not survive.

Americans ought to feel a just pride in this country's support of Israel. The achievements of that young nation make up one of the success stories of human history. Moreover, anyone cherishing the ideals of human freedom and dignity can look to Israel with admiration and respect.

But the recent oil crisis, the cutbacks and threats of cutbacks from Arab nations, made one thing clear. Nations such as France and England and Japan would swap Israel's future for barrels of oil with just the same graceful hypocrisy and cowardice that a British prime minister once displayed in carving up someone else's country to appease Hitler.

Israel's right to exist is likely to be the American test of character in the 1970's.

The Arabs—new arrivals

PALESTINE WAS never, in all history, an Arab state. That area was, prior to 1900, a Jewish state.

Prior to 1922, Jordan was a part (three-fourths) of Palestine.

Prior to 1948, neither East Jerusalem nor the west bank was part of Jordan.

The Gaza area of Palestine was never any part of Egypt.

The Sinai Peninsula was never an Arab state or part of Egypt. For four hundred years prior to 1900 Sinai was a colony of Turkey. After 1900 Egypt, "by acts of aggression against Turkey," dominated the Bedouin in Sinai, but never permitted them to become citizens of Egypt.

The Jews did not displace the Arabs in Palestine. Arabs were displaced by the Arab commanders who ordered them out of Palestine to await return after the Arabs shall have driven the Jews into the sea. Anyway, 250,000 Arabs remained in Palestine, where they live today as equal citizens with the Jews, belonging to the same unions and receiving the same medical benefits and education. All together, 450,000 Arabs are now citizens of Israel, whereas 600,000 Jews left Arab countries after the war of 1948.

The Arabs have now about convinced the rest of the world of an injustice in Israel's occupying the Gaza Strip and the west bank.

When the United Nations talks about acquisition of territory by war, they forget that Saudi Arabia acquired its territory by a military victory against the Turks and Jordan acquired the west bank by a military victory of the Jordanian Legion led by British officers and that the United Kingdom and Egypt acquired the Sinai Peninsula by military victory against the Ottoman Empire and that Egypt claims the Gaza Strip as a result of acquisition by war.

Pressure on Israel that will result in a risk to Israel's existence will not bring oil to the United States. The United States doesn't have to stand idly by while her oil properties are nationalized. The oil was discovered by United States scientists and developed by United States industry. During the whole period of recorded history the Palestinians were never ruled by the Arabs of Palestine.

The rule of the various Arab caliphates, which was a foreign Muslim rule, extended for a period of 432 years. Jewish rule of Palestine extended over a period of some 2,000 years.

The inhabitants of the region consisted of the conquering soldiers and their slaves and only during the Arab conquest of the area were these diverse ethnic inhabitants compelled to accept Islam and the Arab tongue or be put to the sword.

The Jews, in fact, are the sole survivors of the ancient inhabitants of Palestine who have maintained an uninterrupted link with the land since the dawn of recorded history.

Israel, the Soviet Union, and the Arabs

THE SOVIET UNION has sent four billion dollars' worth of armaments to Egypt and Iraq.

It is not merely that Israel is so closely tied to the United States.

Why should the Soviet Union be so concerned over the fate of the Arabs? Ideological affiliations could scarcely be a factor. The Soviet leadership has never allowed the persecution of Egyptian communists to interfere with its support of the Egyptian regime; just as it has backed an Arab cause whose various professing representatives encompass monarchies and military dictatorships of passionate hostility to Marxist ideas.

As with other countries, so with the Soviet Union, the interests of the state are paramount in the development of foreign policy. It is the expansion of Soviet power, through economic relationships, diplomatic agreements, military

115

bases, and facilities, and not moral concern for the Arabs that conditions Soviet conduct in the Middle East.

Having made itself virtually indispensable to the present economy and military posture of Syria, Iraq, and, above all, Egypt, by far the most important Arab state, the Soviet Union has penetrated deep into one of the major preserves of Western power. Its naval and air forces have crucial facilities close to a vital source of energy for the Western economies; and any reopening of the Suez Canal would now make it at least as much a Soviet as a Western waterway. What in the end, for the Soviet Union, therefore, is not the struggle between Israel and the Arabs but an opportunity to diminish American influence and promote Soviet ascendancy?

Israel's survival is a victory for the United States. Israel is fighting for Israel and for the United States in its war against the Arabs. With the reopening of the Suez Canal, the Soviets will have a clear sailing through the canal to the Indian Ocean and onto the east coast of Africa. This is clearly an attempt to diminish the influence of America and to promote Soviet ascendancy.

Red inferiority complex

ONE EXPECTED Soviet authorities to condemn bitterly Aleksandr Solzhenitsyn's *Gulag Archipelago 1918-1956*. Tass reported that Soviet citizens were incensed by Mr. Solzhenitsyn's direct and implied comparisons of Nazi Germany under Hitler and Soviet Russia under Stalin. One is stunned by how vituperative the Soviet authorities are. Communists are the inferior men of the twentieth century.

The uprising at the Attica Prison is no longer hot news; still it occupies the attention of newsmen and commentators, lawyers and reformers. One suspects if Attica had transpired within the Soviet Union, the authorities would have imprisoned everyone connected with it from the inmates through Russell Oswald, the head of New York's Corrections Department, Tom Wicker, the New York *Times* correspondent, and maybe even Nelson Rockefeller, the Governor.

None of these things happened, though indeed Attica will embarrass and annoy the authorities for many years to come.

The Jews collect all of the anti-Semitic material ever published and store it in available libraries. A student of social dynamics could write fifty books on the way American anti-Semitism has manifested itself in the twentieth century from the files of the B'nai B'rith.

The reason Attica is a matter for the courts and anti-Semitism for the scholars is that, basically, Americans and Jews do not feel themselves inferior. But one book distresses the Soviets.

If Stalin imprisoned, as now seems likely, twelve million Russians for a variety of reasons from active dissidence through sheer accident, obviously another 220,000,000 knew they were living through a reign of terror. But to debate this terror, to make its existence a public issue, to perpetuate or end it according to public sympathy, would mean a lessening of control for the Kremlin.

The Kremlin may well be making a mistake. It may prove impossible to continue to terrorize vast millions and punish them arbitrarily simply to perpetuate a system. So far, the inferior men have only to contend with one Solzhenitsyn and a dozen or so of his allies.

Solzhenitsyn in exile

THE EXILE decreed by the Kremlin for the Nobel laureate Aleksandr Solzhenitsyn was headline news around the world.

Solzhenitsyn's courage was of rare caliber. He had won all

117

the honors a writer can win and he had suffered all the indignities and punishments most men can bear. Yet he persevered. He insisted on the truth about injustice. He insisted on describing what can only be called a murrain, a plague of epidemic proportions.

Victor Hugo was banished from France by Napoleon III in the 1860's for persevering and Emile Zola took his life in his hands for exposing the perjured testimony and rigged evidence that convicted Captain Dreyfus. But neither Napoleon III nor the French General Staff was as ruthless or, for that matter, as misguided as the Communist hierarchy. Napoleon III knew the difference between benevolence and tyranny and disliked Hugo for pointing it out, and the French General Staff knew the difference between truth and deceit and dreaded Zola's exposing that difference.

The Kremlin does not know the difference. Terror to the Russian autocracy is as natural a process as, say, employment is elsewhere.

Solzhenitsyn's exile is also unique. Had he been Chinese, he simply would have been matter-of-factly murdered in a counterrevolutionary pogrom. He never would have written. Had he been an American or a Frenchman or an Italian, he might never have been heard because the populace wouldn't have listened.

But he was a Russian, and as often as Russian rulers have tried to isolate the mass of Russians, so often have voices penetrated.

Because he was a Russian is the reason he was heard. The Communist bureaucracy had no idea that someone would say the things Solzhenitsyn said. No American publisher or audience expects someone to write a book proving the Colonists lost the Revolutionary War. What Solzhenitsyn argued was that the very processes of government have turned life into a nightmare. Many men have elsewhere argued as much, but these men hope for reform. Solzhenitsyn proposes nothing less than transformation.

118

That the Russians chose to exile this voice is no indication of their humanity. In the long run they stood to lose more by his murder than he did. Exile to Russians is particularly cruel. Exile to Siberia has passed into the world language. Boris Pasternak, the last Russian to win the Nobel Prize for literature, refused to journey to Stockholm to claim it for fear he could not reenter his homeland. Once out of Russia, Russians experience for some reason a diminution of their energies.

Let us praise Solzhenitsyn for ennobling the race of men.

PART 4

Music in the Movies

Is this the time for Mother Goose?

THE ANSWER is yes.

When I became a grandfather for the fifth time, I posted an edition of *Mother Goose* to my grandson. These verses came into our language about 1700. Though for the most part they are nonsense verses, still they have survived more malignant nonsense, like King George III, unrestricted submarine warfare, and nuclear warheads.

Mother Goose remains a source of satisfaction for the innocent and the sophisticated. Just what would some writers do for titles if they didn't remember their Mother Goose? These nursery rhymes have provided as many titles as Shakespeare and the Bible. *All the King's Men, Come Blow Your Horn, Saturday's Children* come immediately to mind.

About the time I became a father, forty-seven years ago, there was a reaction to Mother Goose because some of the verses were thought cruel; for example, "Little Jack Jelf/Was put on a shelf/Because he could not spell 'pie'. . . ." Just what sort of neuroses we thought this would induce I cannot imagine. We thought at the time, too, that Mother Goose was pointless. But upon review, some of our own folk airs like "Pony Boy" and "I Wanna Hold Your Hand" make Mother Goose as sensible as a primer on electricity.

That's one of the troubles with analysis—we're always talking ourselves out of our own basic needs. There was a time when Beethoven was considered vulgar. His symphonies made too much noise. Out of hand we used to condemn Hollywood movies as childish and simplistic. That is, we used to condemn them until we got an eyeful of television. Even television executives will enthusiastically admit these days that the only entertainment that makes sense on the tube are the old movies.

I recommend Mother Goose. It descends to us from an untroubled time. The untroubled time of infancy. Though psychologists may dispute me, still infancy seems like an untroubled time in contrast to, say, childhood. The psychologists will agree that infants do not learn to smile because they are fed, nor do they learn to smile because they are coddled; they learn to smile when parents talk to them. And that is what Mother Goose is for.

Thomas Paine

THE GREATEST best seller in American history was Thomas Paine's *Common Sense*. This book, the first complete defense for political independence of the colonies, electrified its readers. It sold the then amazing number of 120,000 copies in three months, and Washington and Jefferson viewed it as an indispensable aid to the forging for independence. Paine's *Common Sense* laid the foundation for the Declaration of Independence six months later. Later Paine wrote *The Crisis*, in which he defended the Revolution. "These are the times that try men's souls," began Paine, during a gloomy period of the fight. General Washington ordered that the pamphlet be read to all his men. The boosted morale led to the victories at Trenton and Princeton and militated against all talk of "compromise."

Heinrich Heine, lyric poet

THE CRITIC Georg Brandes wrote that Heinrich Heine was the world's greatest lyric poet. Other critics are inclined to temper this judgment, but all literary authorities have spoken the name of Heine along with those of Robert Burns, François

Villon, Rabelais, Voltaire, and Dean Swift. With Goethe and Shiller, he wrote the finest literature in the German language.

This restless genius was born in the Dusseldorf ghetto in 1797, at a time when no Jew could enter a public park or a pleasure resort, no Jew could leave the ghetto after four o'clock on a Sunday afternoon, and only twenty-four Jews were allowed to marry in one year. In such an atmosphere Heine received his baptism of fire. His father was Samson Heine, a Jewish Micawber who never seemed to make a "go" of anything he tried. After a dozen failures father Heine gave up and surrendered himself to the charity of a brother, Salomon Heine, who, luckily for the whole family, was one of the richest men in Hamburg. The poet may have inherited his father's misfortune of never being able to make ends meet. All his life his mind was tormented by worries over money, springing not only from the demands of everyday living, but from his own deep sense of insecurity. When we realize how much time and energy this genius spent in arranging loans, cashing drafts, pleading for an "advance," waiting for a letter with money, and asking for extensions, it becomes all the more remarkable that he also produced some of the most beautiful lyrics ever written and that he wrote songs that have been sung all over the civilized world.

Heine's name at birth was, of all things, Harry. Harry Heine. While his parents struggled hopelessly to earn a living, they were somewhat above the average intellectually. Heine's mother fancied herself something of a Deist, after the fashion of the French philosophers of the day, although she was a tyrant in the maintenance of Jewish customs in the Heine home. In one of his many (unsuccessful) business ventures father Heine had some dealing with an Englishman by the name of Mr. Harry, and thus, I suppose, to demonstrate their individualism, the parents bypassed the usual Biblical name and named their first-born son Harry. The "Heinrich" came later. When Harry Heine, after a half-dozen false starts, finally won his college degree in law, he found that he could not practice his profession of doctor of jurisprudence unless he became a Christian—at least officially. At his baptism the Lutheran authorities renamed him Heinrich Heine. He came home, waved his baptism certificate in the air, and said, "I now have my passport to Western civilization."

Heinrich Heine was a man of violent passions, but he was also possessed of deep sentimental loyalties. He was as ashamed of his good deeds as most men are ashamed of their sins. He loved to boast of his "wild life" and his conquests among women. Most of it was exaggerated. His marvelous poetry betrayed him at every turn. When he first arrived in Paris, a political exile from Germany, he wrote a dozen magnificent poems, each inspired by a streetwalker, and they betrayed a naiveté about sex that would have been impossible in a "Bohemian," which Heine fancied himself. He tried to create the impression that he was "hard" and that he lacked sentiment, but that, too, was a pose. During a terrible outbreak of the plague in Paris, when everyone fled, Heine remained behind to the bitter end. In writing to his family he gave many reasons for thus exposing himself to danger, every reason but the right one, which was that a friend had been stricken and he wanted to be at his bedside. Again his wondrous pen betrayed him. When his father died, the same father who had never been able to provide a decent living for the family, Heine wrote:

> Of all men on this earth, my father was the most loved to me. I never thought that I must one day lose him, and even now I can hardly believe he is indeed lost to me. There has never been a night when my father has not been in my thoughts. . . . Yes, yes, they talk of meeting again in transfiguration. What good would that do? I know him in his old brown overcoat and I shall see him again in it. He used to sit at the head of the table with salt-cellar and pepper-pot in front of him, one on the left, the other on the right;

126

and if the salt-cellar were on the right and the pepper-pot on the left, he would carefully change them around. . . .

His love for the rich Uncle Salomon is another interesting aspect of Heine's character. Very few people love those upon whom they are financially dependent. Indeed there are times when resentment actually boils over into hatred. Heine's feeling for his uncle was, nevertheless, constant, sincere, and completely loyal. But they spent half their lives in a financial tug-of-war. First came the argument for an "advance," a gift, or a loan. This was followed by an argument over the manner in which the money had been spent, finally followed by a third argument for another "advance." In studying the life of Heine, one must come away with a deep affection for this Uncle Salomon. He was a rich banker in Hamburg, with his own complex affairs, his own large family, his own fears, his own fight for security, and he knew nothing at all about poetry or writing; yet this man literally followed every step of the career of his tormented, restless, and neurotic nephew. He never gave in without a scene or an argument, but he always gave in. First he set Heinrich up in the cloth business in Frankfurt, and that lasted a little less than a year. Then he financed his nephew in two or three different colleges and in two or three different courses of study, until finally Heinrich secured his diploma in law, a profession that he never practiced.

Heine felt that writing was all he wanted to do. And we may well imagine the arguments with Uncle Salomon. How many parents and rich uncles since that day, and before, have said the same thing: "How can you make a living from poetry? Get yourself set up in some business and then you can write to your heart's content." But with Heinrich Heine it was no idle dream. He had genius; and what genius, my friends! He was the sweetest singer of the nineteenth century. From his brain came one of the most popular lyrics in all literature, that beautiful poem *"Du bist wie eine Blume"* (translation by Emma Lazarus):

> Thou seemest like a flower,
> So fair and pure and bright:
> A melancholy yearning
> Steals o'er me at thy sight.
> I fain would lay in blessing
> My hands upon thy hair;
> Imploring God to keep thee
> So bright and pure and fair.

Heine's constant worry over money was not for any desire to live a life in luxury. He simply wanted to be left in peace to write with a clear mind. "My greatest desire in life is a quiet room," he said. He honestly felt that he had a message for mankind—"the Emancipation of Mankind." A dreamer's dream, but when we realize how politically influential this lyric poet became, his works are all the more amazing. But he knew how tough the road was that lay ahead. *"We must be twice as good to get half as much,"* Heine told his fellow Jews. This was during his intense "Jewish" period. He had joined in the activities of the Jewish community, and became secretary of the Verein fur Kultur and Wissenschaft der Juden (Society for Jewish Culture and Learning). He joined with Leopold Zunz, Ludwig Marcus, and other brilliant young Jewish intellectuals who dreamed of bringing about a renaissance of Jewish culture. Oddly enough, it was his impact with another side of Jewish life in Europe that eventually drew his attention away from the "particular" in order to devote all his energies and talents to the "universal." On one of his several side trips financed by Uncle Salomon, Heinrich Heine visited a Polish ghetto, and it made a deep impression on his mind and soul. As degrading as life in the German ghetto may have been, Heine never dreamed that human existence was possible under the conditions that confronted him in Poland. He wrote: "The Polish Jew with his filthy fur, his infested beard, his garlic-laden breath, and his jargon, is still dearer to me than many a German Jew in all the majesty of his Government Bonds."

While Heine continued to work with the Jewish society, he was now ready to enter the broader arena of the political struggle. He felt that a new awakening among the German masses would solve not only the Jewish problem, but all social and political injustice.

"But what is the great question of the age? It is Emancipation. Not merely the emancipation of the Irish, the Greeks, the Jews, the West Indian Negroes, and other oppressed races, but the emancipation of the whole world. . . ."

He became the head of the liberal movement in Germany. "The Young Germany," they called it. Heine's campaign against the Prussian reactionaries was unique and up to a point almost unbelievably successful. The Junkers could be depended upon to take care of themselves against a frontal attack by "radicals." But this was something new. Heine laughed at them. He picked up his pen and laughed uproariously. This satiric strain runs through most of Heine's poems and writings. This Jew dared to laugh at the militarism and nationalism of the Junkers, and thousands of Germans were laughing and singing with him.

He called upon his compatriots to gird their loins and demand the constitution that the King, Friedrich Wilhelm III, had promised. When the constitution was not forthcoming, Heine savagely mocked and gibed the German people for tolerating the tyranny:

> The King of Prussia is a very religious man; he holds strongly to religion; he is a good Christian, firmly attached to the evangelical confession of faith; indeed, he has even written a liturgy and believes in holy symbols. But, ah, I wish he believed instead in Jupiter, the Father of Gods, who punishes

perjury—perhaps then the King would give us that promised constitution.

Heine was yet to experience a torment of a different nature. He was to witness firsthand the working of that mental aberration, anti-Semitism, so dear to the hearts of the German people. In an upsurge of revolt that he and the other liberals had encouraged, the mob, instead of directing its fury against the tyranny, savagely attacked the ghetto. How this sorry event must have sobered Heine! For years the young radicals around Heine had brought the Germans face to face with the tyranny that held them in an authoritarian grip, and finally when the bonds were burst, the German mob turned, not upon its tormentors, but upon the poverty-stricken Jews.

It was now the Junkers' turn to laugh as they were ready to move in. They put a price on Heine's head and he had to flee the country: "I say farewell to this German Fatherland of mine. The ineradicable Jew in me hounds me from the place."

Except for a few stealthy trips back to Hamburg to see his ailing mother, Heine spent the rest of his life in Paris.

He commented often on his baptism: "I am sorry I had myself baptized. As soon as I was baptized I was decried as a Jew. . . . Now I am detested by Christian and Jew alike."

His satiric power never left him. He was surprised at his popularity in certain quarters in Hamburg after his conversion and remarked: "I am getting to be a regular Christian, all the rich Jews invite me to supper."

In Paris Heine continued his struggle for liberal principles and his personal struggle for financial security. His uncle now sent him a regular annual allowance; he received a good salary as political writer for a liberal newspaper, and the French government voted him a pension. Heine fell in love. Madly in love. She was nineteen years old when he met his Mathilde, a strong, strapping Belgian girl. This was the woman Heine loved to the end of his days. He loved her with an amazing and consuming passion. Some of his biographers claim that Heine was probably flattered by this woman's love for him, flattered to think that she loved him for himself. She had no idea he was a famous poet. Indeed she had no idea about poetry at all. But it has been pretty well established that Mathilde was never really faithful to Heine and that the simple truth is that here was a cunning peasant girl who got herself a good thing. Heine was ready to indulge her in her every wish, including her devotion to her parrot. Mathilde and her parrot jabbered away all day long, year in and year out. On one of Heine's secret trips to Germany he took Mathilde along, and Heine's brother-in-law came to meet them. Mathilde handed the cage with the parrot to the brother-in-law, who dropped it, and all hell broke loose. The parrot did not suffer at all, but Heine's trip was a nightmare and he had to send Mathilde back to France. Into their apartment in Paris came such visitors as Dumas, Gautier, Karl Marx, Hugo, Chopin, George Sand, La Salle, but it meant nothing at all to Mathilde. And yet Heine loved her as he loved no other woman.

He never stopped writing, even when he sank into complete invalidism. He was fifty years old when he had a stroke. His right eye was shut tight, and his arm was paralyzed. His last five years were torture. Eventually he had no feeling at all, nor could he taste the food he was eating. He spent five terrible years dying, the last two of which he was completely bedridden. A visitor described how his nurse lifted him out of the bed to change the linen and that Heine's arms and legs, nothing but skin and bone, just dangled helplessly and motionless. Yet that brain never ceased working for a single moment. Heine continued to speak with the fury of a Biblical prophet when he wrote of Germany, nearly one hundred years before "it" happened:

> The stone gods will rise from their long-forgotten ruins and rub the dust of a thousand years from their eyes. Thor, leaping to life with his giant hammer, will crush the Gothic cathedrals. . . . It is

coming. . . . German thunder is indeed German, and it is in no hurry; but come it will, and when ye hear the crash as naught ever crashed before in the whole history of the world, then know that German thunder has at last hit the mark. At the sound, the eagles will fall dead from on high and the lions in the remotest deserts of Africa will draw in their tails and creep into their royal caves. A drama will be enacted in Germany by the side of which the French Revolution will seem like an innocent idyll. Just now all is tolerably still . . . let it not be imagined that the great actors have yet appeared. These restive persons are but little dogs that run about in the empty amphitheatre and bite at one another; the hour arrives when the great array of gladiators must appear."

The restless but brilliant mind encompassed just about everything, including America. His little poem *Dieses Ist Amerika* has given us hope of permanent victory over the forces of evil and bigotry. A few months ago I came across a long treatise by a scholar and philosopher who said that we are safe in America, forever, because "America does not carry the Middle Ages on her back." This was a brilliant thought, one that should help sustain us and our children. When I studied Heinrich Heine and read his poetry, I discovered the source of this philosophy, written by this hopelessly sick genius, this child of the German ghetto, whose mind possessed neither limit nor boundary.

It is astounding how much work Heine managed to do during those last years. Gautier wrote: "Like a dead man, the living poet was nailed in his coffin, but when we bent over him to listen, we heard poetry ringing from under the pall." He died in 1856; his last thoughts were for Mathilde's future, and his last words were: "Paper . . . pencil."

The Nazis searched every nook and corner of their Third Reich to burn the books of Heine, but even the Nazis could not stop their soldiers from singing one of his immortal songs, a song that most of the children of the world have learned to sing. And we may well imagine that perhaps somewhere Heine was laughing uproariously as Hitler published his song—"Lorelei"—substituting "author unknown" for "Heinrich Heine."

Edgar Allan Poe

In 1844 Edgar Allan Poe was working in New York on the *Evening Mirror*. It was this daily that a year or so later carried his poem "The Raven," which netted Poe fifteen dollars. For "The Bells," written in the last year of his life, Poe received a total of forty-five dollars.

In 1845 Poe was invited to read his poetry before the Boston Lyceum. The reaction was mixed. A few persons who were there later wrote that they had heard the marvelous musical voice of the great Edgar Poe, but others in the audience walked out. Then word got around that Poe hadn't written a new poem for the occasion, but had simply retitled an old one. The Boston papers were miffed, and they denounced Poe's performance. In reply, he wrote that he had deliberately gotten drunk before the reading and had delivered a poem he had composed when he was ten years old. In a follow-up story Poe promised to return to Boston and read something he had written at the age of seven months.

Poe nursed a drinking problem for years, though it would be an exaggeration to say he was an alcoholic. He went on occasional binges, got drunk after a few drinks, and did foolish things in public or just kept to his bed.

Poe is popular with many young people today because of his image as a drug addict who wrote weird stories and poems while he was tripping. Try to dislodge this picture from their minds and you will meet with angry resistance.

The fact is, Poe was not a junkie any more than he was a drunk, though it is perhaps comforting to the undisciplined to think so. He was a hard-working professional writer, which means that he sat at his desk for hours at a stretch, reading, composing, rewriting, revising, editing.

The Gettysburg Address

THE ATTRACTION Abraham Lincoln holds is that it was he more than any other President who made us a country. He made us a country because he held onto the single overpowering political idea that the United States was one country and not a collection of sovereign states. He believed in the union of states and he held onto this idea at a time when it was not universally acknowledged, even in the North.

Thus his attraction, and every biographer finds in this an idea so grand that he can separate from it the things he thinks made Lincoln great..

It is because he was a user of words that the poets have always understood Lincoln. The historian Henry Steele Commager pointed out long ago that the supreme tributes to Lincoln came from Whitman, Emerson, Lindsay, Benet, and Sandburg.

Of them, Sandburg probably came the closest to the point because, although he loved the way Lincoln used words, Sandburg also saw him as the master politician he was.

One of the truths we Americans have always hidden from ourselves, or care not to pay heed to, is that our great Presidents have without exception been great politicians. It is probably impossible to do good for the country unless a man will make ultimate use of the political hazards of his time.

Sandburg was the first historian to point out that the Gettysburg Address was at bottom a political speech delivered before fifteen Northern governors to emphasize that the war was not fought for the causes of abolition or state sovereignty, but for union.

It was Sandburg who exploded the notion that the speech was scribbled on a train and instead told us how important a speech it was to Lincoln and how hard he worked on it. Sandburg revealed the whole Lincoln when he uncovered the truth of Lincoln's policy in inserting the phrase "under God" in his speech because it seemed the circumstances warranted it.

Abraham Lincoln was probably the greatest writer among our Presidents. He would have been a very great writer had he decided to follow that calling alone.

Mark Twain, via donkey

THERE'S NOTHING so tiring as a lecture trip, but I'm all right as soon as I stand to face the audience. I shuck the fatigue and the first laugh makes me feel the trip and the receptions both before and after the lecture are endurable. As the audience warms up, I warm up. I forget I have to rise at 5:15 A.M. to catch a 7 A.M. plane that will take me four hundred miles away, where the whole process from the greeting committee to the same chicken dinner will be repeated.

Others on the lecture circuit tell me their experience is the same. The joint complaint of lecturers is that the booking agency reads an airplane schedule different from ours and sometimes arranges transportation that is nonexistent, so that the few hours of leisure are spent on the telephone listening to confused airline clerks tell us you cannot get to Omaha from here.

I can make ten lectures in fourteen days. What cheers me is the memory that Mark Twain would take four weeks to make as many.

135

Mark Twain was the real pioneer of lecturers. Whether there is a patron saint of lecturers or not, I do not know. If not, I would like to recommend he be installed straightway.

Mark Twain went around the world giving lectures. And he did it without an airplane. And not for profit either. Although he had published the *Memoirs of General Ulysses S. Grant* and saved the Grant family from destitution with $500,000, subsequent publishing ventures as well as a substantial investment in a typesetting invention made a shipwreck of Twain's own finances.

At the age of sixty he was dead broke and owed $100,000. In 1895 he began his first worldwide lecture tour to pay his debts. One year later he showed up in England after victorious platform acclaim everywhere with a healthy bank account.

Think of the chicken dinners he consumed and the number of before-and-after receptions he attended! For the harrowing part of lecturing is not the lecture itself, but the three lectures you are expected to deliver: one to the group that escorts you to the predinner reception, the second to those who paid the admission, and the third to the few important people of the community who gather at the postlecture reception.

And Mark Twain did it by boat, train, and donkey cart, and in areas where he was not always sure what language his host would employ.

Music in the movies

ONE OF the curious facts about the movies is that though they started without sound, they were never without music.

In the days before Dimitri Tiomkin, Henry Mancini, or Comden and Green, movie-theater owners depended upon

136

an organist or a piano player to improvise the musical score for the silents.

As movies lengthened from one reel to two, and then to six, these accompanists were hard pressed to suit every film sequence to appropriate music. Sometimes there were three chases in a Western, but, sad to relate, there is only one *William Tell* Overture by Rossini. Matching mood and visual image demanded musicians with extensive repertoires and almost computerized sentiments.

Before the advent of sound, the old Capitol Theatre in New York employed six organists. But in the smaller theaters, say the ones on the Lower East Side, the piano players and organists were often amateurs and rarely did they get the opportunity to preview the picture. In fact, on the Lower East Side the Westerns were always accompanied by Yiddish folk music. It lent the movies another dimension in retrospect.

To help the accompanists, Erno Rapee, then a pioneer composer of scores for silent pictures, compiled a compendium of more than two hundred themes that could depict the mood for fifty-two basic situations. Long out of print, *Motion Picture Moods for Pianists and Organists* has been recently reissued by the Arno Press in New York City. It has proved in the past and will prove for the future a repository past all value and reassessment.

Herein are the tunes that we who are now grandparents and great-grandparents heard when we saw *The Great Train Robbery*, *The Kid*, and *The Gold Rush*.

When Clara Bow chattered in *Mantrap*, it was, according to Rapee, to the strains of Felix Mendelssohn's "Song Without Words." When Richard Barthelmess did battle with Junkers in *Wings*, it was to Beethoven's *presto agitato* of the third movement of the *Moonlight Sonata*. And when Rudolph Valentino strutted before his tent in *The Sheik*, it was to Otto Langey's Opus 58, No. 1, "Among the Arabs."

Anton Dvořak, Frederick Williams, Johannes Brahms,

Zdeněk Fibich, Joseph Raff, Rudolf Friml, Anton Rubenstein, and Ignace Paderewski contributed to the successful love scene. Heroes raced to put out fires to the "Card Trio" from Bizet's *Carmen*, and they mourned at funerals to Robert Schumann's *Andante Pathétique*.

It was always possible to enjoy movies without sound. Some of the finest movies ever produced were silents that still enthrall audiences. It was never possible, however, to enjoy movies without music.

John McCormack's ten encores

JOHN MCCORMACK was one of the world's leading tenors. The great singers of the day, from Caruso down, held the Irishman in greatest esteem, and he gave many a memorable performance. The old Hippodrome in New York was the largest enclosure and McCormack sang there many times to concert audiences. At one of his concerts he sang ten encores. One of the "big shows" like *Happy Days* was playing in the Hippodrome at the time and one of the tame lions had wandered off and just stood for a long time in the wings, watching McCormack and his accompanist. The Irish tenor took one look at the lion (not visible to the audience) and he just kept singing until the stagehands removed the "king of beasts."

Herbert Hoover and George M. Cohan

TIME HEALS all bitterness. Before his death former President Herbert H. Hoover regained much of the prestige and esteem he enjoyed during World War I. He was lucky. If he had passed on in 1932 or 1933, he would have been remembered only as a terrible failure and his name would have been associated forever with economic disaster. People become mellow with years and it's a good thing.

The great actor George M. Cohan also was lucky in that respect. If the famous song-and-dance man had died in 1920, it would have been hard to find a pallbearer for him on Broadway. He tried to break the actors' union, the Equity, in 1919, and the battle was a terrible hardship for many actors and actresses. Mr. Cohan shut down all the theaters under his control and waged a one-man war to starve out the strikers. All through the bitter year he played in his show *Royal Vagabond*, and for a time it looked as if Mr. Cohan had won. Many actors were beginning to waver. The Equity did not have much money to continue the fight, and it became a matter of life and death with too many of them. But they held out, inspired by such people as Bert Lytell, Mary Boland, Ethel Barrymore, John Flood, Francine Larrimore, and others.

The years helped to bind up the wounds and toward the end of Cohan's career, a very strong "union" man, Jim Cagney, played George M. Cohan on the screen in a wonderful movie called *Yankee Doodle Dandy*, and one of the strongest Equity men of them all, the late Walter Huston, played George M. Cohan's father in the same picture. Thus all was forgiven by both sides, and when he died, George M. Cohan was honored by the entire theatrical world for his great contribution to the American stage.

The songwriters

I HAVE whistled and hummed the tunes for so long that it is hard for me to realize I was a contemporary of George Gershwin.

But by the time I was in my twenties Gershwin was an established institution. His melodies and his musicals have

139

passed into the American musical canon and his brother Ira's lyrics have passed into the language.

Not too many boys from the Lower East Side of New York City preceded Gershwin as an American favorite. For some reason the musicians and the songsmiths made it first—Irving Berlin, Irving Caesar, Wolfie Gilbert, and others.

It is easier, I suspect, to plug a song than it is, say, for a Herbert Lehman or a Jacob Javits to plug an election. While the Jews of Europe were musicians, they were never the noted composers. There isn't a Jewish composer the equal, say, of the Englishman Edward Elgar or of Henry Purcell.

But there are few Christians who, as popular composers, are the equal of Gershwin, Irving Berlin, Lerner and Lowe, or Richard Rodgers.

There are several reasons advanced to explain the advent of a George Gershwin, chief among them the truth that America is not only a liberating but a heady experience.

Maybe a last reason is that around the turn of the century pianos were cheaper. There were more pianos in the tenements of the Lower East Side than there were private bathrooms. Now everyone has a private bathroom and they buy their kids guitars and play country music. Folksinging is the result—the music of a nation of amateurs.

Our teachers

AMERICA WOULD not be the same without her teachers. Many of our Presidents were teachers first. The teachers I knew as a boy made citizens out of immigrants within a single generation. They taught us to love our books and our country, to spell, and to say, "Yes, ma'am."

The jazz musicians

PAUL WHITEMAN, the famous bandleader, drank whiskey out of water glasses and never carried any money. He carried no wallet because he wanted the pockets of his coats and pants to be absolutely flat. He was undeniably a man of great talent, wisdom, and compassion.

His death saddened me. I knew him back there in the 1930's when his band was entertaining nightly at the Paradise Club on Forty-ninth Street and Broadway. Mr. Whiteman used the Hotel Markwell, just off Forty-ninth Street, where I was the night manager, as a place to store his instruments and as a *pied-à-terre* where his bandsmen could change their clothes and catch a cat nap now and then.

Bing Crosby and Johnny Hauser were among those who frequented the Markwell with Paul Whiteman. Goldie, the trumpeter, who often conducted the band during Whiteman's absence, was a particular friend of mine and so was Pingatore, the banjoist. Goldie and Pingatore, with their wives, visited us when we lived in Red Bank, New Jersey.

I remember the musicians were greatly impressed with my wife's hamburgers, exclaiming over them as though they were an exquisite delicacy prepared at Maxim's.

Another of the musicians with whom I grew friendly was Jack Teagarten, the trombonist. Teagarten had a marvelous talent for music and an equally marvelous talent for whiskey. I put him to bed several times. He always apologized the next morning. On a lecture tour in New Orleans a few years ago I saw a Jack Teagarten concert advertised. I attended and after it was over, I went backstage and Teagarten threw his arms around me and kissed me.

It was through these fellows I met Jack Amron, who owned not only the Paradise Club but the Hollywood Club and was the financial boss of Jack Dempsey's first restaurant across the street from Madison Square Garden.

One day Jack Amron sighed to me, "I give the patrons a

marvelous steak at Jack Dempsey's for two dollars. I am going broke there. At the Hollywood Club I give them canned food for five dollars and the place is packed every night because, along with the food, I throw in naked breasts."

Ramona was Whiteman's vocalist. Goldie told me that when she left to go to Boston for an extended season, her boyfriends all conspired to send her a joint telegram, which read, "Congratulations on your grand opening."

Now Paul Whiteman is gone. So is Goldie. But I was on the *Today Show* one morning and met Goldie Junior, a dead ringer for his father. He plays the trombone and trumpet just as beautifully, too.

The triumphant lawyers

PAULINE BOYLE was the grand old lady of theatrical stock companies. She was the one who booked young actors into stock companies up and down the Atlantic seaboard. Many of the greatest stars began their careers with job assignments from Pauline Boyle. She was retired and in her seventies when she lived in my brother's hotel, the Hotel Markwell, on West Forty-ninth Street. One day she slipped on a piece of faulty floor covering and broke her ankle. The insurinks man came around and investigated, and he saw this old lady, living alone, who apparently wasn't so sure of herself. So he took out the first of the three checks these adjusters carry—the first one was for $250. She thanked him, but told him to let the matter slide for a while. Then he took out his $350 check but Miss Boyle would have none of that either; and he tried his $500 check, but nothing doing. Finally they went to court and the case was to be heard by a jury of six people. On the morning of the trial the insurance company came into court with two fine-looking lawyers, an elderly man and a younger fellow, each one carrying a bulging briefcase.

After a while in came Miss Boyle, limping on a cane, and behind her came Spencer Tracy, Ralph Bellamy, Pat O'Brien, and Wallace Ford. What a battery of "lawyers"! The jury nearly went crazy with excitement. These were to be her witnesses. The insurinks men settled quick—$2,500, plus all medicine bills, etc., in exchange for autographs for the judge and jury.

Carl Sandburg and the critics

THE GREATEST biographer of all time was Plutarch. Dryden tells us that Plutarch explained his method in these words: "In writing the lives of illustrious men I am not tied to the laws of history, nor does it follow that because an action is great it therefore manifests the greatness and virtue of him who did it; but, on the other side, sometimes a word or a casual gesture betrays a man more to our knowledge of him than a battle fought wherein ten thousand men were slain, or sacking of cities, or a course of victories."

Xenophon tells us, "The sayings of great men in their familiar discourses and amidst their wine have somewhat in them which is worthy to be transmitted to posterity."

My job was harder than Plutarch's in that I wrote a biography or, as I call it, a commentary on a person who was then living and who was a particularly close friend.

Did the late Carl Sandburg ever ask me to write a book about him?

Of course not. Did Carl Sandburg throw his arm around me and kiss me on both cheeks every time we met, even before I was writing a book about him?

Of course he did.

My research, such as it was, was my love for Carl Sandburg and I read everything that Carl has ever written.

When I finished, I went to Connemara, his North Carolina

143

estate, and let Carl read the book. My first idea was to send it to him and just shut the phone off and see what happened. But that would be the coward's way out.

After a drink and a chat Carl made himself comfortable and started reading, with me watching him like a hawk.

This was about three in the afternoon. He was looking at the manuscript, as he put it, "dipping into it." I knew when he said "dipping into it" that this was not yet the real thing. That was to come after supper. About 7:30. I sat opposite him and the Sandburg daughter, Helga, the novelist, sat across the room.

I suggested to Carl that I take out one of the chapters concerning Mrs. Sandburg and let her read it. This was a very smart move on my part. This chapter gets into a lot of personal stuff and I thought I'd be better off if Paula looked at it first. If she brought it back smiling, maybe Carl would wind up smiling, too.

The session lasted until three in the morning, when Carl said, "You seem to think that I'm concerned about critics."

This was the first crack out of the box. "I'm not in the least concerned about critics," he went on. "You write here that I was peeved at Kenneth Rexroth's review of the *Sandburg Range* in *The Nation*. Hell! I never paid the slightest attention to it. Not even to *The Nation* review in August, 1948, by Diana Trilling on *Remembrance Rock*. I never paid any attention to her and I wasn't interested even in the fact that the *Atlantic Monthly* and that editor Weeks did not have enough understanding to review my novel and that Harper's, hah! that Harper's reviewing my book was nothing more than a rehash of the review in the New York *Times*."

"Carl," I protested, "I only intimated that you were pretty well aware of what your critics had to say."

"Hell! I never read any of 'em any more than I can help."

"As you see, Carl, I didn't include only the adverse criticism."

"Yes," he replied, "but you forgot Eric Sevareid. Have you seen the letter Eric Sevareid sent me? Shouldn't that be in the

144

book? Helga, let's get all those letters out from the seventy-fifth anniversary celebration. . . ."

Later on, as I perused Eric Sevareid's letter, Carl boomed, "How many times do you use the word 'Socialist'? Hell, you've got me here as a Socialist a few hundred times—why don't you change it a little bit?"

"Carl, you weren't organizing for the Republican National Committee in 1908, were you?"

"No, I wasn't. I was organizing for the Socialists, but change some of these 'Socialists'—make a few of them 'radical.' "

We changed some "Socialists" to "radical."

So far it was going better than I expected. Then Carl said, "Right about here, Harry, put in my poem 'The Windy City.' It would do the book good. Helga, get the poem off the shelf and read it to us."

"Carl," I said, "you're dictating twenty-five sheets about Ed Steichen. How can I use that in a book about Carl Sandburg?"

"Let's fix it up, Harry, don't worry. But remember: Hell, I'm not interested in critics. You make it appear as though I'm interested in critics. . . ."

"Carl, nothing can hurt you. You are an institution. You are like Albert Einstein and Mahatma Gandhi . . . you're like Paris garters—no metal can touch you."

"But I'm not interested in the critics and I'm not a Socialist—I'm a radical."

Carl Sandburg died in 1967 at the age of eighty-nine.

This poet, two-time Pulitzer Prize winner, biographer, novelist, and Spanish-American War veteran, came to the American scene as a journalist, a reporter for Milwaukee and Chicago papers. He followed the strikes and the picket lines and the race riots, wrote all about the Molly Maguires, the Pinkertons, the IWW's, and the incipient labor unions. From such early conflict this poet later strummed a guitar for a national television audience and wrote books for children.

Carl Sandburg is a symbol not only of our American experience but of our experiments in the last century.

Sandburg was one of the few American writers to succeed as a personality. Only Mark Twain comes to mind. Sandburg and Twain succeeded as personalities because in their writings and in their persons they grasped something essentially American.

But it was more than that, too. In her preface to the *Selected Poems of Carl Sandburg*, Dame Rebecca West wrote, "It is a curious fact that no writer of Anglo-Saxon descent, no representative of the English tradition, has described the break between Lincoln's America and modern industrial America as poignantly as Carl Sandburg."

Sandburg was the first poet to write about the immigrant and to incorporate into his work the everyday slang of the laborer, the itinerant worker, the pushcart peddler, and the black.

Neither of Sandburg's parents spoke English. Yet this son of Swedish immigrants lived to become one of the masters of our language whose poems are read in schools all over America.

To the thousands of students who wrote him asking how to become a writer, Carl replied, "Solitude and prayer—then go on from there."

Camus and Kreisler

APPARENTLY THE car was going more than ninety miles an hour when it rounded the curve, shot out of control, and smashed headlong into a tree. In the back of the wreckage, dead, was Albert Camus, the French philosopher-novelist, the second-youngest man to win the Nobel Prize for literature.

Whatever the automobile has brought in comfort, it has also caused us loss in greatness. Auto accidents are robbing civilizations not only of the Albert Camus but also of the Kreislers.

146

Fritz Kreisler, until his death from natural causes in 1962, was the world's greatest violinist. But he gave the world a shudder on April 26, 1941. This gentle artist was on his way home from luncheon with his wife at his New York City home on Sutton Place. At 12:15 he was crossing Madison Avenue at Fifty-seventh street. While he was in the middle of the street, the traffic light changed. Confused, Kreisler hesitated, took a step forward, then a step backward. A half-ton egg-delivery truck was unable to swerve. It struck him hard and hurled him to the curb. Anyone who remembers the photo that appeared the next morning in the newspapers remembers the terror of the world's great musician sitting numbly on the sidewalk, blood pouring from his head, while passersby stood by helplessly waiting for the ambulance.

Luckily the world did not then lose Fritz Kreisler, although he remained unconscious for three days with a fractured skull. Kreisler recovered to play for two more decades. How much poorer the world would have been if Kreisler had died that noon on Madison Avenue! How much poorer the world is for losing Albert Camus!

But how many "Kreislers" are there who do not recover? How many men and women identified simply as "musicians" are wheeled into the hospitals with sheets covering their faces?

Getting a fresh start

WHEN A man finishes a book, as I just did, he wants a few days off to catch up with the mail, go over all the magazines to which he willy-nilly subscribes, and put in some long-distance calls to pals scattered about the continent. Then back to work.

A blank sheet of paper in a typewriter is as discouraging to a writer as a chain bolt on a door to a salesman. What you have to do is start early on a Monday morning, preferably after a hearty breakfast, and figure that by Friday there will be ten sheets covered with words.

Making a fresh start in this world is one of the privileges denied me. Promptly at 9 o'clock Monday morning the neighbor's cat got stuck on my roof. I learned of this by the caterwauling of several children at my front door, each of them holding me responsible for the plight of the cat.

Let me tell you how the Fire Department saves marooned cats. The firemen wrench the air conditioner from the bedroom window. They pry up the frame with a jimmy. A booted fireman steps outside, coaxes the cat to his arms, and returns smiles to the faces of children who should be in school. Then it is up to me to return the air conditioner to the window. I cannot even maneuver the venetian blinds back down.

The air-conditioner serviceman looked at it and said casually I needed a new one. While I was at it, he suggested, I might as well call a glazer for a new window frame.

All right. It was now 11:30. I missed a few hours' work but I could make it up. It was then suggested that since I had time, I might devote myself to fixing the sink, which had leaked since Christmas. I spare myself the repairing of sinks with the excuse that I have no zwicken. I have no idea what zwicken is but I have heard plumbers bandy the word about. I called a plumber. Repairing a sink is literally an operation. I stood beside my plumber like a surgical nurse, handing him a basin wrench and his soldering iron and his washers upon instruction.

Monday was going down the drain, so to speak. I still hoped I could get one or two sentences committed. But my accountant called to tell me the Internal Revenue Service wanted to audit my tax return. I said that was impossible, I had just filed it. He said they were auditing last year's return. He had already set up the appointment for Tuesday.

Prizes—win one, lose one

I WON an Emmy, an East Coast Emmy, one of those awarded for television news and documentaries that come out of New York City.

The last time I won a prize I was in grade school. The prize was awarded to a New York City seventh-grade boy or girl who submitted the best patriotic theme.

I submitted a sentence enabling a boy to memorize the names of the first eleven Presidents of the United States. It read: "When a just man makes a just bill he takes pay." The first letter of each corresponds to the first letter of each President's name: Washington, Adams, Jefferson, Madison, Monroe, Adams, Jackson, Van Buren, Harrison, Tyler, Polk."

If they had had Emmys in those days, I would have won one for that certainly.

What won me the prize for the Emmy was a program beamed on NBC for five minutes every night for five nights. I read from portions of my book *The Greatest Jewish City*.

I have often watched these awards for Emmys, Oscars, and Tonys. I knew what to say. I said, "Thank you. I never thought anyone would ever give me anything. But the award belongs to my producer," whose name I did not mention since I couldn't remember it.

Ordinarily I am against all prizes unless they are awarded to me. For the past decade I have annually filled out an application mailed me by the Mayflower Prize Committee of North Carolina. The Mayflower Prize goes to the best book written by a Tar Heel (North Carolinian to you up North).

The application annually comes with a letter informing me of my nomination and would I please fill it out. While there are several Mayflower repeaters living in Charlotte, I have yet to win at all. I confess I have despaired of winning this prize, which I believe carries with it a plaque, twenty-five dollars, and the chance to lecture (without a fee) before the annual meeting of the Mayflower Club (all of whose ancestors came

149

over on said-named ship). In fact, I have so despaired that instead of filling out the application the last time, I told the Mayflowers I wasn't sure I could qualify for their award since I was a *Graf Waldersee* boy. The *Graf Waldersee*, however, beat the *Mayflower* to America. In 1905 the *Graf Waldersee* took only eleven days to bring us from Hamburg to New York and the *Mayflower* took a lot longer to bring Pilgrims to Plymouth Rock.

Liza Minelli

My FRIEND Joe Lapid, reporter for Israel's largest afternoon paper, *Maariv*, wrote to me about his interview with Liza Minelli. This actress, then only sixteen years old, played the role of Anne in the Israeli production of the *Diary of Anne Frank*. According to all of the critics, she gave a moving performance.

Lapid asked her, "How can you, an American girl, whose father is an Italian Catholic and whose mother [Judy Garland] is a Protestant, understand so accurately and poignantly the life, thoughts, and fate of Anne Frank and present them as beautifully as you did?"

Answered Liza: "Every young girl has the same problems with parents, with the lack of parental understanding. Every young girl has her first love. . . ."

"And what about the persecution?" asked Lapid.

Judy Garland's little girl made an interesting observation: "The audience here is quite different. At the moment in the play when the Germans come to pick up the Frank family, I looked at the audience and do you know what they seemed like? Like the Germans were coming to pick them up, too."

This way to see the naked lady

 EROTIC PASSION is a No. 1 editorial topic these days. It has come to the attention of journalists that naked ladies flit across the screen and prance upon the stage and "streak" in the streets. Television panelists discuss the arrival of clinical sex if not its artistic portent.

Fortunately for the history of sculpture, the Greeks did not call conferences to decide whether or not the artists should clothe or unclothe their statues. No one bothered to determine whether Myron was in good taste or bad taste in sculpting the *Discobolus*. They ascertained immediately that in a colossal statue Myron had achieved balance and symmetry and that was enough for them.

No one thought Rubens or Titian was starting a revolution when they painted nudes. The last painted nude to stir a controversy was Marcel Duchamp's and that because no one could find her descending the staircase.

No one should insist it is all the Supreme Court's fault, that the Court invented pornography, which a majority of my fellow Americans believe is sex before marriage. Eros and passion were with us long before anyone invented the concept of an obscenity law.

It is interesting, however, to speculate why the emphasis came now.

I often boast that I never include four-letter words or describe sex in clinical detail in my work, but that is because in my formative years no one thought to do so, let alone dared.

World War II brought a general loosening of language, a mixed blessing, for now we must tolerate *Portnoy's Complaint* and *The Love Machine*, so the loosening had better come up with something good pretty soon.

The advent of television is certainly in many ways responsible for *I Am Curious (Yellow)* and *Behind the Green Door*. The American public stopped paying two dollars to see a bedroom comedy with Cary Grant and Irene Dunne as soon as one

151

could see Lucille Ball as Lucy for nothing. Hollywood tried 3-D to lure the shut-in from the tube with limited success and then discovered, as Hugh Hefner had discovered, that a naked woman is not only front-page news but hard-ticket box office.

Let me offer also that the censors and would-be censors, those who would bowdlerize and those who would suppress, are always wrong. They always overestimate their hand. If the public gives them leave to track down hard-core pornography, they feel compelled in the process to knock down Steinbeck's *The Grapes of Wrath*, Faulkner's *Sanctuary*, Joyce's *Ulysses*, Henry Miller's *Tropic of Cancer*, and Edmund Wilson's *Memoirs of Hecate County*.

Make a nice ordinary businessman like Arthur Summerfield postmaster and he immediately bans mailings of *Lysistrata*, a play that enjoyed continuous publication since Aristophanes wrote it.

Unalterable plots

PROBABLY THE greatest plot in all literature is the Cinderella legend—the story of the little glass slipper. Just who wrote it makes little difference. Perhaps it was never really written in the sense we recognize authorship. Very likely, the legend in some form was born in that dim era where legend hardly ends and history barely begins. I am sure that after primitive man satisfied his bodily needs, he began to imagine coming upon good fortune—suddenly—and he kept changing this legend to fit his environment as he wandered across the face of the earth.

Essentially the Cinderella story is the story of getting something for nothing, of finding the crystal spring in the desert or redressing cruel fortune's blows. It is the story that lets us believe there is retributive justice in the universe, that the good will be rewarded and the bad punished.

Cinderella exists in many forms. Sean O'Casey tells the Cinderella story in his masterpiece, *Juno and the Paycock*, in which the oppressed captain comes upon a windfall only to have it vanish at the play's end. The Cinderella legend is applicable to all times and all places.

Man's everlasting hope to come upon good fortune suddenly is reflected every time he buys a lottery ticket or places a bet on a twenty-to-one shot.

Lord Bacon wrote, "The carrying of men from hope to hope is the greatest antidote to the seeds of discontent."

Next in the order of great plots is Daniel Defoe's story of Robinson Crusoe, the shipwrecked man on an uninhabited island, only his ingenuity between him and extinction.

There would have been no story at all to Robinson Crusoe unless there was a witness to his individual worth. That witness was, of course, his man Friday.

In the Cinderella story we have the chance at hope for a better life and in the Robinson Crusoe narrative the story of human relations.

No matter how many stars we explore in space, we will never alter these two basic themes.

The art of writing

ANYONE WHO writes will confirm that writing prompts three species of complaints. Of course sometimes writing invests the constituency with joy and sometimes with understanding and sometimes amusement. But no matter how hard the scribbler tries, there are those ready to weigh in with criticism.

The first of these, the one most commonly charged against

a writer, is that whatever he wrote, he wrote for money. Or Samuel Johnson observed that only a blockhead would write for no money but the fact that a man in the twentieth century gets paid for his efforts as logical constructs outrages some. He is placed in the category of the baseball player who holds out: Everyone knows a center fielder should be out there for the sheer love of the game. Royalties for a book or payment for an article somehow demeans the prose. Which is a comment on our society and its shabby values. If a writer is to be dismissed as a genuine contributor for receiving monies, it leaves us with the truth that the only worthwhile folks in our society are the PTA vice presidents and blood bank donors who rap their gavels and open their veins for the love of rapping gavels and opening veins.

The second criticism is "You should have asked me first." When I wrote a book about the South some years ago, I got a letter from a Mayor in Mississippi, saying that if I had talked to him I would have understood that the Southerners cannot change their way of life; when I wrote a book about Israel, I got letters from Tel Aviv cab drivers stating that if I had but sought them out I would have spared my readers grievous errors; and recently, when I published a book about Jewish communities in different American cities, at least ten rabbis wrote to inform me that since I hadn't interviewed them about Hartford or Cleveland or St. Louis I didn't know what I was talking about.

The last complaint, the one that hurts, is that your prose is journalistic. I do not know why it hurts, but it does. There is nothing wrong with journalese. Some of the most profound truths in this world have been issued in the newspapers. But the readers get annoyed if a writer writes as though his composition would grace a page of the daily. It means he does not write like Mark Twain or Ernest Hemingway or William Faulkner. Alas! It is hard to write like Mark Twain, Ernest Hemingway, and William Faulkner. In fact, toward the end of their careers Twain, Hemingway, and Faulkner were each trying in his own way to copy his younger efforts.

I remember a reviewer who complained that what he missed in my books was the profundity he got out of Thoreau and Emerson. It is useless to explain I didn't set up as Thoreau or Emerson. All I could reply was that the critic didn't sound like Sainte-Beuve or Edmund Wilson to me.

The library stiff

I WROTE an article for the *New York Times Book Review* in which I described how the tramps used to come into the lectures that were held free at the Cooper Union Institute. These tramps used to come in to escape the cold but after a couple of winters of listening to Clarence Darrow and Will Durant and Eugene V. Debs and Margaret Sanger these tramps were amazingly erudite—more so than many in the respectable audience. About two weeks after this little piece appeared, I received a letter from a hobo who had read the article and wanted to introduce himself.

He was still happily on the road, he said, but he was what the Wobblies used to call "a library stiff." Most of the hoboes, he said, used to find out on what track the slow freight left and at what time and make off to the poolrooms or the town bar until they could highball out. But this made them easy prey for the "town clowns" (cops) who would daily raid these two places and "vag" all the hoboes. This fellow used to make for the library, where the cops never made an arrest, let alone thought a hobo was taking refuge there. It was a good, warm place to sleep. But the curious thing that happened was that this fellow began reading the books he hid behind. He has spent much of his time in libraries all over the country and he recalled some of the famous ones. He was sorry to learn that the old Rivington Street branch of the New York Public Library had been torn down, but he was glad Cooper Union was still standing and flourishing.

How to weather the workshop

Do YOU have any idea how many hours the classroom teacher is required to sit and listen to what is usually a lot of pompous hogwash about the Whole Child, sometimes on weekends or after school, sometimes during school hours, while twenty-five to thirty "whole children" are left with busy work, which, at the junior high level, shortly turns into mayhem, and who can blame the kids!

Teachers have different ways of enduring these lectures. After one high-salaried "English consultant" informed them that "reading is a language skill"—and proceeded to develop this ludicrous statement—one smart teacher acquired a transistor radio with earplugs and sat out the rest of the "workshops" that year with Chubby Checker, whose "message" made as much sense as, if not more than, the vacant terminology of the "In-Service Program" and the big paper on the "Culturally Disadvantaged," prepared in all seriousness by a big educator at a Stanford University "workshop," you should pardon the expression.

Reason triumphs

SOME YEARS ago I remember reading a report that concerned the philosophy department of a reputable Ivy League school. The teachers were all in conference trying to outline teaching methods when the logic professor got so mad at the

156

ethics professor that he punched the latter in the nose, thereby proving logic wins again.

My degrees

I RECEIVED honorary degrees from a Catholic college, a Methodist college, a Presbyterian college, and a black university, and now from a Lutheran college, Thiel College in Greenville, Pennsylvania.

All I get from the Jews is a pledge card.

The event at Thiel College on May 25, 1974, was exceedingly gratifying to me. The administrators, the faculty, and the students were highly receptive and the campus is beautiful. Here is an excerpt from my commencement address:

It is a great honor to be here. I hope I can avoid the usual platitudes of the occasion, platitudes which include such things as "Today I am a man," or "Go forth and conquer," or "Graduation is only a commencement," and so forth. And yet this does not mean that you will necessarily remember anything of world-shaking importance out of my commencement address.

When I graduated from the East Side Evening High School of New York in 1919, I remember that the commencement speaker was an Annapolis man who had been in the first graduating class. He had sailed with Admiral Dewey into Manila Bay in 1898. While I was writing this speech I tried to remember what this speaker had told my class but I could not. All that stands out in my mind is a fellow looking trim and smart in his blue commander's uniform, and one phrase. He told us that before Dewey had beaten the

157

Spanish fleet, Manila was spelled with two *l*'s. But Admiral Dewey had knocked the *l* out of Manila.

I wonder if this is to be my fate. Some of you undoubtedly will be commencement speakers, and you'll have to make up a story of your own, and such originality is all to the good.

I suspect you will forget what I have to say to you. You see, you are the toughest audience any speaker has to face. It is simply terrifying to stand up and speak to a body of college students. I say this advisedly, you are the toughest audience in the country. You are all smarter than I am. All of you see things more clearly because you are more willing to accept them. You are stronger than any one of us in this audience of forty and over. Some of you, within the next few years, will make decisions that would leave me and all of my fellow elders weak and nervous. You are going to decide what to do with your lives while the rest of us are wondering what we did with ours.

Thoughts on spring

OF ALL the seasons, poets have devoted most of their verses to the spring. Chaucer begins *The Canterbury Tales* with, "Whan that Aprille with his shoures sote/ The Droughte of Marche hath perced to the rote . . ." and T. S. Eliot begins *The Wasteland* with the observation, "April is the cruellest month, breeding lilacs out of the dead land. . . ." The choice of April is not haphazard for either poet. For Chaucer spring was the season of growth and life and for Eliot spring was the season of decay.

And some of our prose writers are as dour. Cyril Connolly said spring is a call to action and hence to disillusion and

Samuel Butler said that youth is like the spring—an over-praised season—delightful if it happened to be favored but more usually rainy and gloomy.

Nature will have its way. The spring cannot be denied. It is a time of hope. It is what Shelley meant when he wrote, "If winter comes can spring be far behind?" and what Vachel Lindsay summed up in his line, "The spring comes on forever."

PART 5

Blacks, Jews, Gradualism, and Breakfast in Texas

Life in these United States

A YOUNG girl entered an Orlando, Florida, department store and selected a blue bathing suit. She went off to try it. The dressing rooms were marked "white" and "colored" and she entered the "colored" dressing room.

The salesgirl said, "Why did you go to the wrong dressing room?" The young girl replied, "I bought a colored bathing suit. Where was I supposed to go?"

Above all, human dignity

How DID the struggle against the "separate but equal" doctrine develop? Remember that all the early black lawsuits never challenged "separate," their attack was on "equal," because nothing was "equal."

While Earl Warren was still Governor of California, it was the Kentuckian Chief Justice Fred M. Vinson who set the new direction for the social revolution of the American black. While the blacks were still suing for "equal" in the Sweatt and McLaurin cases, Justice Vinson said "separate" was immoral and unconstitutional. This was the big moment in the civil rights movement of America's mid-twentieth century.

The Vinson Court was stating a philosophical truth in deciding that the black law school in Texas was not equal to the University of Texas at Austin, by the mere fact of being separate. Facilities had nothing to do with it. The Supreme Court said that education also involves the reputation of the faculty, the status of the alumni, the prestige of the university, the size of its library, and the ability to communicate with the other students.

Enunciated here is the truth a man is more than body and mind. He is also spirit.

But the resistance continues, and it continues only because of the need for a caste system.

We must be clear about this because I believe it is the basis of the entire problem. In the South as elsewhere it is a matter of caste and nothing else. All the other factors involved are pretexts. The blacks, as a matter of fact, do live in the finest homes in the country. In the South they live in the finest mansions in the most exclusive neighborhoods. In New York they live on Park Avenue and in Chicago they live on Lake Shore Drive. But in all these places they live in peace and in harmony because they do not pay rent—they are servants.

The moment the black wants to become a payer of rent, the backs arch and he is denied admittance. If it were a matter of anything else but caste, he would not be sleeping in the same room with the children in the fancy house and neither would he be the janitor in residence in the finest apartment houses on Park Avenue. A black with a white coat and a black leather bow tie has access to every room in the finest hotel in the South.

And the reason for the caste system goes much deeper than habit or what the Southerners call "the way of life." There are 1,850,000 industrial workers in the South who have been getting from 60¢ to $1.10 an hour less than the workers doing the same jobs for the same number of hours in the North. We are a school-oriented society; once the schools are integrated, the entire pattern of segregation collapses and this includes the places of employment of these industrial workers. He will say, "I've been willing to work for from sixty cents to a dollar ten an hour less than the fellow who does the same job in Pennsylvania. I've been willing to do this because of racial segregation. Now the blacks are going to school with my kids and I want that sixty cents to a dollar ten an hour more than I'm getting now." You multiply this by 1,850,000 industrial workers and we can see what tremendous stakes are involved in the maintenance of a caste system.

When you draw a line so that certain people may not cross that line, you'll find yourself spending the rest of your life watching the line. As the black makes his drive for middle-class status, the Southerner will find outside his door the largest untapped consumer's market in the country. And the South may again become a source of poetic creativity. Its Senators and Governors will no longer worry night and day whether a black is moving from the back of the bus to the front.

Interestingly enough, it is precisely in the South where we now have evidence that Americans can live together constructively. We do not get much of this good news because a bully-boy sheriff is more sensational. But the amazing paradox here is that the ones who have won the immediate victory out of the civil rights movement have been the white Southerners. They are picking up all the marbles especially where integration has been accelerated, as in Charlotte, Winston-Salem, Durham, Richmond, Nashville, Atlanta. The money is rolling in. The streets are paved with gold. In these cities and in at least another dozen we see the proof of the late President John F. Kennedy's aphorism: "The rising tide lifts all the boats."

We must smile at those who say that law cannot do it. They would negate the foundation of the Anglo-Saxon ethos. Was it not law itself that established segregation? This did not come down from heaven; it was law that decreed the back of the bus, and separate schools, and bus stations, and it was law that shut the black out of the mainstream of the American civilization. Law made it and law is unmaking it.

The Southerners themselves came to the Constitutional Convention—Tennent, Gadsden, and Pinckney—demanding a provision for religious freedom. The Presbyterians had gone underground with their first seminary

165

and the Methodists built their first churches with a fireplace so that when the Anglican sheriff came around to arrest them, they could hide their prayer books and say they were visiting the sick. In arguing for law guaranteeing religious freedom, Rev. Tennent paid his tribute to the great libertarians of the day, but he said, "The hearts of men doth change." Today in the Deep South there are blacks working in cotton mills performing a white man's job for the first time in history and these white men, mind you, were those who were the fiercest in their resistance to integration. The blacks were there because of the federal government's directive. If you discriminate, you lose your government contract. And even the poor white of the Carolinas, Georgia, and Alabama, said, "Bring them in."

When you consider this, you'll realize that the American Southerner can answer in the affirmative: "Can Americans live together constructively?" It will take some time to remove the myths and backstairs legends. In our ghettos at the turn of this century we did not like each other; a Jewish kid would not dare walk through an Irish neighborhood; an Italian would not dare come into the Jewish ghetto. But Tammany Hall taught us that we didn't have to marry each other or visit each other or even say hello to each other. But if we voted together, each of us would achieve equity. If the white American wage earner and the black voted together, our race problem would be purely academic; we wouldn't even be conducting meetings because the answers to our questions would be coming from the eighty thousand voting precincts. The grandeur of America is that we are a politically oriented society.

But a vast political coalition of white wage earners and blacks appears to be a long way off. And so the civil rights movement must go on.

People in New York tell me about the Puerto Ricans; the tenements smell bad, they hang the wash on the line, they leave the baby carriages in the hallway. And my reply is, they said the same thing about your mother fifty years ago.

166

Proust has a line in his great book, *Remembrance of Things Past*: "The hatred of Captain Dreyfus opened the doors of the aristocrats to the bourgeoisie." Of course it is better to be a superior white than a mill hand or a letter carrier.

And we fortify this illusion by an evil myth—the myth that "they are pushing." This fake makes of us poor harassed martyrs and sets us up as big shots, such big shots that people are falling all over themselves to live next door to us. The worst evil nonsense of all, "They are pushing," was said of the Irish in 1880, of the Jews in 1900, of the Italians and Poles in 1910, and now of the blacks and Puerto Ricans. And none of these people was pushing. They were escaping, escaping from filth, degradation, and early death.

We have wonderful projects, privately financed for research: polio, heart, cancer, tuberculosis, muscular dystrophy, all worthwhile projects that perform great services to the people. But did you know that the third-biggest killer in fourteen of our states is pregnancy—black pregnancy? There are no drives for that. In fact, no research is even necessary. We have the facilities and the know-how to remedy the situation, a situation due to segregation and discrimination. The fact that tuberculosis, which is twelfth as a cause of death among whites, is third as a cause of death among blacks is due to the slums.

What is actually involved is the recognition of humanity. Because above all else is human dignity. A human being can go without food longer than he can go without human dignity.

Here is a true story. It was on an intelligence test for black children as part of an antipoverty project. One of the pictures on the paper was of a window with a crack in it. "What's wrong with this picture?" was the question. And none of the black children gave the answer. A crack in a window was not a "wrong" to them. They had cardboard for windows or rags, or they had no windows at all.

We must not permit the wonders of science to obscure the greater wonder of human kindness.

These are the common enemies that underlie all forms of tyranny—racism, authoritarianism, McCarthyism. They are no less enemies when being sold or offered as truth or salvation by blacks, yellows, or whites.

If blacks and whites who understand this can make it clear, we can help to save America. For America cannot survive if blacks do not. And blacks and no other group of human beings are likely to survive if America does not.

The scattered ghetto

I RATHER smile at the "restrictions" against Jews. The discrimination in housing and in country clubs and in summer resorts is a fit subject for humor, because the Jews are largely in the middle class, perhaps even in the upper middle class.

Each rebuff results in a new development far more opulent and far more luxurious than the restrictors ever dreamed of. I think back to my weekend visits to Jennie Grossinger's in the Catskill Mountains and to the Concord (which Jennie's people call "*dortens*," meaning "there," not deigning to mention the name of the competitor). Neither Julius Caesar nor Augustus nor Kublai Khan ever dreamed of such magnificence. So I should worry about a few joints around the country restricting Jews? A few joints with insects, and with no hot onion rolls for breakfast with cream cheese and herring and wine sauce? Phooey. This you call discrimination? Compared to Jewish resorts, Jewish country clubs, and Jewish residential sections, one feels sorry for the misery of such places as Camelback Inn and White Sulphur Springs and The Cloisters down in Georgia.

The day the blacks have a Grossinger's and a Concord, I will cease in my agitation against housing discrimination.

This is not because the Jews are more ingenious—nonsense. We are all the result of the conditions to which we've been exposed. Jews have Theodosius to thank. If the Emperor Theodosius had scattered the Jews throughout Europe as slaves, as was done with the black man, the result would have been the same for us. Instead Theodosius and the early church fathers made the mistake of their lives. They relegated the Jews to the ghetto—a spiritual, mental, and physical fortress, a homogeneous society that allowed only one avenue of self-esteem—the practice of human dignity—and with only one avenue of escape—reading books.

If Jewish survival was partly based on confinement in ghettos, why did the blacks not do as well when they were in ghettos? The big difference is that since the middle of the seventeenth century until the end of the nineteenth century the blacks were scattered and not in ghettos; they were scattered as slaves. Under slavery they were enjoined. Whenever the plantation owner saw a close attachment between blacks, he sold off the wife or the husband or children. The secret of survival is the family. The Jews made their religion a family religion. This is the big difference.

As it is, the black has done well enough. His intellectual advancement with both hands tied behind his back has been nothing short of phenomenal.

A spectacular advance in the field of desegregation came when I addressed a Roman Catholic meeting at Lexington, Massachusetts, with Msgr. Casey, the chairman. The young priest who introduced me told the audience of two thousand people that they would find cards on their seats. He instructed them, "After the speaker gets through, ushers will pick up those cards, which we hope you will sign after reading them." I thought this was church business and paid no further attention. After the lecture the lights went up and the ushers went down the aisles and picked up the cards and brought them to the platform.

Out of the two thousand in the audience some seven hundred signed cards that read: "I hereby promise that if a Negro family moves into my neighborhood, I will not move out, but will visit the Negro family and welcome them. I give permission for the use of my name and address and telephone number in any way the bishop decides to use it in an attempt to break down racial discrimination in housing."

Southern womanhood

THE MOST interesting aspect of the celebrated Montgomery bus strike revolved around the attitudes of the whites toward their black domestics. The husband came home from his meeting with the white citizens' council and he saw the black domestic who had joined the strike and he said, "Get out." The next morning the fellow's wife drove to the domestic's home and took her to work and said, "Don't you worry what my husband tells you, I'm going to come for you every day."

It was essentially this that won for the blacks. The Southern woman would not do without her domestic.

She does not speak of mongrelization but she uses the term "biggity." "She is biggity" is an expression of resentment against the possibility of losing a domestic. The domestic reaches the point where she may want a job as a nurse or department store buyer or a secretary and she is automatically "getting biggity."

Vast thousands of Southern women for nearly three-quarters of a century were never accustomed to work because the black domestics did it all and were easily obtainable in an agricultural society. Many Southern women would joke, "If I ever try to make up a bed, I'll fall in it."

Southern password

MANY WHITE Southerners, for one reason or another, found it inexpedient to express their views for integration publicly. But quietly they developed a system of communication that spread throughout the states of the Old Confederacy.

When these people met a black on the street or if a black came to the door for one reason or another, these white Southerners whispered, "We shall overcome," and the black replied, "Someday."

Many housewives greeted their black cooks in this manner, and it was the first "communication" of its kind as citizen equals. You noticed it particularly in the elevators of business and professional buildings. "We shall overcome," whispered a white-coated doctor, and without turning to the speaker, the black whispered his amen, "Someday."

The two greatest singing movements in American history have been the Wobblies (Industrial Workers of the World) of the 1890's and the Negro "freedom" movement of the 1950's and 1960's.

The Wobblies gave trade unionism its most important song, "Solidarity Forever," as well as a hymn of mourning for the greatest Wobbly of them all, Joe Hill:

> I dreamed I saw Joe Hill last night
>   Alive as you and me.
> Says I, "But, Joe, you're ten years dead."
>   "I never died," says he.
>   "I never died," says he.

This is gradualism?

NOWADAYS A surprising number of our Southern seg-
regationist friends are paying homage to Booker T. Washington. How they love Booker T. Washington! They have a
reason. Back around 1905, Booker T. Washington told blacks
they would have to wait, things weren't going to come their
way. Whether he would have voiced these sentiments in 1960
or 1970 is a moot question. Fortunately for the segregationists, Booker T. isn't around.

What helped the revival of Booker T. Washington's popularity was the news about Dr. W. E. B. Du Bois, who died at age
ninety-five, in Ghana, an African citizen.

Dr. W. E. B. Du Bois was the impetus behind the Niagara
Movement, which later became the National Association for
the Advancement of Colored People. Dr. Du Bois also joined
the Communist Party at age ninety-three, an incident that
brought sobs deplorable from a few Southern editors who
mourned the fact that Dr. Du Bois had replaced that "fine
Negro, that wonderful citizen, Booker T. Washington."

These few Southern editors forget that when President
Theodore Roosevelt invited Booker T. Washington to the
White House, their editorial forebears screamed, "The most
damnable outrage ever!" A New Orleans newspaper was led
to question, "White men of the South: how do you like it?" Of
course, the ancestors of these indignant journalists write
today and recall, "Oh, for the good old days of Booker T."

This is gradualism.

In the 1950's Du Bois was brought handcuffed into an
American court and was charged with advocating peace while
acting as an unregistered foreign agent. After a week's trial
the case against him collapsed. Dr. Du Bois urged: "Let us be
humble, not arrogant or boastful in the awful crisis. My words
are not a counsel of despair. Rather they are a call to new
courage and determination to know the truth."

Dr. Du Bois deserves better of all Americans, white and

black. Perhaps he gave us a clue as to why he took this desperate step and joined the Communist Party at so advanced an age and why he left to become a citizen of Ghana. It is in something he wrote in 1934:

> It is a peculiar sensation, this double-consciousness, this sense of always looking at one's self through the eyes of others. One feels his twoness, an American, a Negro; two souls, two thoughts, two unreconciled strivings: two warring ideals in one dark body, whose dogged strength alone keeps it from being torn asunder.

Jews in the black ghetto

THE JEWISH peddler filled a great need of the Southern black. The Jewish peddler supplied the blacks when the whites wanted none of his trade. The peddler extended credit and peddled necessities like mattresses and shoes and clocks. Also, he let the black try on clothes he might wish to purchase, a practice still forbidden in many stores throughout the modern South.

Much the same might be said of the Jewish storekeeper who set up in the black ghetto.

The relation between the Jewish shopkeeper and the black continued right into the 1930's.

It is quite true that in some cases the shopkeeper exploited the dire poverty and ignorance of the black. But there was more to it than that. The Jewish shopkeeper was a center of communication. He knew the names of lawyers when the black needed one, he knew the names of doctors when a child was ill, he had a much more tenable relationship with the police. And he sold everything the black needed.

Sometime around the 1930's, however, the white "uptown"

stores began beckoning to the black. It was in these stores that the black found better quality at cheaper prices. These stores beckoned to the black because they realized that with the New Deal the black had found a bonanza. For the unemployed white man a relief check of $23.86 was a dole; for the unemployed black, a weekly fortune. The "uptown" stores offered easy terms; often they let the black take home goods with no down payment or with only a token down payment. To this day the Southern black is the largest credit buyer. Hundreds upon hundreds of blacks who had never left the ghetto before were now going uptown to the big stores.

But it was in this process that the black found how dismaying sitting in the back of the bus was, how humiliating and uncomfortable it was not to have rest-room facilities, how cruel it was not to be able to sit at the snack bar in the very store that was making a profit on his purchase. And it was on these trips back and forth to the beckoning uptown store that he found out he could not even go to a movie, and that if the child had to go to the toilet, the black woman had to take the kid all the way back home.

The civil rights movement was no sudden impulse. It had been building up for forty years.

Nobody here but us Aryans

MRS. TOBIN, the real estate saleswoman, was very upset because she met with resistance in a very wealthy suburb when she tried to sell a house to the Reuben Ecksteins. Only Aryans were acceptable. She blandly bought the house herself and the neighbors shook the martini cobwebs from their eyes as they saw a tribe of Gypsies move in.

The Gypsies hung their wash from the beautiful front balconies; a score of bold-eyed handsome Gypsy lads ogled the neighbors in giggling delight. Noble Aryans, one and all. Mrs.

Tobin ultimately sold the house to the richest family on the street, the family that had five daughters. Mrs. Tobin made a handsome profit on the sale.

The liberal Turks

ON MAY 16, 1963, the United States concluded a treaty with the Ottoman Empire, Article 46 of which contained a provision that no consul resident in Turkey would recognize the claim of any American citizen to hold any person in slavery or in bondage within the limits of the Turkish Empire.

Breakfast in Texas

No WHITE man, South or North, is ugly or discourteous to an individual black on a face-to-face basis. It is only when fear, fostered by myths, legends, and stereotypes, overcomes white men that they resist admitting 11 percent of the American population to the responsibility, joys, and life in the industrial age of the twentieth century. Sometimes, however, the black is able to wage his fight as an *individual*.

An example: Dr. Benjamin Mays, a great and recognized black educator, entered a grill-type restaurant in Texas. It was a small place and uncrowded, but when Dr. Mays sat down at the counter, the waitress approached him with a worried look. While she was polite, she had come to whisper that she couldn't serve him. "If I do," she said, "the other diners will leave."

Dr. Mays rose from his place and clapped his hands for attention. The patrons turned to him. Dr. Mays announced that he would like to eat there, but if any white patron wanted to walk out if he were served, he promised he would leave immediately. No one got up. Several of the diners applauded. Dr. Mays ate his breakfast.

Duke, 100, Carolina, 0

A STUDENT group at the University of North Carolina at Chapel Hill invited two speakers to the campus—Herbert Aptheker, a self-proclaimed Marxist theoretician, and Frank Wilkinson, a long-time supporter of leftist movements.

The students were testing the Speaker's Ban Law, which the North Carolina Legislature had passed, then repealed in the face of a threat to both the university's accreditation and its reputation.

But the legislature, in its repeal, added an amendment that though anyone could be invited to address the student body, only the university trustees could pass on who could appear.

The students wanted to see if the ban was still in effect.

The trustees met and, after serious deliberation, said no, the students couldn't listen to either Mr. Aptheker or Mr. Wilkinson, it was too dangerous.

Within hours of the decision, Duke University at Durham invited the same two men to speak.

Duke is thirty miles from Chapel Hill and the Duke students extended invitations to the Chapel Hill students. Duke, of course, is a privately endowed university. Formerly it was known as Trinity College and was a devout Methodist school. There was a time when the liberals of the University of North Carolina at Chapel Hill laughed at the stuffed shirts of the fancy Duke University. But as fast as Chapel Hill has declined, Duke has now become the best-equipped and best-staffed university in North Carolina, perhaps in the South.

Once this was Chapel Hill's boast. That was in the days when President Frank P. Graham made Chapel Hill a byword for Southern liberalism.

176

And the academic freedom at Duke is no accident. Where would you look for the official papers of the American Socialist Party? At the Rand School maybe? At the New School for Social Research? Or the New York Public Library? Or in the private library of Norman Thomas?

Not at all. The official papers of the American Socialist Party are in the library of Duke University, a school endowed with the millions of Buck Duke, the symbol of big-business buccaneers. Buck lies buried a few yards farther than the library in the Gothic splendor of Duke Chapel. And I wonder what would make him turn over in his grave quicker: that Duke entertained Aptheker and Wilkinson or that the University of North Carolina has its academic activities screened.

The Irish and organized labor

I WAS the guest speaker at the annual dinner of the Friendly Sons of St. Patrick at Middletown, Ohio, one St. Patrick's Day. Middletown, between Cincinnati and Dayton, holds a prosperous population of some forty-five thousand and the principal industry and influence is the Armco Steel Company.

It was a grand night for me and Frank Parker, the Italian who sings Irish ballads. It is good to relax once a year in the feeling that God and everybody else loves the Irish; that their ancestral home is a land of saints and scholars; that the Irish won the Revolutionary War for George Washington and the Civil War for the North; and that they have defended and saved every country in which they have taken root.

And this has great value for our democracy. The Irish contributed as much as anyone to American democracy, probably more. They were the first to articulate the pluralistic principle upon which our country rests. The Poles were tithing for a free Poland at the turn of the century, the Pennsylvania Czechs were hoping for a free Bohemia, the Jews were arguing Zionism, but it is the Irish who helped confirm the principle. They were helped by the fact that they were immigrants but they spoke English and could explain that their roles as Catholics and as partisans for a free Ireland in no way affected their disposition and loyalty toward the United States. If you ever question an Irishman about "dual loyalty," he shouts, "Up Sligo."

I told the Friendly Sons of St. Patrick in Middletown that I believe the Irish are one of the ten lost tribes of Israel. My facts are good facts. I listed them while the good Irish whisky flowed after Frank Parker sang "When Irish Eyes Are Smiling." These facts are that Jeremiah had come to Ireland; that he died on the Holy Hill of Tara (Torah), the Law; that the British royal standard (which precedes the days of "The Trouble") has David's harp in a field of emerald green with the image of the lion of Judah and the whelps.

Despite the occasion, it was not a completely happy day for *all* the Irish. It was a sad day for a friend of mine, David MacDonald, head of the steelworkers' union. Although I saw no point in telling these upper-class Irish at the Middletown dinner about it, David MacDonald and I are good friends and the day before the dinner he and his union had suffered an overwhelming defeat in attempting to organize Armco Steel.

Middletown (like Kannapolis, North Carolina) is a one-company town where all the employees are well treated. The company participates in all the community activities and in religious life and both Armco and Mr. Cannon (who owns Kannapolis) have found this participation and activity the best defense against encroaching unionism.

And this is the big union problem today.

It is no secret that trade unionism has been at a standstill in recent years. In fact, the movement is losing members. The drive is gone. When people get too rich and too comfortable, they go to the horse races. They do not think of themselves as organizers anymore.

The rest of the problem is with philosophy. Labor has not adjusted itself to the new demands of organization.

Some of the boys are still preaching "class war," and there is no "class war." Workingmen are joining civic clubs and private swimming pools and buying luxury items and they do not listen to that nonsense. The fellow's wife has a bridge club and the insurance companies sell him policies that will enable him to send his kids to college.

Look back several decades to one of the early strikes the steelmen won. Their demands were for a nine-hour day and an increase of fifteen cents an hour. Today such demands are out of the question. Wages and hours are regulated, more or less, and no organizer can recruit a member by promising him fifteen cents an hour more.

The companies themselves give employees many of the same benefits the union once offered. In many plants the employers take this initiative when they learn the union has started campaigning. Right away they raise wages to union levels. This takes all the steam out of the organizer.

What he cannot convince the workers of is that the raises they receive and the benefits they enjoy are directly due to strong unions elsewhere.

Organized labor must find a formula of communication between itself and the unorganized workers. The organizers must convince the worker that what he has today he has because other union men gave it to him. If this worker does not join in organization, he shirks his responsibility and he will lose what he has as soon as the employer thinks he can shave it down. Until the unions find this formula, they must face decline.

But what I started out to say, from the bottom of my heart, is long live the Irish.

Revelations of a strike

IT HAS been forty-five years since the general strike at the Loray Mills in Gastonia, North Carolina, twenty miles west of Charlotte.

The first textile mill in the South had been built on the banks of the nearby Catawba River fifty years before the strike. Gaston and Mecklenburg counties were the pioneering counties in importing the New England textile mill and mill town into the South. The mills had helped the South recover from the crippling effects of the Civil War. But in fifty years abuse had piled upon abuse.

The strike against the Loray Mill, the largest single mill in the South, was led by Communists. (I gave Fred Beal, the Communist strike leader, a job selling advertising for *The Carolina Israelite* sometime after he was paroled from the North Carolina penitentiary in the early 1940's.) Fred Beal and some other Communist leaders were tried and convicted for conspiracy in the murder of Gastonia Police Chief Aderholt at the height of the strike violence.

After their conviction Beal and his codefendants skipped their bail and fled to Russia. They were welcomed there as American labor martyrs. But Fred Beal was no simple, Stalinist personality. What he saw in Russia deeply disillusioned him. He returned to America, surrendered himself, and served his sentence. He became an anathema to the Communist Party in America. He was truthful about what the Communist Party in America did. He was truthful about what the Communist aim in Gastonia had been and what the aims in Russia were. When he was asked how much better were the workingman's conditions in Russia than America, he laughed and said, "To think that I was fighting for workers who eat flap jacks and bacon for breakfast!"

Beal might have become the new sort of American celebrity, the recanting, confessing celebrity. But instead of going from the deep "left" to the far "right," he went from "left" to the "center." He tried lecturing, but was unsuccessful. People were ripe for the McCarthy-type informer, and this Beal could never be. Fred Beal became the forgotten man of the labor wars. He had one last brief flurry of publicity before he died when he petitioned the courts to have his citizenship restored.

To talk of the Gastonia strike means necessarily to talk of Dr. Liston Pope's classic, *Millhands and Preachers*. Dr. Pope was a professor at the Yale Divinity School. His book, published in 1941, is a profound study of the role of the churches in the Loray Strike. *Millhands and Preachers* leaves no doubt that Gastonia was one of the two genuine class wars we have had in America (the other being the Montgomery bus strike). In fact, Gastonia was more than a class war, it was a small revolution, a shooting revolution. Guardsmen patrolled the streets, there were barricades, and under kerosene lamps strikers and managers plotted battle strategy.

The Loray Mill was surrounded by a large picket fence. When the mill hands reported for work every morning, the gate was locked. The Loray Mill was called "the jail." The mill hand put in twelve hours a day. He worked the "stretch-out" system where he kept himself ever on the run caring for more and more looms. Mill hands say six looms is all the stretch-out system can ask of a man. In the Loray Mill the men watched twelve. When the mill hand's wife went to the washrooms, she was timed to the second by the foreman. Children were impressed into the mill at the age of six or seven because, said management and the preachers, they liked work better than school.

When the cage was unlocked, the mill hand went home to the mill village owned by the mill management. He rented a four-room shack from the company, bought at the company store, attended the company church. Malaria, pellagra, and typhoid fever were ever present. For many years the mill hands had been petitioning for window screens, toilets, and bathing facilities. Company police, called "social workers," patrolled both mill and village. In March the Loray Mill cut the workers' pay. In a burst of spontaneous agitation, the workers left the mill. It was April Fool's Day, 1929.

I say it was a revolution for the simple reason that company management never considered arbitration. Strikers and managers lived in two different cultures and once the strike was called, each threatened the other. The millowners treated the strike as a species of treason and, under the protection of the National Guard, began to import workers from South Carolina. The day after the strike began, the mill superintendents began to evict workers from the mill shacks. There was no more credit at the company store. The National Textile Workers Union, a Communist-dominated organization, had infiltrated the strikers and was in command of strike strategy.

The mill women attacked the Guardsmen. The mill hands ambushed the scabs. The police arrested everyone. The strikers were forced from the mill property to adjacent fields, where they set up a tent colony. The severe deprivation, coupled with the clear knowledge that the company was not going to yield, had diminished the strike force from several thousand to a hard core of militant agitators.

One night in May the Gastonia police force made a raid on this tent colony. The police were asked by the strike guards to produce search warrants. When police refused, the strikers would not let them pass. There was a scuffle. Soon firing broke out. One striker and several police officers were wounded. Police Chief Aderholt died of wounds the next day. This broke the back of the strike. It unleashed a wave of vigilantism and led also to the arrest of all the strike leaders.

Another slaying took place a few weeks later. Vigilantes, chasing strikers from the county, opened fire and killed Ella May Wiggins, one of the strike leaders and the mother of seven. Although the shooting took place in broad daylight with fifty or more witnesses, no one was ever indicted or tried. All over Gaston County there were beatings, floggings,

182

and kidnappings. Bit by bit the strike was crushed by force.

The strike failed in one sense because the Communists had an invincible ignorance about the mill hands. The mill hands were not educated in the ways of dialectical materialism. When the managers accused the Communists of atheism, they proudly admitted it. This is a sudden-death admission in the Bible Belt. The mill hands were absolutely incapable of measuring their own interests with atheism. And, of course, the Communists were exploiting the strikers for whatever vague aims the Communists had. Much of the money raised for strike relief by mass meetings elsewhere in the country never found its way to Gastonia. (Fred Beal estimated that at least one million dollars was collected from audiences around the world, not a dollar of which ever reached Gastonia.)

Gastonia served this purpose for other strikes that broke out over all the mill communities of the South: When Communists appeared, the strikers invariably ran them out of town. Very probably the inability of the Communist Party to recruit members in the South may be laid indirectly to the way its members conducted themselves in Gastonia. They had tried to make the mill hands into their image instead of themselves into the mill hands' image.

By the winter of the year, of course, the Great Depression had set in. For many years the mill was idle. Eventually it went into bankruptcy and was bought by a rubber company and converted. The Depression, which brought new problems, dimmed the memory of Gastonia's violence, as did the New Deal reforms. World War II made the strike ancient history. But Gastonia will never be completely forgotten.

It made another South. For there have been two Souths in the American imagination—the South that existed before the Gastonia strike and the South after it. Before 1929 the South was imagined as a place of the sweet magnolia, the many-pillared mansion, the cavalier, and the manners of a soft-spoken aristocracy. After 1929 America and the rest of the world knew that the South was a place, too, of the ugly mill villages and of the millowner who controlled body and soul of every one of his thousand workers.

Before the Gastonia strike the novels of William Faulkner or Robert Penn Warren or Erskine Caldwell would have been incomprehensible. Gastonia taught Americans that the last of its indigeneous cultures—the old South, with its deep agrarian roots and culture—had vanished.

Understanding your neighbors

THE OBVIOUS function of a society, wrote Samuel Butler, is to get along with itself. For so simple a statement, this remains a hard lesson for society to learn.

A friend once said to Charles Lamb, "Why do you dislike that man? You don't even know him." Charles Lamb replied, "And I don't want to know him for fear I may get to like him."

It should be perfectly clear to us from our experience throughout the world that the way to get along with others is to know them.

I hasten to add that this does not involve the violation of one's privacy. But what it does involve is an understanding of the point of view of others, their ideas and their aspirations.

I gave the commencement speech at the Bethesda-Chevy Chase High School in Maryland. I told the six hundred graduates, "At this very moment millions of parents in Asia, Africa, and Europe have the same dreams for the welfare of their teenage sons and daughters as your parents here have for you; and if you understand that you will have won a great victory both for yourself and for America."

When William J. Gaynor ran for mayor of New York City around the turn of the century, only one newspaper backed his candidacy—Joseph Pulitzer's New York *World*.

Arthur Brisbane, one of Hearst's editors, had a brilliant

idea as the race grew hotter. He proposed to Mr. Pulitzer that the pro-Gaynor *World* run one column a day sympathetic to Hearst and the pro-Hearst *Journal* run one column a day sympathetic to Gaynor.

Pulitzer agreed. He saw that this gambit would not only build circulation for both papers, but allow Gaynor additional publicity, which he badly needed.

Mr. Pulitzer plastered the city with six-foot posters with Brisbane's picture announcing this campaign innovation.

Arthur Brisbane's articles that ran in the *World* were so hot against Gaynor that after he was elected, Mayor Gaynor filed suit against the *World* for libel. Mr. Pulitzer handled the distressing matter beautifully. "Now the *World* is glad that it was the only paper in New York supporting Gaynor," he said. "Any man who can sue his only friend for libel is the kind of Mayor we need. He will show the same courage in suing the corporations for delinquent franchise taxes which they have been avoiding for years. We need a man who is not afraid of lawsuits, not even against friends."

Mayor Gaynor was never noted as a man who got along with people and did not win subsequent reelections, good mayor though he was. He just didn't see where his interests were parallel with those of Mr. Pulitzer, though indeed they were.

People have refused to get along with each other for so long that it is no longer a cause for despair, only wonder.

Chief among the reasons they don't is that they already believe they do. Those white men in the Southern city quite truthfully would insist they have no malice in their hearts.

It might seem at first that some of the ills in this world occur because we have too little communication with each other. But it is hard, nevertheless, to believe listening will solve these ills, particularly when love has not. The love of our fellowman is supposed to pay off in large premiums, but love has never been an attractive investment. Because it is so unattractive, we have substituted concepts like "togetherness."

Anyone who has lived on the Lower East Side of New York

or in a tar-paper shack in South Carolina knows the disadvantages of togetherness. Togetherness means sleeping with your brothers on the fire escape on a hot July night or squeezing into the cool milk porch—that's togetherness.

No society or historical sect has ever been without a formula for ensuring it will get along with itself. Perhaps the Hebrews gave the succinct appraisal with: Do not do unto others as you would not have others do unto you, which the Christians, with characteristic clarity and brevity, reduced to: Do unto others as you would have others do unto you.

Certainly I have no better formulation to offer.

Free speech—the ultimate weapon

IF WE can explain free speech, we explain simultaneously the concept of the democracy of freedom, the entire concept of our Western culture.

Free speech is some sort of license. But not complete license. Free speech, said Oliver Wendell Holmes, does not yield the privilege of yelling "fire" in a crowded theater when there is no fire, nor does free speech yield the privilege of slandering a neighbor.

By free speech, I suppose, we mean the unimpeded dissemination of ideas, ideas unimpeded by fear of punishment. "The civilization of the dialogue," Robert M. Hutchins called it, "where everybody was content to abide by the decision of the majority as long as the dialogue could continue." Free speech, narrowly defined, is the right to express ideas that run contrary to popular opinion.

While free speech aids such ideas, these ideas are not necessarily the greatest ideas expressed by men. Indeed, the greatest ideas are usually those that advance the interest of the majority by slight modification.

186

Free speech also means that the majority has the right to override and ignore certain ideas.

Contrary opinion has always been with us. Athens did not have such a thing as free speech, yet it produced great thinkers, most of whom at one time or another went against the grain of the majority.

The Achilles heel of Athens was the fact that though she could produce great men, she could not tolerate them. This should not be a surprising fact. The Inquisition burned the works of Dante, and eminent Englishmen thought William Blake only a loony printer.

For many centuries the men who had the only interest in free speech were the philosophers. Whether or not they would be put to death was the gamble they took.

The gamble worked for St. Thomas, but not for Galileo. When Galileo begged the bishop to look in the telescope and see for himself that the earth revolved about the sun, the bishop said he wouldn't dare. If he saw what Galileo said he'd see, he knew the devil would have put it there.

Here was the crux of the problem: Free speech was not a concept. The dissemination of ideas was a struggle rather than a privilege.

What changed this was the invention of the printing press. St. Thomas and Maimonides and Luther agreed on the truth of a monotheistic God, but there was no longer a parochial audience to hear them out. It was a universal audience. Monotheistic God or not, the audience disagreed. How can you sanction truth? And philosophers for the first time realized you can't. You can sanction only speech.

Free speech in the beginning served the interests of the theologians and the philosophers. But the whole of society was affected. An aristocratic society with a new middle class that produced commercial ideas in direct conflict with the tenets of the Catholic Church—this battle was fought in the realms of books and sermons. After a century of burning bodies at the stakes, of wars, of tortures, society began to realize the need for speech without punishment. Punishment did not deter speech, nor did it silence men. Philosophers began to dedicate themselves to a minute analysis of free speech as an abstract concept.

The classic statement on free speech evolved at the beginning of the nineteenth century. John Stuart Mill in his pamphlet *On Liberty* offered three irrefutable reasons for allowing free speech. They were: (1) you may be wrong; free speech will eventually let you hear the truth and set you right; (2) you may be only partially right; free speech will correct your errors; (3) you may be totally right; free speech will let you hear the contrary view and confirm your truth.

Such modifications as the United States courts have made since Mill have always been to enlarge and define speech —really to give a better shake to the minorities.

It has been a custom to proceed along these lines with a long recital of the accomplishments and contributions the minorities have made with free speech.

But what a pity the majority does not recite its own accomplishments and contributions. It was the Protestant majority in Virginia and North Carolina, after all, that sanctioned free speech and made it a cornerstone of American democracy.

We often overemphasize the "equality" of man when the basic idea of America means the "acceptance" of man. It is by accepting them and hearing them out that we have finally achieved a wide and free dissemination of ideas—because we have allowed for different men.

The Dutch in Holland did not produce a Franklin D. Roosevelt; nor did the Irish in Ireland produce an Alfred E. Smith. Nor did the Germans in Germany produce such humanists as Wendell Willkie and Robert Wagner, Sr. It was not geography that produced men of genius. When they left the country of their origin, they encountered here this American idea—the meaning of the Founding Fathers.

The Jewish people made their greatest contribution to

188

civilization after the ghetto walls had been destroyed. In the Dark Ages, when millions of people lived and died without ever having seen a written word, nearly every Jew could read and write. Yet it was not until the door was opened upon the open society that the Jews produced a Spinoza, a Mendelssohn, a Disraeli, a Brandeis, and an Einstein.

With more than two centuries of free speech behind us we have learned that where there is resistance to freedom, the resisters lose as much as the resisted. Because today we are still struggling to perpetuate this unique American idea—the freedom to speak and the freedom to enter the open society. And it is only through this freedom of speech that we may hope to eliminate the greatest of all evils—prejudice against people with common characteristics that are independent of their specific behavior.

The greatest weapon in this fight to eliminate prejudice is free speech. The guarantee of free speech in the South has done more to aid the black in his cause than anything else. For it is the majority who speaks now and questions, just as it is the majority who will step aside and allow another minority group to enter the open society and participate in the interchange of ideas that is as necessary to civilized man as food and water.

Atlanta and Philadelphia

WHILE ATLANTA has elected a black as its mayor, Philadelphia had other thoughts on the matter. One of these thoughts was the stoning of a lone black woman who had moved into a white block in the southwest section of the city. The woman, Mrs. Lillian Simpson, whose husband is in the military serving in Germany and who works and cares for her brother's four children, was driven by violence from her home at 2601 S. 73rd Street by angry white mobs and a silent mayor.

189

"Sure, we believe everybody's equal. Certainly, we think every person has a right to better his condition. Yes, we believe in democracy," the people in the North often say. But when a decent, hard-working black family tries to move into a better home, the hatred comes alive and the rocks begin to fall and the hypocrisy comes out of hiding.

"Just think," Mrs. Simpson said after she moved away. "My husband holds a Silver Star and Bronze Star for bravery, with two tours in Vietnam. He has fought for his country overseas and I have to fight here at home for a decent place to live."

Sterilization in the South

IN ALABAMA a white doctor made incisions in the abdomens of twelve-year-old Mary Alice Relf and her fourteen-year-old sister, Minnie Lee. Hours before their sterilization surgery, Minnie Lee had borrowed a dime from a patient in Montgomery's Professional Center Hospital to call a neighbor who would fetch the girls' mother to the phone.

That afternoon a family-planning nurse had gotten Mrs. Relf's "X" (she can't read or write) on a form authorizing the sterilization of her minor daughters, then returned her to her apartment in the project.

"Mother, we're scared. Y'all come get us."

"Minnie, you stay down there and take those shots like they said. You know we don't have a car to come get y'all."

"They're not gonna give us shots," Minnie cried, her voice beginning to waver. "A lady in the next bed said they gonna operate on us."

"That nurse said they was gonna give y'all shots," reassured Mrs. Relf. Mary Alice and Minnie had been receiving Depo-provera injections, an experimental birth-control drug, for several months. But it had recently been banned by the FDA

190

because it produced cancer in laboratory mice. No proof existed that these children even needed birth-control assistance. Little did the Relfs know they had been human guinea pigs for experimental drugs. And less did they know that when the operating room opened the next morning, their two daughters would be made forever sterile.

Sterilization is fine—but only for consenting adults.

Dr. Benton told the press he insists on sterilization of all welfare mothers with two or more children because ". . . my hard-earned taxes go to support these children." Justification for the Relf girls' sterilization was "because boys were hanging around and we could no longer give the shots."

Reports of involuntary sterilization have since been discovered throughout the South. And they all have a common theme. Each was obtained by coercion, threats, or misrepresentation. Several women were even told their tubes would come *untied* in about two years, allowing pregnancy. But, in truth, each operation is *final*.

We are all agreeable to a little friendly deception. We play practical jokes on friends, laugh at bigger-than-life movie plots, and so on. I am urgently concerned that the projects our government undertakes don't result in permanent harm to others.

The project about which I'm concerned is federally financed sterilization of the poor—and it is far from ended.

After the Southern Poverty Law Center filed suit to require constitutionally acceptable guidelines for the sterilization of minors, illiterates, and the mentally incompetent, the Department of Health, Education, and Welfare issued woefully inadequate regulations continuing its policy of illegally sterilizing the poor.

Health care for the poor will be the legislative concern of the 'seventies. Before we launch massive bureaucratic health and family-planning programs, constitutional standards must be written.

Violence in Brooklyn

SOME TIME ago a group of black teenagers waited outside a Hebrew school on Bedford Avenue in the heart of the Bedford-Stuyvesant section of Brooklyn. According to the witnesses and the police, the group included about forty blacks who beat the young kids of the Lubavitcher Yeshiva. These Hebrew students were ten-year-olds.

Some of the folks have written me, "What do you say about civil rights now?"

Here is what I say:

I was heartsick when I read the story of the Lubavitcher Yeshiva on Bedford Avenue. And yet this terrible incident calls for a maximum of maturity—intellectual maturity. What is involved is an untruth we ourselves have fought against for centuries—the identity of an entire race of people with the delinquency of one or several of its members.

A father some years ago was convicted for raping his daughter down here in Carolina. It never entered my mind for a moment that Southern white Baptists rape their daughters. All I thought of was a poor, mentally ill human being who needed institutionalization and treatment. When I read of the terrible incident outside of the Lubavitcher school in Brooklyn, I did not think of the black people, but of a group of juvenile delinquents who need treatment and perhaps punishment, too.

I understood, too, that the ignorance of the young blacks on top of their frustration could result in a lashing out against what they sense is the weakest point of the white structure —the Jews. We bear this burden and that is why we must be in the forefront of the struggle for *law*.

Will love ever unite us?

No.

Some years ago a rumor spread through a small Southern town that the blacks were arming. The community was afflicted with fear and the whites began arming. This little town suddenly became a concentration camp of fear. There wasn't a grain of truth in the rumor, and but for intelligent action by some well-informed officials, the town might well have succumbed to its urge for violence.

Now if a rumor spreads that a sick child needs medicine or a budding genius a scholarship, perhaps there are three citizens in every town who will lend an ear to this, but one could hardly say the community would be galvanized into action. The hope for help is not a unity-producing hope, only the hope for hate or fear.

Hatred has always united mankind. Every great movement that has succeeded has succeeded precisely because it was able to exploit hate for someone, something.

When England entered the war against Germany in 1914, Woodrow Wilson found it necessary to proclaim our neutrality (although common sense and, I might add, our own welfare demanded we declare war on Germany one hour after England). No one would go to war out of love for England, but we were mobilized for war against Germany and out of hate.

Can we survive without war?

BETWEEN THE years 1815, which marked the end of the Napoleonic wars, and 1914, when World War I began, Europe was described as an armed camp. The phrase was the nineteenth-century equivalent for "cold war." In 1886 the Prussians proved their point to the Austrians that they were to be reckoned with, and in 1870 Bismarck proved his point to Louis Napoleon that Germany was to be reckoned with.

There was some real killing in 1877 when Louis Napoleon set out to destroy democracy in France by the simple expedient of calling all the democrats and liberals "subversives." In preparation for this slaughter he even took possession of the bells of Paris so that no democrat would sound the alarm. He forgot, however, to take care of one witness, Victor Hugo. Victor Hugo went into exile and talked up the slaughter and soon enough Louis Napoleon was deposed.

Still, there was peace in Europe as a whole. My father, who came from Austria, told me there had been men there, fifty years of age and older, who not only had never gone to war but had never been affected by one. Nevertheless, the Austro-Hungarian Empire was an armed camp because everyone knew this is what kept the economy going.

In all these villages and cities of Europe the favorite election platform of burgomasters, or mayors, or provincial deputies was the promise "to bring a regiment."

The candidate most likely to have influence with the general staff got the job and tried to persuade the generals to post a regiment in town. You see, it made no difference to the general staff where the troops trained, and so they scattered them throughout all the towns and cities.

Often a humanitarian spirit prevailed and a regiment would be posted in a depressed area, much as though we were to locate an airplane factory in West Virginia, to help the economy get back on its feet.

Only the terms have changed, really. The difference between the metaphors of an armed camp and a cold war distinguish the difference between primitive and technologically advanced war processes. Setting up a missile factory in West Virginia does not differ from posting the 12th Hussars to Lemberg, now called Lvov.

The first thing that happened when the 12th Hussars came

was that the servant girls suddenly had some spending money. Everybody had more money.

Nothing, of course, is simple. The 12th Hussars brought problems with them. The young lieutenant stationed in the fine mansion waltzed every night with the mistress of the house to the consternation of her husband. But the mistress was hoping to preserve the chastity of her two virgin daughters with her overt display of friendliness. Alas, all too often the mistress found her sacrifice had been in vain. But the lieutenant was a harbinger of prosperity, tangible, real, and pleasant.

Now, in our civilization the defense workers don't waltz with the servant girls nor does the mistress waltz with the engineers. Instead we have bowling leagues and professional football games and cheeseburger drive-ins, but then we are, of course, more free from sin than the armed camp of the Europe of 1905.

Our purposes are no different: A President expresses concern at closing a naval base and Franz Josef was sorry when he had to pull the 12th Hussars out of Stanislav.

When the 12th Hussars left, there was another election and this time a candidate who promised to bring a regiment of Uhlans won because the Uhlans had horses and that meant grain and fodder had to be imported and the leather workers had a field day.

Capitalism has yet to face its crucial test: whether it can survive without the naval bases, without the 12th Hussars, without war.

PART 6

Key Precincts and the Red-Hot Stove

The press giveth back

FORTY-FIVE YEARS ago I heard a judge sentence me to five years in jail. I spent three years, eight months, and twenty-two days in prison, during which time I catalogued the prison library at Atlanta.

In the years that followed I told only three men in the South about this episode. I told Josephus Daniels, Woodrow Wilson's Secretary of the Navy and the publisher of the *Raleigh News and Observer*; Frank Littlejohn, the Charlotte chief of police; and Hermann Cohen, a Jewish textile merchant.

In 1958, when my book *Only in America* had made me a celebrity, an anonymous letter to the editors of the now-defunct *Herald Tribune* revealed this prison record.

I remember repeating my story with a dry throat to reporter Judith Crist in the offices of my publisher.

For the second time in my life I made the front pages. When the story appeared on September 19, 1958, I thought I was a dead man.

I was wrong. Many editors said in their columns that the past was over with, that the only reason to hold me in contempt was if I let this exposure keep me from functioning. The moral of my story is: *The press taketh away and the press also giveth back*.

That was not the end of the story, though.

In early December last year, when dusk was falling, I had a call from the White House. The call was from White House attorney Leonard Garment. Richard Nixon had granted me a full and unconditional pardon. Legally I was never in jail.

For any man who's ever been in prison, a pardon never comes too late. Not only has the President restored my vote to

199

me, he has freed me to run for the Charlotte City Council, a prospect I make more as a threat than a promise.

As for Richard Nixon, I silently wished him the happiest of new years and hoped he would be able to lay his troubles successfully to rest as I laid mine. The important aspect of this story is that the most conservative Republican President of our generation gave a pardon to a most left-wing liberal Democrat.

Richard Nixon and Ajax

I SAW the Watergate scandal preenacted in vaudeville half a century ago.

It was a skit called "Pay the Man the Two Dollars," and it starred Victor Moore, of sainted memory.

Victor is arrested for a parking violation. When he offers to pay the two-dollar ticket, his lawyer dissuades him and he assures him that he, the lawyer, can get him out of it.

Well, the lawyer gets him into obstruction of justice and contempt of court and troubles heap upon troubles until, finally, the guards are leading Victor to the electric chair and he turns back to the lawyer and begs plaintively, "Pay the man the two dollars."

If President Richard Nixon had promptly fired certain close associates at the outset, that would have been the end of it. But someone—there is always that someone—decided that the whole group could cover its tracks and get away with it.

The Watergate crew consists of law-and-order boys, with their no-knock proposals and searches and preventive detention. These are the people whose candidate was elected on a law-and-order program with a guarantee by the candidate, "Now things will be different. I will replace the Attorney General [Ramsey Clark] with a new Attorney General." And he gave us John N. Mitchell.

200

President Nixon has seriously compromised the Presidency. He reminds me of Ajax of Greek mythology who thought he was killing soldiers, but all he was doing was killing sheep.

Carbon paper in the suburbs

A HUMORIST could make his reputation and fortune gathering his materials at weekly meetings of suburban city councils, aldermanic boards, and county commissioners.

The exclusive concern of these bureaucrats is money—not the big money, but the niggling amounts. Why do the food trucks of the Welfare Department use so much gasoline? Why is the audit from the parking meters so long delayed?

About the worst thing that can happen to the bureaucracy is when the Public Works Department gets the Public Health Department's bill by mistake.

Imagine the pain of admitting to the director that the files do not reveal who bought twelve gallons of gasoline on April 15. Back and forth the letters fly. The gas station says, "Yessir, our pump register shows twelve gallons; therefore you owe us $4.44, less ten percent discount if paid before the first of the month, and since this is the third, it is $4.44."

"We got ordinances in this town to take care of guys like you," says the public works director. "In addition to which, our budget does not include that $4.44. It was never authorized by this department."

After two years of protracted wrangling, a sharp-eyed clerk discovers it was not Casey, the road engineer, who got the twelve gallons; it was O'Casey, the assistant sanitarian, who by this time is complicating the records of Tucson, Arizona.

It is said of the Nazi bureaucracy that clerks sat estimating the tons of paper clips the general staff would require for a new offensive while Russian tanks clanked through the streets below. But of course that is typical of the Germans. As the novelist Richard Condon has remarked, the German soldier is eager to die under orders so that no one can blame him for having died in the first place.

What keeps the bureaucracy going is carbon paper. Asking it to do without carbons in triplicate would be like asking the bureaucrats to go without oxygen. Every bureaucracy has its own madness, as Tolstoi liked to remark of families, and no red-blooded American mayor would ever tell the town clerk that the minutes of the council ought to be indexed alphabetically. He would never get away with it, since the land grants of George III and deeds of sale of 1789 are indexed chronologically.

Counterproductivity

SOME OF the folks despair that only rich men can become President in these affluent times. None of the reforms the folks propose seems dedicated to putting a poor man in the White House, but rather they are aimed at relieving the financial burden of the rich in campaigning.

Man on a horse

THE MAN on a horse is the fellow who sweeps up the people in a frenzy of enthusiasm and becomes their leader.

The first man on a horse was Alexander the Great, the son of Philip of Macedon. Philip wasn't too keen on Alexander as an heir. While Alexander had the advantage of Aristotle as a tutor, he had the disadvantage of Olympias as a mother. Olympias played with snakes and, in as polite a euphemism as I can muster, misbehaved egregiously with the court. Consequently, Philip banished both. But when Philip died, Alexander decided he was king of the cats and mounted a white horse and set off alone. Two weeks later, when he showed up at the castle, he had an army behind him. Alexander kept right on riding that white horse until a species of classical virus laid him low in Babylon.

A modern man on a horse was the French general Georges Boulanger, who used to ride through the streets of Paris on a coal-black steed named Tunis followed by three hundred generals. This information is readily accessible in Richard M. Watt's excellent history *Dare Call It Treason*, a survey of the conditions that led the French Army to mutiny in the trenches in 1917. Boulanger planned to seize power and abolish the Constitution. He gained overwhelming support and enthusiasm when he ran for four seats in the Chamber of Deputies at once and won all four handily.

Boulanger let his moment slip past and before he knew what happened, the Chamber of Deputies was about to indict him for treason. He fled to Belgium, where two years later he committed suicide over the grave of his mistress, which led Clemenceau to remark, "He died as he lived, like a subaltern."

"The real thing"

LORD BRYCE, the Englishman who knew a lot about American politics, said that neither a "liberal" Republican nor a "conservative" Democrat can win an election. On a broad basis this is true. However, as with all truths, there are exceptions. For example, we have had two Republican Presidents who were really "Democrats"—Abraham Lincoln and Theodore Roosevelt. And we have had one Democrat President who was really a "Republican"—Grover Cleveland. In recent years this was repeated in the situation of two defeated candidates—Wendell Willkie, a Republican nominee, who was really a "Democrat," and John W. Davis, a Democratic nominee, who was really a "Republican." However, in its broadest sense the Lord Bryce thesis holds good. If the voters are confronted with a liberal Democrat and a liberal Republican running against each other, they are inclined to vote for "the real thing." The same is true when a conservative Democrat runs against a conservative Republican.

On reform

IN THE old days of the hansom cab on Fifth Avenue one of the popular dogs was the coach dog, a white dog spotted with black spots somewhat in polka-dot fashion.

Once a fellow did a thriving business in coach dogs—for a few days. Those who bought an animal from him found that if the newly purshased coach dog stayed out in the rain, all the spots came off and he was just an ordinary hound dog.

In politics the reformers come along every ten years or so and say the markings are genuine, but it would be wise to expose the *new* Tammanyites to a bit of rain. Tammany boss Dick Croker once said: "Maybe the people can't stand corruption but they can't stand reform either."

Politicians' credo

THE GENIUS of a politician manifests itself in his election and reelection.

The politicians' credo has been summarily stated by the famous Vicar of Bray, who kept office in good old King Charles' golden days.

"The Vicar of Bray," wrote Disraeli in his *Curiosities of*

Literature, "was a Papist under the reign of Henry and Protestant under Edward. He was a Papist again under Mary and once more became a Protestant in the reign of Elizabeth. When this scandal to the gown was reproached for his versatility of religious creeds and taxed for being a turncoat and an inconstant changeling, he replied, 'Not so neither; for if I changed my religion, I am sure I kept true to my principle which is to live and die the Vicar of Bray.' "

During the Eisenhower Administration the politicians affected blunt speech in which they mixed up a sufficient number of uh's and dangling participles to prove they were level-headed, ordinary folks. Under Kennedy there was more rhetoric around, but not to the extent that John F. and Jacqueline drove any of the politicians to poetry because there is a limit as to how far they will go. However, it was evident that they dressed better.

Nixon and Jerry Ford have made the football metaphor compulsive.

Campaign financing

THE UNITED STATES SENATE has passed a bill that would prohibit large donations to candidates for federal office and instead would finance election campaigns from the federal Treasury.

There is little likelihood it will affect Congressional or Senatorial races in 1974, which makes all the incumbents breathe easier. Federal financing would give their opponents a break.

I seriously doubt that the bill will become law. There are 535 Senators and Representatives and it is incredible to believe that a majority of this number will vote a bill that directly threatens their welfare.

If the country wants to reform election financing, I strongly recommend it change Election Day from the second Tuesday in November to the second Tuesday in September. That is two months less in which to spend money and it means not so much must be raised. I recommend further that all primaries, whether Presidential, gubernatorial, or whatever, be held on the second Tuesday in April in every state. This also reduces the expense of potential Presidential candidates.

Instead of trying to limit donations, we would be wiser to limit campaigning.

It is absurd to imagine rich men won't try to buy favors from elected officials with money. One might as well tell a rich man he has no expectation of heaven.

Big-city politics

I HAVE always been fascinated by the story of Peter McGuiness, Tammany boss of Greenpoint, a densely populated section of Brooklyn. Mr. McGuiness plastered the area with road signs that proclaimed that his section (which included a sizable city dump) was "the Garden Spot of the World." Of course Boss McGuiness always called it "Greenspernt," and he was otherwise a most colorful character.

Boss McGuiness was register of the county, and he was also sheriff—the two most lucrative plums in New York politics. According to the law, neither the register nor the sheriff could succeed himself, so the boss made an arrangement whereby one year he would be register and the following year he would become sheriff—and he kept alternating the two offices through most of his highly profitable adult life. Another colorful character was one of Peter McGuiness' assistants, Hyman Shorenstein, who was assistant register. The Seabury Investigation revealed that this official who handled the records and archives of the county could neither read nor write.

The ultimate jail

BETWEEN 1917 and 1918 the United States government jailed thousands of pacifists, anarchists, draft dodgers, and Communists who would not go to war. We jailed no number near as many during the years of the Vietnam War, although there were more people and many more dissidents. Society was not as outraged over Muhammad Ali's refusal to step forward for induction in 1965 as it was over Grover Cleveland Bergdoll's attempt to evade the draft in 1917.

None of the usual reasons for jailing men applied in the case of Spiro Agnew. Society no longer needed protection from a disgraced Vice President and Spiro out of politics forever is an instantly rehabilitated man. Jailing him to assuage our outrage is futile. Senseless murders outrage us far more than shakedowns.

If there is an inutility to a jail sentence for Agnew, obviously there is an inutility to prison sentences for thousands of other men. But no one has yet to venture a program that even tentatively would suggest a way to achieve justice without the existence of jail. As far as jails go, the best of them was Botany Bay in Australia, which, as a matter of fact, was not a jail but a place of exile.

St. Paul and Zeno Ponder

IN ACTS 17:19 we are told St. Paul appeared before the intellectuals of Athens. The Gospels say he thereupon delivered the "Address on Mars Hill."

Another council convened on Mars Hill, which these days is the name of a charming town in the western North Carolina mountains. The State Election Board met there to investigate alleged voting frauds. The council was looking into the vote for Zeno Ponder, who had been declared winner of a primary for state senator. Zeno Ponder is the political boss of Madison County, of which Mars Hill is the most populous municipality. (Mars Hill was born at a time when North Carolina was the center of the Bible Belt. These good people were thinking of St. Paul; they did not anticipate Zeno Ponder.)

What brought the board to Mars Hill was the charge that a fourth ballot box, filled with ballots allegedly premarked for Zeno, had been secreted in the polling place, and when the polls closed, this very box had been substituted for one of the other three.

Some of these Tar Heel boys are better at this game than the Tammany Hall experts of the 1900-1920 era. I remember when the Socialists were coming along strong on New York's Lower East Side and they usually had four poll watchers at each of the voting places on Election Day, each an emotionally dedicated volunteer. But it didn't do them much good. The Socialists had the watchdogs but Tammany had the cop.

Before the count began in a district with strong Socialist support, there was a sudden power failure. When the lights went on, two ballot boxes were missing.

There must be many ballot boxes on the bottom of the North River. Once by accident they discovered two boxes off the Pike Street pier filled with votes for William Randolph Hearst for mayor of New York in an election of twenty years earlier. If Hearst had not been robbed of that election, he might have gone on to become the first Socialist President of the United States.

Tar Heels are not that crude. Three ballot boxes come into the polling places and three go out. We are never quite sure about the fourth ballot box, which comes in with the fog and goes out with the fog and no one is the wiser.

Occasionally the trick is not accomplished with finished dexterity. At another investigation, in Raleigh, while the State Board of Elections held hearings, a big woman burst like a hurricane into the committee room and shouted, "I'm from Swain County." She forthwith reached into her enormous

208

bosom and drew forth one hundred and seventy ballots, which she threw on the committee's table with the announcement: "I found these in the ladies' rest room."

Happier than hippies

THE ELECTION bonfire was an eagerly awaited event on the Lower East Side of New York. It was not spontaneous. The location had to be selected carefully. It had to be near the vicinity of the Tammany precinct house but it could not endanger the neighboring tenements. Backyards were out. They were littered with debris and all too many of them still had the outhouse sheds. A square or a park was the best bet.

I can remember building one on Tompkins Square on the night Woodrow Wilson was elected President. Tompkins Square when I last saw it was the home of the hippies, who didn't seem to be having as much fun peddling and smoking their marijuana as we did lugging old carpentry to the pyre.

Kids eight to twelve began to accumulate wooden packing cases and fruit crates and every piece of wood they could find in empty houses and in houses that weren't so empty. The kindling was heaped on the bottom until it measured perhaps two feet high and ten feet in diameter. Then the old chairs were added and the lighter lumber. Then the big pieces.

The fire was lit when the polls closed, by which time Tammany had the results of the precinct anyway: The local candidates had won, as usual, and the national candidates were leading. The bonfire was meant to spur Woodrow Wilson on, since in New York we wouldn't know the results of the election until the morning, and the late morning at that.

Tammany alerted the Fire Department and you heard the siren and the fire bells all over the city. The kids started the fire and invariably the engine arrived to put it out. Then the older fellows took over, the big boys between fifteen and twenty. This one the fire engine didn't put out. It was fueled with kerosene. The firemen would stand and watch it, not even bothering to chase the other spectators.

It was a brilliant sight.

The big bonfire on election night probably came from America's first colonists. On the coronation of new kings, the English built bonfires, and while I am not sure of this, it seems reasonable that the American English continued the custom when they were electing new Presidents instead of shouting, "Long live the King!"

My days as a Socialist

I WAS almost sixteen years old when I joined the Young People's Socialist League (YPSL). Algernon Lee of the Rand School inducted about eight of us one night. Though young, I was already familiar with the pamphlets of Carl Sandburg and Eugene V. Debs, which the YPSL's used to distribute free. I believed in them. These were the days, of course, of the Molly Maguires and the Pinkertons and the Homestead Strike. When Morris Hillquit, the No. 1 Socialist of New York, addressed an audience, all he had to do to capture their attention was shout the name "Rockefeller." Imagine the days when Rockefeller was the No. 1 villain?

There were Socialists I knew whose vision of the emerging America was compelling. But I never met one who vaguely suspected that the sons of the robber barons would march in the vanguard of liberals within a generation.

There were many other issues we Socialists underestimated. We agitated for an eight-hour day and for unemployment insurance but we never suspected that Prohibition was a political issue. A disciplined party man like Al Smith did. Though Smith lost the election in 1928 by six million votes, that election marked the first time a Democrat had carried the

210

cities. One of the reasons Smith broke the Republican hold on the big towns was that he campaigned as a wet.

It is true we young Socialists used to heckle Communists in the days when the mass of Americans had no idea what the Third Internationale was. Capitalism was an enemy we Socialists thought we could correct through legislation. Communism was the enemy we could never contain. And we knew it. I remember my father writing in 1934, "The Nazis burn our books and the smoke spirals to the sky for all to see. The Communists bury us in a dungeon. When you write a Russian ambassador about a missing poet, his answer is he never heard of him."

Neither Communists nor Nazis did the Socialists in but a rich man, Franklin D. Roosevelt. The first one hundred days of his New Deal were essentially the implementation of the Socialist Party platform of 1908. It is naïve to suppose the Socialists could have accomplished these reforms. What the American people would take from a senior warden of the Hyde Park Episcopal Church, a fellow who wore a Navy cape, they could never accept from a polemical Socialist who wore a beard and spoke with an accent.

Wondrous Wendell Willkie

At 1:47 a.m. on June 28, 1940, a political miracle of major proportions took place. On the sixth ballot the Republican National Convention nominated Wendell Willkie for President.

It was wondrous—not so much because a dark horse had won the nomination, but because, in the middle of a world crisis, the American people were about to go to the polls in a position where they couldn't lose. It would be Willkie or Roosevelt.

Willkie was nominated on Friday. On Monday of that week

the French government had signed an armistice with the Nazis ceding half their territory to German occupation. England had only recently evacuated its army from Dunkirk.

Thunderous events had shaken the world. These alone explain why Wendell Willkie, a nonprofessional, was able to overcome the choices of the politicians.

Willkie was an Indians lawyer and Meyer Berger of the New York *Times* once remarked that *all* Indians lawyers are by nature prospective Presidential candidates. Forty-eight at the time of his nomination, Willkie was the president of Commonwealth and Southern, a giant utility. He had gained national prominence in his spats with the Tennessee Valley Authority, the New Deal venture into electric power. But Willkie was not an anti-New Deal diehard. And he was not an isolationist. He simply disagreed. He was a well-informed citizen who realized that the war in Europe meant hard times ahead. His platform was "peace, prosperity, and preparedness," but one-third of the platform was wiped out before the campaign got under way when the overwhelming majority of Republican Congressmen voted against giving the Air Corps six thousand planes.

Willkie won the nomination over three of the shrewdest and most adroit politicians ever to grace the national scene.

The front runner was Robert A. Taft, Senator from Ohio. The fifth ballot of the 1940 convention was as near as the good Senator ever came to winning the nomination. District Attorney Thomas E. Dewey was the second-strongest candidate. And the real dark horse was former President Herbert Hoover, who, in his address, virtually challenged the delegates to nominate him if they wanted to call themselves Republicans.

But the nation was captivated by Willkie. All through the convention the gallery kept chanting, "We want Willkie." Willkie's *W* was a most fortunate choice of letters, for it lent itself easily to alliteration. The official Republican slogan was

"Win with Willkie." Dewey and Taft were neck and neck on the first ballot. When Dewey released his delegates after the fifth ballot, seventy-five of them went for Willkie and the stampede was on. Willkie was nominated unanimously.

Perhaps Willkie was the most romantic figure ever to enter American politics and lose. He certainly was one of the hardiest. He fought in a grueling, bitter campaign. But Willkie gave as good as he got. In defeat he gained great stature. Against anyone but Roosevelt, he would have won.

Joe McCarthy and Charles E. Potter

IMMEDIATELY AFTER the Army-McCarthy hearings I observed, "The moment Joe McCarthy told General Zwicker that the general wasn't fit to wear the uniform of the United States, it marked the beginning of the end for Indian Joe."

Ex-Senator Charles E. Potter, who was a member of the committee that held the Army-McCarthy hearings, confirms this observation in his book, *Days of Shame*. What Joe McCarthy did was to attack the elite a year or two too soon. It was a crucial and fatal mistake. Hitler knew better. Hitler kept after the trade unionists and the Social Democrats until he had won the wholehearted support of the upper-middle class. Joe should have waited until he had the whole middle and lower-middle class behind him. He was certainly given enough time and opportunity. When some Senators confronted Robert A. Taft with Joe's excesses, Taft shrugged them off with the comment, "He's hurting Democrats." When Joe started to hurt Republicans, it was a different matter.

Had McCarthy waited and made his move against the Tafts and the Eisenhowers and the Army sometime later, the gambit might have succeeded. The Gallup Poll showed that 50 percent of the American people were cheering on Joe's pursuit of the demon. Joe should have kept chasing the demon until he hit upon a program that would have ensured another 25 percent of the people. McCarthy was eminently successful in whirling the people away from themselves in hysteria. He created a devil and then told the people, "I will save you from this devil." Over and over, he told the American people the Communists "had a razor at the throat of America."

But when the hearings ended, McCarthy did not go tangling with the razor-wielding nemesis, he went to the Southwest for a two-month vacation and to hell with that razor.

Senator Potter's book has its humor. Senator McCarthy was so desperate to find one Communist he could call his own. Somehow he could never catch up to one. He somehow obtained documents from the FBI and the Pentagon, directives that were three or four years old, and he used these to make headlines for himself. The headlines gave the false impression that Indian Joe had initiated these inquiries. But Joe initiated nothing. He never found that one Communist—a single, solitary Communist he could call his own.

Toward the end he was lashing out in panic. He had his assistant, J. B. Matthews, accuse the whole of the Protestant clergy. When that didn't work, he found an anti-Semite who told him General Marshall's deputy, Anna Rosenberg, was a Communist. Senator Potter reveals that some of the "research" in this field was done by Gerald L. K. Smith. When the charge proved a monstrous lie, Gerald L. K. Smith closed down his "research" headquarters and quietly left Washington. But McCarthy couldn't leave. He had to sit in the Senate and eventually vote "yes" for Anna Rosenberg's confirmation.

Sadly, too, Potter's book reveals that it was not only the people who were caught up in the hysteria but elected officials as well. Senators feared McCarthy. They were afraid to speak out. President Eisenhower, if not afraid, was more than inept. Dwight D. Eisenhower enjoyed tremendous prestige and he could have smashed the McCarthy image with a few well-chosen words. The words never came. It had to be done the hard way, albeit with the lesson that it can happen here.

Herbert H. Lehman

WE ARE not sure that Al Smith lost the election to Herbert Hoover because he was a Roman Catholic. A few years earlier John W. Davis, an Episcopalian, had done no better against Calvin Coolidge. It is extremely unlikely that a Democrat who had walked into Kentucky with Dan'l Boone could have won the Presidency against the Republicans in the 1920's.

But we are sure that Herbert H. Lehman was never given a chance for the Presidency because he was a Jew.

A governor of New York, Republican or Democrat, is automatically a contender for the nomination to the Presidency. Samuel J. Tilden, Grover Cleveland, Theodore Roosevelt, Charles Evans Hughes, Al Smith, Franklin D. Roosevelt, Thomas E. Dewey were either nominated for or won the nation's highest executive office.

Nelson Rockefeller is still a contender for the 1976 nomination. Herbert H. Lehman was four times governor of New York, yet he was never considered, even briefly, as a possible nominee.

This was a strange decision for the country to make, not only because of his excellence as an administrator but because he came closer than any other political figure of my generation to being what our Methodist brethren call "unspotted from the world." In addition to which, Mr. Lehman in his time beat some of the top Republicans of all history. He beat Dewey twice and John Foster Dulles once (for the Senate).

Mr. Lehman had been called the giant among liberals of America, but one day this good man knew sorrow. His ancestors had been bankers in Germany and his father had worked actively for the Confederacy during the Civil War. He himself had brought New York through the Depression and the exigencies of World War II. But while he sat in the Senate, Joe McCarthy got up and in a speech said Herbert H. Lehman was "soft on communism." Only Senator Wayne Morse of Oregon rose to defend this honorable and aged veteran. In the Senate cloakroom later Herbert H. Lehman, sunk in a chair, confessed that he was surprised that at least sixty of his colleagues did not rise up to defend him against this outrage. But we were living in fear—the McCarthy era of amnesia.

Once the Tammany bosses tried to withhold Mr. Lehman's credentials as a delegate to the Democratic National Convention. They did this because Lehman had been fighting bossism in New York politics. But their action backfired. Too many people remembered Herbert Lehman's era of honest government, his generosity, his consistency, and his unswerving loyalty, which helped both Al Smith and FDR spend many peaceful nights. "My good right arm," Roosevelt called Lehman. "I love him like a brother," said Smith.

Life in the middle class

I VENTURE out into the middle class only when it is absolutely necessary. My house insulates me perfectly. Margaret comes in at 8 A.M. to prepare breakfast, tidy up, make the lunch, and we wave good-bye. My secretary is here at 9 A.M. and she keeps us all in touch with the universe of publishers, newspaper syndicates, and lecture bureaus. After I walk my dog Gaon and his mate, Dubah (which means "Little Bear" in Hebrew), there's no other reason to involve myself in the giddy affairs of ordinary everyday living.

But Margaret had no scouring powder the other day. I volunteered to make the expedition to the supermarket. There I bought three canisters of Ajax, getting free Handi-Wipes with each. Since they were marked two for forty-nine cents, I figured I owed seventy-four cents. I waited in the express line (five items or fewer) and displayed my purchase to the big hippie who was punching buttons on the register. By mistake he included among my three Ajaxes a head of lettuce belonging to the lady behind me.

"That's mine," she said.

"You owe her twenty-nine cents," the clerk informed. I was about to hand over the change to this charming lady when I realized I didn't owe her twenty-nine cents. "I only bought three cans of Ajax. I owe you seventy-four cents. Why do I owe her twenty-nine cents?"

" 'Cause I rang it up on the register," said the clerk. Then he added, "You're right. She owes you twenty-nine cents."

"Why do I owe twenty-nine cents?" she asked.

The clerk started to explain. But she cut him off. "I know *that*. I understand. I thought the lettuce was nineteen cents."

He twirled the lettuce around to show her the twenty-nine cents inked on the cellophane.

"It says nineteen cents in the window," she insisted.

The clerk buried his head in his hands as though it were our fault.

Later, arriving home with a head of lettuce I didn't need, my secretary informed me that a local VIP Democrat was on the telephone.

What he asked was, "Harry, do you know a Democratic piano tuner?"

"Do you mean a registered Democrat or a piano tuner who mixes with all classes of pianos?"

"Registered," he said.

"Why do you want a Democratic piano tuner?"

"We need a piano for the band at our Columbus Day Democratic Ball. If we rent one, it will cost twenty-five dollars. Ray Discepolo has an old piano in his garage. I thought if I could locate a Democratic piano tuner, he'd tune it for nothing, thereby saving the party twenty-five dollars."

I did not know any Democratic piano tuners.

"Well, at least," he asked, exasperated, "do you know anyone with a bust of Columbus? I want to take a publicity photo beside it to advertise our ball."

"Why don't you ask Discepolo?" I suggested.

"No good. He's from the north of Italy."

"I don't think I can help."

"That's the trouble with the party this election," he complained. "Everybody lets me down."

Spiro Agnew

"I FEAR the Greeks though gift on gift they bear," wrote the poet Homer about ex-Vice President Spiro Agnew.

Spiro Agnew was going to end the permissiveness of the courts and clamp down on the excesses of the press. He promised a panacea of reforms. But a couple of shakedowns perpetrated several years ago did him in.

What amazes me is that the man thought he could fight back, that though there was no chance of vindicating himself because he had indeed taken the money, somehow he could continue to serve.

Mr. Agnew is another example of the truth that you cannot have it both ways.

Mr. Agnew wanted to be the Vice President of a nation of two hundred and ten million people but he thought none of those two hundred and ten million had a right to know anything about his private life. He wanted to be Vice President and private citizen all at once.

Instead of those fervent promises that brought Republican women to their feet in a frenzy of admiration, Spiro should have thanked God for six years of getting away with it. The *Times* had broken the story in '68 and charged that he was in receipt of bonds that constituted a clear conflict of interest. Agnew replied that his father had left him the bonds but the newsmen proved Agnew's father had died five years before the bonds were issued. The only reason Richard Nixon didn't dump Agnew in '68 was because Eisenhower hadn't dumped Nixon in '52.

There are a lot of questions that President Nixon swears he never asked but if he didn't ask Vice President Agnew, "Ted, did you ever take any money?" then President Nixon ought to be sent back to college to study political science. I am willing to bet the President did ask and I am willing to bet he said, "Ted, if you took a dime, it's all over." So much for the Agnew aides who cursed Nixon and the Justice Department.

These are indeed sad situations. It was sad about Abe Fortas and sad about Thomas Dodd and sad about a variety of mayors in New Jersey and sad about Schuyler Colfax and sad about Albert B. Fall. But what more does a man need than to be county executive of Baltimore with a widening political horizon ahead of him? What more does he need than to be Supreme Court Justice, mayor of Newark or Jersey City, Secretary of the Interior?

Republican errors

MR. WILLIAM E. COBB of Morganton, North Carolina, was the state chairman of the Republican Party. He ran afoul of the press, which discovered not only that he was a happily married lumber executive in Morganton but also that he was virtually a happily married family man in Roanoke, Virginia. Mr. Cobb was keeping a second woman.

Mr. Cobb, to my way of thinking, made two mistakes. First, he should not have kept the second woman in Roanoke. Miami would have been a far likelier place or Washington or New York City. As hundreds of thousands of tycoons and executives could have told him, Roanoke, Virginia, is the last place in the world to stash away the *other* woman.

His second mistake was to have resigned from his party's

chairmanship and from his race for the North Carolina Senate. The worst that could have happened to him was that he might have lost, which would have happened to him anyway in what was then a Democratic Southern state, but Mr. Cobb might have attracted a lot of votes he didn't expect to attract. He might have elicited a great deal of admiration from the men in the community. And he was good to the "other woman" and there are lots of wonderful ladies who would have given him their ballot just so long as the ballot was secret. Most women secretly imagine themselves the "other woman" and they will go—hook, line, and sinker—for the fellow who stands by the consort.

But, anyway, Mr. Cobb has made his two mistakes, and I wish him luck. He'll beat this because he is a man of talent and decency. Politics had much to do with it.

When a Southern Democrat becomes a Republican, he finds it very difficult and this leads often to a split personality.

The budget and the red-hot stove

Down here in North Carolina we have perfect examples of that amazing political contradiction of our times —the "conservative" politicians who rap government spending and then take the federal money.

It can be said that the public in general agrees with its conservative "watchdogs" in Congress and in private conversation denounces big government, but that same public takes from the federal government with both hands from sunup to sundown. They will take a red-hot stove from the federal government. They go to the mailbox to get their check—the cotton check, the peanut check, the soil-bank check, and the checks from forty-seven other federal agencies. They take the checks to the bank and as they make the deposit, the bank clerk says, "The government is getting too big," and they nod in silent agreement as they take away the duplicate deposit slip.

There was a terrible fight against the Rural Electrification Administration when that federal agency began to string power lines in the remote farm areas of the state. But the very people who fought this project have been its greatest benefactors. The power lines resulted in nearly a million new customers for electrical appliances, everything from radio and television sets to washing machines and toasters.

Then the "conservative" establishment fought against the expenditure for the building of secondary roads that New Deal Governor W. Kerr Scott constructed, roads that led right up to the back door of the farmhouse. The "conservative watchdogs" in the large cities were able to accumulate vast fortunes because of this development. The people of rural areas were able to go to the movies in the evening and patronize the stores on Saturday and get their eyeglasses fitted and visit the doctors and dentists in the medical buildings. And of course the farm people could line the streets by the thousands during a visit of a celebrity, watch the annual Thanksgiving Day parade, and buy tickets to the prizefights, ice hockey, and football exhibitions.

Thus one of the great dilemmas of our political lives—the demand that the budget be balanced and the demand for a share in the welfare state.

Governor Wallace

THE LARGE vote Governor Wallace of Alabama received in the Wisconsin, Indiana, then Maryland primaries in 1972 came as no surprise. As a matter of fact, we ought to be gratified that the vote against Mr. Wallace was a decisive majority.

The people who voted for Wallace knew that they were not

221

voting for a potential or possible President of the United States. Thus he became a convenient symbol for the dissenter, the disenchanted, the bigot, the racist. There are enough of them everywhere.

But there's more to it than that. A candidate like Wallace comes into a state in these years of uncertainty and crisis, as he plans to do again in 1976, and he is not responsible to a major party. There is no platform to which he must adhere, no program to which he is committed. He literally asks the folks, "What's troubling you? I got everything."

Any man who runs for President and offers the people a promise of no taxes, no sit-ins, no foreign aid, etc., will get all the disenchanted, including even those who believe in free love. We had a fellow like that run on the Lower East Side of New York many years ago. And I remember he distributed cards with his slogan, "No Hurry, No Worry, Moe." It never worked for Moe.

The black mayors

ATLANTA HAS elected a black man as its mayor. Maynard Jackson, a thirty-five-year-old lawyer, formerly the vice mayor, defeated Sam Massell, a Jew, who was the incumbent.

One could write a stirring piece about the ascension of black men to the mayor's chair in Newark, Los Angeles, Gary, once Cleveland, and possibly, in 1979, Chicago. Political brotherhood has arrived. But I am not sure that that is what the election of a black mayor betokens.

The elections demonstrate departure of many whites for the suburbs and creation of large and decisive black voting blocs. But there are whites who vote for black mayors because these fellows are the nominees of a political party, after all.

I think one of the reasons blacks are nominated and win is

that municipal elections mean less than they used to to the constituency.

For many years municipal elections directly affected the constituency in a way national elections did not. Municipal elections determined what proportion of the citizen's tax dollar the city would collect and what services the city would provide. These services were not remote services, like trade agreements with Russia, but the visible garbage collection, public-school systems, health programs, water supply, and protection to persons and property.

But in the last two decades municipal employees have increased their numbers by 83 percent. Voting for one candidate or another makes little difference in the citizens' taxes. Boards of education are locked into salary contracts with teachers and the city is locked into salary agreements with the police, firemen, sanitation workers, public-works employees.

It was once thought that blacks, relatively new to the political process, might make a difference. But in Cleveland Carl Stokes couldn't make a difference.

Many of the blacks who are succeeding as chief executives in the cities and going to the state legislatures and to Congress are the very men who should have attended integrated schools as boys, for Brown vs. Board of Education is now twenty years old. That they did not attend such schools, although segregated schools were unconstitutional, should teach us at least that politics does take turns unsuspected.

Senator Sam Ervin

SENATOR SAM ERVIN, after eighteen years as a United States Senator from North Carolina, has decided to retire to his home in Morganton.

Senator Ervin has been a consistent fighter for constitutional adherence to civil liberties. This goes back to the McCarthy era when the Wisconsin Senator was up for censure and Senator Ervin's work was decisive in the Senate's affirmative decision.

Senator Ervin has been the chairman of the select Senate committee investigating the Watergate matter.

Senator Ervin uncovered the Army's snooping and collection of dossiers on everybody who thought the Army ought to start innovating on the policies it drew up in 1863. This kind of criticism is enough to mark a man a dissident, and among those so marked evidently was Senator Adlai Stevenson III. Who is more suspect than a man whose grandfather was Vice President of the United States and whose father ran for the Presidency twice? The Army, I suspect, defends itself with the proviso that its agents even check up on the sons of Republican Presidential candidates.

Senator Ervin's Senate committee also opened up the can of worms on the data banks wherein all the information a citizen supplies his draft board, his credit company, his employers is collected in one huge file so that the folks can tell in a glance whether he pays his bills in ten days or in three months.

For two of his terms Senator Ervin's interpretation of the Constitution was that it did not insist black children go to school with whites. Now that he is off that subject, it is much more interesting to listen to him question bumbling lieutenant colonels.

What is important are the truly outstanding Southerners who sit in the United States Senate, men with fine minds, good hearts, wonderful characters, and enlightened patriotism. If racial segregation dehumanized blacks, it dehumanizes these Southern Senators, too. Many of their constituents aren't even aware they elected great men and they couldn't care less. All they are interested in is that their Senator "holler nigger" right before he announces for reelection. And they do not much concern themselves if the hollerer is a great statesman or a semiliterate backwoodsman.

224

Senator William Fulbright of Arkansas has the character and the brilliance to have long ago been considered for the United States Presidency were his name not irretrievably construed with racist policies. The same is true perhaps of Senators Lister Hill and John Sparkman of Alabama.

Sam Ervin is one of the best legal minds in the Senate, an engaging personality, and a raconteur of rare ability—a combination that should have endeared him to the whole country.

But outside of North Carolina, Sam Ervin, until Watergate, had no "public."

Most of the Senators I have mentioned are men of such character that it is quite obvious they must be ashamed of playing the roll of a Claghorn and they have clothed this process in more palatable subterfuges of "states' rights," "the Supreme Court's abuse of power," and "the Southern way of life."

Goldwater and a Jewish secret

WHEN I was writing my book *Mr. Kennedy and the Negroes*, I was invited to visit the President as often as I found it necessary. One morning in his office he pointed his finger at me and said, "Harry, that's the best thing you've ever written."

He was referring to my comment in the *Carolina Israelite* on Barry Goldwater and his Presidential nomination. I wrote, "I always knew that the first Jewish President of the United States would be an Episcopalian."

But the Jews did not vote for Barry Goldwater; they voted for Lyndon B. Johnson.

Jews are essentially "liberals." There's an age-old reason for this. I'll let you in on the secret.

The Roosevelt New Deal did not affect the American Jews too much, one way or the other. Essentially the New Deal started out as an agrarian reform: farm moratorium, CCC camps, and agricultural subsidies. In some respects the New Deal even hurt Jews as it hurt many small businessmen, especially in its initial stages.

But the Jews swore by Franklin D. Roosevelt as they swear by all liberals. By experience, the Jew has learned that when the society in which he lives is in trouble—with a devastating war, unemployment, depression, social upheaval—the Jew is always in real trouble.

This everlasting vulnerability is historic fact. Only a few years ago the police in Paris demonstrated in the streets for more pay. Did they curse the French government as they marched? Not at all. They shouted, "Down with the Jews!"

So the Jew likes to see everybody healthy and happy, getting Social Security and old-age pensions, medical care and hospital insurance, free eyeglasses, even a guaranteed annual wage, if possible, including complete civil rights and for everybody at least six weeks' vacation with pay. The prosperity of the nation and its people has been the Jews' most reliable guarantee of personal security.

The fact is that LBJ went to war against Vietnam with an intensity never thought of by Barry Goldwater. But his liberalism remained intact. Lyndon Johnson's war on poverty and his ending the race war in America and his contributions in the field of education were the greatest since Roosevelt's. This is what the Jews voted for.

But Barry Goldwater of the United States Senate is a tower of strength. His integrity is unquestionable. Jimmy Reston in a recent column noted that Barry Goldwater is a decent man, to which I say, "Amen."

Nixon, Goldwater, and Pompey

THE QUESTION before the Watergate investigators, as Senator Howard Baker put it, was, "What did the President know, and when did he know it?"

This reminds me of the case of the California actress in the 1964 Presidential campaign of Senator Barry Goldwater and, also, of Sextus Pompey.

The actress threatened to sue the Republican National Committee because some member corrupted her. Said committeeman talked said actress into posing nude for a television drama that the Goldwater forces intended releasing as campaign propaganda. The actress in her nudity was supposed to represent the low moral state to which the electorate had sunk after four years of the Kennedy-Johnson Administration. It seems to me a logical mistake to presume you can condemn nudity among our women by portraying it, but who am I to advise the Republican National Committee?

This half-hour production also depicted the litter that disgraces our highways, the knifings that terrify our citizens, and the motorcyclists who tear up our towns.

Senator Goldwater previewed the film and said nix. He said it was a racist film. It wasn't until later that we, the public, discovered that a group of dedicated Goldwater women had financed this exposé of American morals that the Senator's good taste kept them from showing. The Senator in this matter acted a lot like Shakespeare's Sextus Pompey.

After the murder of Julius Caesar the Roman Empire was divided into three parts. Anthony, Octavius, and Lepidus composed the triumvirate that ruled this empire. Anthony controlled Egypt and the East. Octavius controlled Rome, and Lepidus, Africa. But they faced the problem of dealing with the fleet of Sextus Pompey. Sextus was the son of the great Pompey whom Caesar had defeated. Now the son wanted the empire and the vast wealth that Caesar had confiscated from his daddy.

Anthony, Octavius, and Lepidus didn't want to fuss with the strong Sextus at the moment so they arranged a summit conference, which they held aboard Sextus' flagship.

The triumvirate kept bargaining and drinking wine and soon enough Anthony and Lepidus were roaring drunk. Octavius, unaccustomed to strong spirits because of his tender years, needed but three sips to put him off his feet.

Along about midnight the three of them passed out and Menas, Sextus Pompey's second in command, sidled up to his chief and said, in effect, "Boss, I can make you master of the world. All I need to do is cut the cable and split the throats of these three." Menas was on pretty solid ground. There was no question about his ability or chance for doing it.

But Menas made a mistake, a serious mistake, confiding in Pompey. For Pompey had to reply, "Why the hell didn't you do it without telling me? Now it's too late. I can't sanction such a deed."

As Shakespeare noted: "In me 'tis villainy/In thee't been good service."

The ladies who produced the Goldwater film made the same mistake. They asked Barry's permission. If they really wanted to condemn American nudity, they should have gone ahead and shown the film and let Barry disavow it afterward.

The thrust of John Dean's testimony, of course, is that President Nixon, approached for villainy, proved no Barry Goldwater or Sextus Pompey.

Watergate may be a blessing

RATHER THAN regard Watergate and its attendant dislocations as a disaffection, I think we should regard it as a blessing. In fact, Watergate may eventually take its place in the development of the American dream with the Constitutional Convention of 1787.

It may well be that politicians will again try to deceive the electorate, will try to fix the election, and try to enrich themselves. But they will never again trust so many subordinates in any of these efforts. So widespread was the Watergate conspiracy that it was foolish to suppose all involved would keep their mouths shut when the crunch came. A man can embezzle by himself, he can hold up a bank alone, but he cannot fix an election by himself.

What makes Watergate a blessing is the vision of just how tough and inexorable due process can be. Far from lynching Richard Nixon, what his critics have done is to force him to rely on the law. Richard Nixon could offer the American public no better example of law and order than he provides by his own ordeal. He had promised the constituency that law and order was simply a matter of decision and attitude when in fact law and order is a process, sometimes a slow process, but often a final one.

Another reason Watergate is a blessing is that it reassures us that there is bite and vigor in our institutions. Watergate was opened by the judiciary in the person of Judge John Sirica. It was further exploited by the press. Then it was acted upon by Congress. Now all the institutions of government and information are working cohesively together and they do seem awesome. But it is also true we did not write a Constitution, establish a judiciary, elect a House and Senate simply to badger and ruin Richard Nixon. When he complains that it seems to him as if we did, we ought to remind him we didn't elect him to defend the Presidency. We thought he was going to lead.

Carl Sandburg on Watergate:

WHY DOES a hearse horse snicker hauling a lawyer's
bones to the graveyard?
—"The People Yes"

Great day in the morning

EARLY ON Election Day is a time like none other in
America. Is the country going ahead with a sense of strength
or is it going to stick its head into the dustbin of the past?
The people go early to the polls. They know the answer.

William Shakespeare on Watergate

"THE FIRST thing we do, let's kill all the lawyers."
—Henry VI
Part 2, IV

230

PART 7

What Happens When We Die?

America needs the devil

WE BELIEVE in one God.

It follows naturally that we believe in one devil.

In 1918 the one devil was the Germans. In 1931 the one devil was Wall Street. In 1952 the devil was Communism.

Of course, in 1918, if you happened to be Irish, the devil was England and in 1931, if you happened to be Herbert Hoover, the devil was the missing pot in which to put the chicken and the missing garage in which to put the car. In 1952, if you were a reasonable man possessed of liberal attitudes, the devil was Joe McCarthy of Wisconsin.

No matter who, there was one devil and as soon as you exorcised him, Eden would return.

We have finally returned to the real thing. We have turned to the devil as the prince of evil. Millions of people are lining up to see his cunning power in the movie *The Exorcist*. I think the popularity of arcane cults is due precisely to a dearth of visible devils.

It is hard to imagine Russia as a devil when Communists are only cornering the wheat market. It is true that if you are Richard Nixon, the devil is Special Prosecutor Jaworski but since we have seen Richard Nixon exorcise other special prosecutors, Jaworski can be only a minor devil indeed.

No, things are going from bad to worse and as a nation of God-fearing men we need Mephistopheles, Beelzebub, Lucifer, Satan in a popular, return engagement.

Personally, I think it is all to the good. I think we are better off with the real devil than with his other manifestations who excite and empassion rather than frighten us.

Satan has been a drawing card ever since an overly imaginative Bedouin invented him and cast him as one of the central characters in the Book of Job, where he loses his bet to God over Job's patience.

The devil has a literary history all his own, as extensive and voluminous as books about Robert E. Lee.

One of the first of these was *Witchcraft and Satanism* by Jules Michelet, the mid-nineteenth-century historian.

In Michelet you find the first graphic description of the Black Mass, in which the congregants repeated the offices of the daily Mass backward—their altar, the body of a naked woman. Sacrifices were made of the last dead and the last born. A toad was torn to pieces, which represented the breaking of the Communion wafer.

Michelet took great pains with this description because it enforced his thesis that the Middle Ages was a grossly inhibited time and people redressed their needs furtively and illicitly.

Satan, Michelet concluded, represented always nascent reason. Suggested Michelet, "If people fear devils, surely it isn't because there are devils but because people need devils."

That is why the folks are lining up for *The Exorcist*.

I suggest there are a great many things in which we used to believe and now can't. But the devil remains immediate and menacing and diabolical. It is fun to tease ourselves with his supposed existence.

There are devils of all variety; one of them tempted Faust with Helen and another stood on the lowest pit of the Inferno chewing Judas, Brutus, and Cassius.

Our present-day devil goes about his work in his own mysterious, invading way, just the kind of devil we need these days. The sad aspect is that once upon a time the devil used to pay you a price for the possession of your soul. These days he is as peremptory as the IRS with a delinquent taxpayer.

The gift to Western man

I RECEIVED a letter from a Baptist lady in Charlotte who told me that I am now on the list of her prayer circle and that the circle will pray for me to see the light and come to God.

"Come to God," indeed! In a sense I have always been jealous of the Christians.

Here it is we who developed the idea of Jehovah, who started out originally as a minor tribal god, and it is they who get all the benefits. It is they who are having all the protection, security, joy, comfort, success, and perhaps even fun. Just think of the tremendous gift we gave to Western man (and how they hate us for it) through the happenstance that the early Jews, who had first thought of the idea, were constantly on the move searching for grass and water for their flocks.

Because of this mobility these early Jews took their god with them wherever they went. The idea caught on, that God was not necessarily a "stationary" god, and thus Columbus could take Him along on his voyage westward. Lindberg could fly with Him eastward, and He could watch over all the armies—Eastern Front, Western Front, north and south, and in every single foxhole on Guadalcanal—all at the same time.

And all of this because up to the time of the establishment of the monarchy in Judea the Jews were on the move, "and God was on the water as He was on the land."

That is why Wotan, Jupiter, Zeus, Neptune, Mithra, Isis, and any of the other eight hundred gods could not make the grade. Each of those fellows belonged to a particular place, to a particular people, often to a particular cave, mountaintop, temple, or building.

But, more than that, the deeper you go into it, the more you wonder at the brilliance of the idea the Jews developed. They made Jehovah a personal God, so personal that you could even argue with Him and often win the argument. Think what this has meant to Western man in his lonely journey westward with an ax in one hand and a rifle in the other. What a comfort.

You remember when He was fed up with the Jews, actually gave the order to have them exterminated and Moses argued with Him, "Now look here, I know these people are bad, but, after all, if they didn't really love You they would have stayed in Egypt with all that wine, women, and song, but here they are, they did go into the wilderness and suffered, and does not that prove something—that they deserve some consideration?"

And Jehovah saw that Moses had a point and relented.

Then we have that wonderful scene with Abraham, which never ceases to fascinate me. Here again, Jehovah was all set to wipe them all out and Abraham began a wonderful selling job. "After all, You are not an ordinary God, like them pagans have. You are special, You have wisdom. Look here, suppose there are only five good people there, why kill them along with the bad?"

Jehovah couldn't answer that argument. He gave in. This is perhaps the most wonderful aspect of this entire Jewish idea of Jehovah!

The GI Jewish converts

I ONCE wrote about several Baptist and Lutheran members of the United States Air Force who announced they were converting to Judaism. The converts announced this from Saudi Arabia, where Jewish soldiers are proscribed, and soon enough these smart fellows were transferred from the blazing heat of the desert to the air-conditioned comfort of a Frankfurt bar.

Each of the fellows had bought a mezuzah and a star of David hung around his neck, and each told all and sundry he was engaged to a Jewish girl and taking correspondence instruction in Judaism.

An Air Force official pooh-poohed my story. I pay him no attention. For now I have additional evidence that several military personnel of the United States have converted to Judaism in Portugal.

The "innocence" of the unmarried Portuguese women is considered sacrosanct and valuable. All American personnel arriving in Portugal go through a lengthy briefing session about the proscribed moral and ethical practices of Portuguese courtship.

A soldier has to include a duenna, a chaperone, on every date. Invariably this is a member of his girlfriend's family. She is very hard to bribe. A boy gets to talk seriously to his girlfriend only through a heavily screened window, as the convicts in the old James Cagney movies used to talk to their mouthpieces. But once the girl invites the fellow in for a cup of coffee, his acceptance is automatically a proposal from which there is no chance of reconsideration. There is even less chance of reconsideration if the fellow is an American.

One of these fellows either by bribe or chicanery made the most of his time. And the girlfriend filed a formal complaint.

She wasn't an "innocent" at all, insisted the soldier.

She was, too, insisted Mama and Papa.

The military authorities explained to this embryonic Don Juan that he had broken two laws at once. One was a Portuguese law that makes "deflowering" a criminal offense and carries with it a five-year stretch in a Portuguese jail. The other is a military offense that makes having "carnal knowledge of a woman not a man's wife" a criminal offense and carried with it ten years in the post stockade. There is only one way and the soldier grabbed it.

"All right, I'll marry her," said the errant GI.

"Si, si," said Mama and Papa.

"But I'm not a Catholic," said the GI.

"A civil wedding will do," said the military provost.

"Si, si," said Mama and Papa.

"But I want to get married in my own faith," said the GI.

"Si, si," said Mama and Papa.

"We'll do anything we can," said the provost.

"It will take about two months for the rabbi to convert her," said the GI.

When the translator hit the word "rabbi," Mama and Papa said volubly, "Ixnay on the eddingway."

Moral of the story? Forty other GI's bought transcripts of the testimony.

Miracle treatment

MOST LAWS legislating welfare work assign patients and recipients of welfare monies to the care and instruction of workers who share the same religious beliefs. There was a problem recently raised in a large Eastern state about this method. One woman needed welfare help. Formerly she had been Jewish and was reputedly now a Jehovah's Witness. They asked her which kind of worker she would prefer. She said she couldn't decide. "It was this way," she said. "I was pretty sick and about the time I went to the hospital I met these people with a new religion and I joined them. But in the hospital they gave me shock treatments and then, see, after that I was Jewish again."

It figures.

The Jewish culture

OUR MODERN Western world derives its jurisprudence and system of government from Rome. But when we turn to the Jews, we perceive almost at once that our modern laws and social structure and the very foundations of our manners and usages are set very deep in Jewish monotheism, and this is particularly true of the Anglo-American world. From the borderline where fable scarcely ceases and history begins, the Jews make their entry upon the world scene with the moral precepts from which have come not only Christianity and Islam but the entire code of human conduct and human relationships.

Before you can have "culture," obviously you must have "life." First there is life and then there is the survival of that life. It is from this "culture of survival" that all other cultures emanate. What "culture" matches the "culture" of an uninterrupted continuity of history from the moment the curtain rises on this drama to the present day? If by some miracle a Roman legion under Vespatian were to suddenly appear on the streets of Charlotte, North Carolina, there is only one thing the Romans of two thousand years ago would recognize—the synagogue. As a matter of fact, Vespatian would take off his helmet, scratch his head, and say, "The last thing I remember is burning that thing down."

Is there a Jewish culture? When most of the men of Europe and Britain were still painting their bodies blue and made little distinction between their own daughters and other women, Jews were already sitting on a hard bench arguing for hours and hours whether a chicken was fit to eat if the servant girl by mistake happened to have splashed a drop of milk on it. No wonder Heinrich Heine once said that if people had a proper historic perspective, they would travel a hundred miles merely to see a Jew.

Where are the knishes?

THERE IS not one truly Jewish restaurant in Tel Aviv.

Many a tourist is disappointed by this lack of Jewish food. So much so that the Government Tourist Corporation has announced a big drive for improving the food in hotels and restaurants—with an emphasis on the traditional Jewish cooking.

Most of the restaurants are kosher. Gefilte fish is on the menu. And, of course, chicken soup. But what is the trouble with knishes? Borsht is rare. Salami is not Katz. And even on Chanukah, some restaurants do not serve blintzes.

"Exodus" without blintzes?

The Wailing Wall

AN AMERICAN visitor to Israel noticed an elderly Jew crying at the Wailing Wall, as if his heart were breaking. Overcome by such an outpouring, he approached the old man.

"My good man, may I help you? You seem to be crying bitter tears!"

"I want to be with my people!" groaned the old man.

"But you are with your people here . . . in the Promised Land!"

"No! . . . I want to be with my people . . . in Miami Beach!"

Upward mobility

THERE WAS a poor Presbyterian family living up the road and some of the kindhearted ladies of the church took pity on them and sent the family a big box of secondhand clothing for the children. But for the next three weeks none of the children appeared at Sunday services. The minister and the elders of the church were concerned. They made a personal inquiry and the mother said that the children looked so handsome in the clothes she decided to send them over to the Episcopal Church.

The ardent Jewish scholar

A JEWISH merchant recently established himself in a very small town not far from here. The only Jew in the town, he has been bombarded with tracts and invitations to join one of the local Christian churches. The fellow now travels forty miles to attend synagogue services on the Sabbath. On Wednesdays he travels the forty miles back and forth again to attend an adult class on Judaism. "I must get as much information as possible," he says, "so I can say a few words when I am asked to join the church."

A new cause for the Jews

To COMBAT anti-Semitism, the Jewish social-action societies should triple their budgets immediately. And I do not urge this because of any growing threat of anti-Semitism. As a matter of fact, organized anti-Semitism is at its lowest ebb in the history of Western civilization. While there has been tremendous upheaval caused by the Supreme Court decisions ending racial segregation in the South, there has been no increase in anti-Semitism at all. The South remains the hard core of philo-Semitism in the English-speaking civilization.

But what has happened is that the professional hatemongers outside the South are trying to exploit a vacuum. The vacuum was caused by Southern political leaders who made clear they meant to put as many blocks as possible in the way of the Supreme Court directives. The Southern politician did

241

not know he was lending any support to these professional haters. But the hatemongers stepped into the breech that was widened by the fight about segregation and they substituted the word "mongrelization" for "Bolshevism" when they talked about Jews.

The bombings and attempted bombings of the temples and community centers were the work of disorganized crackpots and bore no relation to the race question. There was an attempt, for instance, to bomb a temple in my home city of Charlotte. Now, these are all good people in this temple, but I do not know of one single expression by the rabbis or the trustees or even the laymen that could have been constructed as participation on the side of integration.

If this attempted bombing had had anything to do with the race question, it would have been attempted at the churches of the Rev. Dr. Jody Kellerman of the Holy Comforter Episcopal Church, Dr. Claude Broach of St. John's Baptist Church, Dr. Sidney Freeman of the Unitarian Church, or the Roman Catholic bishop of a North Carolina diocese, Vincent Waters. These four clergymen have openly spoken out against Jim Crow.

My point is that despite the absence of a discernible heightening of anti-Semitism, the social-action groups of the Jewish organizations need a budget three times today's so that they may expand their activities into the entire field of civil rights.

The battle that gave the Jew civil rights was fought in many corners of the world by good friends and improbable allies as well as by Jews themselves. Now that we know we can defend our own rights, we also have the opportunity to fight for the rights of others. For the first time in 1,500 years we are not the target.

Paradoxically, this is the true integration in the American milieu. I would like to see all the societies lend themselves to these causes. I would like to see them use their tremendous resources and send their trained workers into the Southwest,

242

where the migratory workers stand beleaguered. What a moral thing if the Jewish community of America were to fight for the rights of the Mexican wetback!

And there is the ever-increasing problem of winning rights for the black and for the Puerto Rican. No matter where civil rights are threatened, we should be there. This would not only enlarge our spiritual vigor but relieve our own fear. And I have seen this fear all over America. After a lecture I've been invited back to the home of my host, invariably a rich man. He has a beautiful home. It is obvious that he is respected throughout his community. But toward midnight he will lean over to me and ask softly, "Harry, what do you think will happen to us here?"

I am amazed at this kind of fear. It has no basis. But the same man will light up when I tell him of the efforts we must make to help raise 26 percent of the Southern population to first-class status and citizenship.

Let me cite an example. A few years ago a woman resigned her job in the Cannon Mills in North Carolina. She was a spinner, and the shifts had been changed so that she was now required to work on Saturday. This woman, a Seventh Day Adventist, refused and was discharged. When she applied for unemployment insurance, she was turned down. She was not turned down because the North Carolina administrators are unkind. She was turned down because the law said she could not refuse available work and still receive unemployment compensation. There was a job available for this woman. But she could have it only if she violated her religious principles. She sued. The case came to the attention of the American Jewish Congress, which asked me to help. Together we engaged a distinguished lawyer, Mr. Mayne Albright, of Raleigh, North Carolina, who decided to handle the case without a fee. We won the case. The Supreme Court of North Carolina ruled that the woman was unemployed because to accept work offered her meant a violation of her rights as a citizen in following the dictates of her religious conscience. The Supreme Court discovered, in fact, that this woman had never worked a Saturday in her life.

What did this mean to Jews? Let me present some of the evidence. The letters are not only from Quakers and Unitarians but from Roman Catholics and from dozens of Methodist, Episcopalian, Presbyterian, and Lutheran clergymen and laymen who extended the glad hand of fellowship and gratitude to Jews in this matter. To some of the folks who live in fear, it might seem Jews were not minding their own business. But we were minding our own business, because we helped greatly to enlarge the prestige of our own people by this act.

This is the avenue now for Jewish social action—the field of civil rights.

And it would not be hard to get the money. We have only to state the case intelligently to the American Jewish community.

The greatest antidote for anti-Semitism is for the Jews of America to devote their energies and their resources to the struggle for civil rights for Christian Americans.

The tablet of Siloam

WHO KNOWS what crypts remain sealed to this very day with wonderful secrets of the past? The Hebrews, "people of the book," were constantly concerned with archives. Who knows what the Israelis will yet uncover once they really begin to develop their natural resources? We are all familiar with the Dead Sea scrolls, which after twenty-five centuries were found by accident. Julius Caesar had a very keen sense of history, and he was the most "archive-minded" man of antiquity. Perhaps in some sealed crypt we may yet find his book of apothegms, which we know he wrote. Today, thanks to the "boondoggling" of Roosevelt's New Deal, we have magnificent archives facilities in every state in the Union. It will not be in the "sealed crypts" but in these permanent state archives where the people of 2074 will find our story.

I have spent some time in these buildings, and North Carolina's is one of the best. What a treasure, too, for future scholars in the Library of Congress, the Harvard Library, and the New York Public Library, to say nothing of the British Museum. The British began early to keep their documents and records systematically. Many original documents are there, including the order of Edward I expelling the unconverted Jews from the realm in the year 1290. But the year 1290 is nothing at all compared with the Dead Sea scrolls of twenty-five hundred years ago and the Siloam inscription found in Jerusalem in the year 1880, which antedates the scrolls.

Mr. Azriel Eisenberg, writing in the *World Over* (Jewish Educational Committee), tells the interesting story of this, the oldest Hebrew writing known. In 1880 two Arab boys waded into a tunnel in a rock wall in what is today the Old City of Jerusalem. One of the boys slipped and fell into the water. When he rose to the surface, his eye caught something on the rock wall. He saw that it was "writing" and ran to tell his teacher, Dr. Schick, a German architect. Six months later a group of scholars began to work. They built a dam and drained off the water. Eventually they discovered the writing was actually a tablet set in the rock. The inscription in pure Biblical Hebrew tells how some workers dug a tunnel—how they started at both ends and met at the middle and broke through to one another, and how the water began to flow through the tunnel. The writing explains an exciting story that is briefly mentioned in the Bible, in 2 Chronicles, chapter 32.

The tunnel of the inscription was dug at the time of the Assyrian conquest of the Kingdom of Israel, about 2,700 years ago. King Hezekiah of Judah ordered workmen to seal up all the springs outside the city. He knew that the enemy needed fresh water. He also knew that his own people could hold out only as long as they had a steady supply of water. At the Spring of Gihon, on the temple mount, Hezekiah had an underground tunnel dug to bring the water into the Pool of Siloam inside Jerusalem. The inscription cut into the tunnel wall tells the story of the great "dig." The fact that the inscription was cut into the rock indicates that the tunnel was very important and may have had something to do with the victory. The Assyrians turned back and did not attack the city. Through the centuries the pool and the tunnel were forgotten until two Arab boys went wading. The tablet of Siloam is now in a museum in Constantinople.

Jesus with the elders

WHEN JESUS stood before the elders and argued with them on points of law, I am convinced it was when he was bar mitzvah. It had to be his bar mitzvah. There is no other way for a young boy to get close to the elders, let alone argue with them.

If the elders discussed the Scriptures among themselves, they would almost come to blows about some finer points of interpretation; *but* when a bar mitzvah boy stood before them, they were all smiles. They beamed, and they let the boy put forward all his ideas, and no matter what the elders thought, they continued to smile with tolerance and pride.

This was the one time when a boy was not considered an *azzes ponim* (one who shows lack of respect for his elders). This *azzes ponim* idea involved only your *secular* life, and you had better watch yourself. But when it came to *learning*—or the Scriptures—the most intolerant of the elders was indulgent, kind, and generous, and he would never put the boy in his place. At this stage in a boy's life it was far more important to *read* than *interpret*. The elders were tolerant about

246

interpretation, but make a mistake in reading and one of the old gents would reach out and give you a pinch and many of them had a special corkscrew pinch that they called a *knip*, and you did not make the same mistake twice.

Threat to the Church of Rome?

EMINENT CATHOLIC authorities have cautioned their laity against joining Biblical arguments with any of the missionary Jehovah's Witnesses. The Jehovah's Witnesses are missionary with a unique zeal. They ring doorbells in their search for converts and, as any salesman knows, if you ring enough doorbells, you make your quota. The bishops and priests suspect their parishioners just won't know enough to slam the door. Catholics apparently aren't well enough versed in the Bible to give reasonable argument to the Jehovah's Witnesses and might succumb to conversion.

Though no Catholic, I would like to remind Catholic authorities of Christ's injunction to Peter: "On this rock I will build my Church."

Some years ago two of these Jehovah's Witnesses missionary workers visited me (I believe all Witnesses are actively involved in conversion work). It was a Sunday afternoon. I greeted them cordially and chatted with them awhile. Both were women, one middle-aged, the other a little younger. I told them I was too busy reading and hadn't much time to converse. The ladies studied my bookcases and one of them replied, "If you will read this pamphlet, *The Watchtower*, you won't have to spend so much time reading books because the whole truth is here and makes these thousands of books just so much paper and ink."

I excused myself in order to take a healthy shot of bourbon, felt a little better, and accepted their *Watchtower*. I shook hands with the ladies and they departed in a wreath of happiness that they might have won me. But they hadn't. What makes a Catholic any different from me?

Why should a Jehovah's Witness, whose Biblical scholarship is rather crude and primitive at best, endanger the Church of Rome?

My mother had faith and she believed in the ritual and laws of Judaism with no deviation. I smile to think of what would have happened to an army of evangelists who tried to storm her citadel. Yet she was an illiterate woman.

Actually, the evangelist and missionary, be he Jehovah's Witness or whatever, is not trying to spread joy as much as he is trying to convince himself of his own faith. Faith alone will not sustain him. He must have numbers.

If this were not so, there would be great kindness in the world. People who would not give you three dollars for bus fare in a moment of dire distress are still more than willing to give you a share of all eternity and will hold your lapels and plead that if you only believed as they do, you would be free for all future life and attendant benefits. Why such generosity about eternity?

Were there no hatred in the world, no bigotry, if there were universal acceptance of one's neighbors, I might believe the evangelist when he appears to tell me he is eager to save me.

But with things as they are, I don't believe him. Why should anyone share such a secret? If the evangelist found a gold mine in South Dakota you can bet your life he wouldn't tell anyone until he had filed his claim. He wouldn't tell his mother, let alone his neighbor. Still less would he confide in a stranger. But eternal life! He can't wait to pass the news on.

A man's religion is much like his boudoir. An evangelist has a lot of nerve to come into another man's home and say, "You must believe as I do, your religion is wrong and mine right." It is arrogant and unkind.

Nothing can prevail against a secure faith. Thus, why the Catholic prelates' worry? They have a religion that has been

248

around a lot longer than the religion of the Jehovah's Witnesses.

Don't get me wrong: I love the Jehovah's Witnesses. I am for any religion that imposes its metaphysic as an ethic for everyday life. The growth of a new sect or the reinvigoration of an old one makes me happy. The great strength of our democracy is in the fragmentization of our culture. Hundreds, perhaps thousands of associations, fraternities, sects, and clubs meeting behind closed doors and deciding their rituals or observing their faith form the rock bed of a practicable democracy. But the more intense the sect is in evangelizing, the greater the members' doubt. They are uncomfortable until everybody has joined them.

The beard and the *sheitel*

FIRST WE, the children of the immigrants, shamed our orthodox fathers into shaving off the beard. We thought a beard was not American. We no sooner got rid of all the beards than Madison Avenue discovered it was the perfect thing to sell fizz water, shirts, and mutual funds.

After we got rid of the beards, we started on the *sheitels*. The *sheitel* is the wig worn by the orthodox Jewish woman after she is married. Her hair is shaven right to the scalp and from then on when she ventures to the *shul*, she wears a *sheitel*. In the first two decades of this century every letters-to-the-editor column of the Jewish press was filled with distressing pleas—"Please advise our mothers to give up the *sheitel*," and "It is about time your newspaper told the old-fashioned women that the *sheitel* isn't worn in America."

And now the *sheitel* is all the rage among the fancy ladies of America. It did not become the rage until the very last of the old folks capitulated. Every lady has wigs today, from the movie star right down to the suburban shopper.

249

I went into a salon operated by a world-famous stylist and saw no ladies under the dryers. There was none of the usual chattering, the gossip about how much the new ballet master charges, or how rude the local school principal is. But in the back of the shop were eight beauticians busy as little bees, prettying up the wigs. Indeed there were more than twenty wigs on twenty blocks with stylists going from one to the other, primping here and cutting there. The lady does not waste her time under the dryer anymore. She deposits her wig in the salon and goes about her supermarket perambulations and comes back in two hours and picks it up. Of course, she loses out in the gossip and this deprivation may drive her back to the salon.

The women and pants

I HAD thought the pants suit a mere vogue of erratic twentieth-century women's fashion. I am wrong. Once the orthodox rabbis begin to debate the subject, to argue pro and contra, one knows the pants suit is here to stay. The pants suit has occasioned the rabbinic divination about the nature of woman, clothes, and God.

One rabbi has quoted the Talmudic injunction: "The apparel of a man shall not be upon a woman and a man shall not put on a woman's garment; for an abomination to the L-rd thy G-d is everyone that does these."

But another rabbi has argued that a pants suit is wrong only if the woman dons it to mingle unrecognized among the men. If she wears it to keep her pipes warm, it is okay in the eyes of G-d.

If I were to voice an objection to the pants suit on religious grounds, I would hazard that it should be banned principally because of the anatomy that the L-rd thy G-d has conferred upon us. Women have a front and a back. The pants suit never looks as nice going as it does coming.

It is wrong to dismiss the preoccupation of the rabbi, however. Most of us view everything in terms of whether it is good or bad for the Jews; the rabbi whether it is pleasing or displeasing to G-d.

Heaven help the L-rd because according to rabbinic concerns, he has had H-s eye on a multitude of things besides the sparrow.

Did He ever anticipate chocolate-covered matzohs and kosher Girl Scout cookies? Let alone Friday night KP for Jews in the armed forces?

I remember living in Red Bank, New Jersey, lo almost forty years ago when women's slacks became a vogue. The Red Bank City Council dealt peremptorily with the matter and passed an ordinance that women were not to be seen on the main thoroughfares in pants. This ordinance went by the boards the next summer when shorts gained popularity. The City Council was beside itself with anxiety. But G-d knew what He was doing because in 1939 He sent King George VI and Queen Elizabeth to Red Bank, from whose railroad station the royal couple motored through Monmouth County, New Jersey, to Hyde Park, New York. And there wasn't a pair of slacks or shorts along their entire route. G-d sent them to Red Bank because the mayor's name was English and the road they would travel was King's Highway.

Let me advise the rabbis, He moves in mysterious circles His pleasures to be made known.

Who has all the money?

I WAS on the Bob Raiford show, station WIST, Charlotte. Bob conducts this show every day and allows questions

251

from the listening audience. So one fellow asked me a question, "Why do the Jews have all the money?" This old anti-Semitic canard has always puzzled me. I could have answered the question by saying, "Because God loves them since He was one of them."

But it is not as simple as that.

Take Charlotte, which is a microcosm of middle-class America. Who has all the money?

Start with the banks: North Carolina National Bank, Wachovia, First Union, First Citizens, and all the others. No Jews, not even a Jewish employee in any one of them.

Then we go to the department stores: Ivey's, Belk's. No Jews, not even a Jewish employee.

Then come the utilities: Duke Power Company, Carolina Power and Light, Piedmont Natural Gas. No Jews, not even a Jewish employee.

These are the people who have all the money in Charlotte, as their prototypes do all around the rest of the country, particularly in heavy industry. U.S. Steel, Ford, General Motors, Chrysler, General Dynamics, IBM, Xerox, Allied Chemical. No Jews.

And I often wonder what the anti-Semite means when he says why do the Jews have all the money? Does he contemplate confiscation of private property or does he recommend massacre?

The unsettling blond influence

THE EASIEST way to be a Jew is to live in a big city. That way you're just a Jew. You are not caught up in the activities of the new ranch-house synagogue, the frenzies of the local Hadassah, the machinations of the cultural committee, and the countdowns of the fund drive. The city provides anonymity. You're just Jewish. You don't have to speak Hebrew or even know what the Talmud is. Except that it doesn't always work.

I knew a city family and the woman began to watch her children come along, each child a little blonder than the one before. These children were born in the late forties. At age sixteen the boy was the most Aryan-looking fellow in the world. At twelve the girl was blonder than the boy, in addition to which she had blue eyes.

All of this can be explained by the fact that Roman legion-naires were always eager to teach Latin phrases to some of the Palestine girls they had brought to the Rhine River.

The family in question was very proud of its blond off-spring. Like most American-born Jews living in the city, they paid very little attention to their *shul* or temple. But the blondness of their children made them jump in with both feet, not into the temple, but into the orthodox *shul*. They were afraid that when their children got to college, they would be mistaken for supermen and, flattered by their blond looks, might become racists.

The parents involved them in every aspect of Jewish life, even going to the trouble of maintaining a kosher home. They saw to it that the family name was on as many cornerstones as they could manage in an effort to insulate their children against Nazism through a very wide endowment of tribal loyalty.

Redemption from Israel

SOME THIRTY years after the massacre of six million Jews by the Germans, a bitterness still comes to me while I write of it. A people to whom I belonged had been turned into an exterminator's quarry and there was no outcry against the

253

dead; no statesmen or journalist struck out; art also was silent. Was the Jew so despised that he could be murdered en masse without protest from the onlookers?

The political outcry had been entirely missing. There was no protest against the Jewish massacre from Roosevelt, Churchill, Stalin, or other official heads of government.

The war that rescued humanity from German defilement ended triumphantly, but with all the Jews of Europe exterminated, and the great victory still indifferent.

During the few weeks of rebellion the Jews of Warsaw had issued their communiqué over a single radio. They were standing firm but the need for guns and bullets was growing. Nobody in the world answered; not even a cap pistol fell out of the sky. Thus the Jews of Warsaw were finally reduced to fighting with stones, hot water, and sticks.

I felt the most deeply shamed by the silence of the American Jews.

The unassimilated Jews—the Yiddish Jews—were speaking their horror in the Jewish newspapers. In the synagogues the Jews were weeping and praying. In thousands of homes where Yiddish was spoken the German murderers and their deeds were cursed. But these were the locked-away Jews who had only the useless ear of other Jews and, possibly, of God.

The Americanized Jews who ran newspapers and movie studios, who wrote plays and novels, who were high in government and powerful in the financial, industrial, and even social life of the nation were silent.

That silence, finally, was broken when David Ben-Gurion announced the rebirth of the state of Israel in 1948.

It is not only the clearing of the marshes, the building of the universities and museums, and making the desert bloom, but a spirit. The Germans thought they had killed the Jews, but here was Israel.

We often wonder what Israel has done for the American Jews in return for the United Jewish Appeal Fund and the

Bonds for Israel we have bought, all of which is nothing compared to what Israel has done for us.

It has redeemed an entire generation of Jews out of silence with the thundering voices of David Ben-Gurion and the Histadrut and Moshe Dayan and Golda Meir and Teddy Kollek of Jerusalem. They have given us a new dignity. They have redeemed us all.

A speech to the Presbyterians

I was not particularly flattered, nor did I think I was over my head, when I was invited to address a banquet of Presbyterian church educators early this year at Williamsburg, Virginia.

We live in a time when the American Medical Association listens enraptured to an address by TV's Dr. Ben Casey, and the lawyers at their annual convention listen to an address by TV's Perry Mason.

Thus there is no reason why a Presbyterian church educator shouldn't listen to Harry Golden. I am no less versed in Presbyterian education than Vince Edwards in medicine or Raymond Burr in law.

On the other hand, I might underestimate my qualifications. First of all, I love Presbyterians. I love Presbyterians not only because I believe the Scots are one of the lost tribes of Israel, but I love them because Scotland is the only country in the entire world that has never had an organized anti-Semitic movement of any kind.

The theme for the meeting was "Creative Restoration" and putting it back together again. It was in this context that the educators were concerned with "wholeness" of life and sought guidelines to cope with the physical and psychological overload of today.

I told them that I believe that the Protestant "God is dead" movement is a direct result of the fact that the Protestant churches backed away from a moral issue. "Stick to religion" was the word that was passed down from the congregations to the pastor. "Stick to religion and stay away from social and political questions." And thus they backed away from the great moral issue of the twentieth century. The Jews, denying the basic philosophy handed down by the prophets for social justice, imitated the Protestants. And the members of the congregation passed the word down to the rabbi, "Stick to religion." We will never know how many Protestant clergymen were dismissed because they refused to "stick to religion."

The Protestant minister or rabbi in the South who followed the moral impulse to speak out against racial segregation ran the risk of losing his pulpit.

The number of clergymen who lost pulpits because they supported the Supreme Court decision of May 17, 1954, is hard to determine. The number fired outright because of their "moderate" or "liberal" views are but a handful of those who found themselves out of work because they were "too controversial" or because they "devoted too much time to community affairs." One minister in the South, a personal friend of mine, condemned racial segregation one Sunday; the next Sunday his congregation let him out because "he wasn't visiting the sick as often as he should."

And the question is: Why did the local clergy and the local Protestant church of the South withdraw? Why did neither church nor churchman see that the struggle would envelop them just as it enveloped John F. Kennedy and Lyndon B. Johnson and all America?

The middle-class parishioners remade their church in their own image. One consequence was to rob the minister of his authority. He no longer made more money than the members of his congregation; he made less. He no longer accounted to the officers for a charity financed by men of great wealth; he accounted to fuel-oil distributors who had once been mechanics and to contractors who had once been carpenters.

As the middle-class proliferated, their need for self-expression also grew. Lacking the talent or inclination for politics, traditionally the province for the rich man's personal ambition, the well-off layman found that he could fulfill his hunger for expression by managing his church.

Eventually he began to oversee the content of the Sunday sermon, since he wanted the church to reflect him, not the minister, who was but an agent.

When the race issue began intruding on Southern life, the middle-class deacons, stewards, elders, and trustees told their clergymen, "Stick to religion."

As a result, the Protestant church throughout the South is rarely the champion of the unpopular cause, not even the unpopular cause remote from the racial crucible. The church conforms in almost all respects to the prevailing beliefs and sentiments of the overpowering majority.

All political candidates in the South proclaim their belief in religion—Christian religion, as they call it. In all political advertisements the candidate's most important boast is, "He is steward of the Second Methodist Church," or "He has been a member of the First Baptist Church for forty-three years." "He teaches a Sunday school class" is the most effective of all.

But in the South religion does not instruct the middle class; the middle class instructs religion.

The new uses to which people put religion are manifold. Mr. W. W. Taylor, a former member of the North Carolina House of Representatives, appeared before a legislative committee in March of 1959. He came as a representative of small businessmen who opposed passage of a seventy-five-cent minimum-wage law for the state. Said Mr. Taylor, "Jesus Christ would be out of place if He returned to earth where employers were told what they could pay their employees." Clearly, he implied that Jesus would have opposed a minimum wage of seventy-five cents an hour.

257

The Presbyterian educators asked me to give them an insight into my life-style. I told them of the *Carolina Israelite*, a journal that I ran from Charlotte, North Carolina, for more than twenty-six years.

The personal journalist is the only hope for an occasional outrageous opinion. When E. W. Howe, the sage of Potato Hill and publisher of *E. W. Howe's Monthly* in Atchison, Kansas, was considering elective office, William Allen White wrote him: "Why don't you run for the Legislature on the platform, 'Down with Love, it's worse than whiskey. . . .' " Hundreds of Howe's aphorisms have passed into the language and when some of his fellow liberals questioned his abiding belief in God, Howe said, "Religion is not an intelligence test, but a faith."

Elbert Hubbard, the sage of Aurora, was certainly the most colorful. His newspaper, *The Philistine*, was a national institution. "I propose to write every single article and paragraph in it, including advertisements," promised Hubbard. "A Message to Garcia" was first printed almost casually in *The Philistine* in March, 1899, and Mr. Hubbard had no idea of the excitement he would create. The New York Central Railroad alone ordered one hundred thousand reprints and in the next fifteen years "A Message to Garcia" sold in the millions. What impressed the business community with "Garcia" was Hubbard's advice to young men: "It is not book learning young men need, but a stiffening of the vertebra which will cause them to be loyal to a trust, to act promptly, concentrate their energies; do the thing, carry a message to Garcia." As the orders poured in, Hubbard announced: "I am now the voice of American business." But the subtitle of the *Philistine*'s masthead remained "A Periodical of Protest." Hubbard lives on, revered for his profound observation that "Life is one God-damned thing after another." He went down with the *Lusitania*, unfortunately, before he could fulfill a lifelong ambition of one day throwing an egg into an electric fan.

Another personal journalist was the Socialist Oscar

258

Ameringer, whose *American Guardian* was for many years the only Oklahoma newspaper with a national circulation. This was during that period when Oklahoma had more registered Socialists than New York. It was Oscar who wrote, "Cannibalism gave way to capitalism when man discovered it was more profitable to exploit his neighbor than to eat him."

I started my newspaper because the South gave me a ready-made subject, namely, the fight of the black for first-class citizenship.

I had no credentials as a Southerner, for in 1940 and 1941 I was new. Nor was I qualified by knowledge or inclination to run a Jewish parochial newspaper. Not at all. Yet my paper was successful, in a way, precisely because I was a Jew. Had I called my newspaper *The Tar Heel Gazette* or the *Carolina Journal*, the native population would have asked: "What is this little fat Jew doing, coming down here from New York to tell us about the Southern way of life?" Calling the paper the *Carolina Israelite* insulated me because, when they read it, they said simply, "Oh, well, it's just a Jew paper." By the time they realized the *Carolina Israelite* was not what it looked like, it was too late. I had become a big shot and they were stuck with me. I've even detected in recent years that they have acquired a sort of proprietary pride in me. And I achieved the result I sought originally. In North Carolina, for instance, we had 4,622 paid subscribers, of whom 315 were Jews, and 4,307 were Angles, Scots, Saxons, Picts, blacks, Moravians, Greeks, Waldensians, and Irish.

In the beginning I had trouble. Some of the Jews in North Carolina organized a "Golden Go Home" committee. They used to complain, "What kind of Jewish newspaper is this, that talks about the Scottsboro boys in Alabama, that urges the textile workers to join the union?" To be fair, they had a point, because we Jews do indeed carry a burden of history. We won't go into that except to say that even at the most intellectual level of the Gentile world, I have observed there is an idea, however, vague, that all the Jews meet in some cellar once a week. I did succeed in destroying the stereotype. There was no doubt anywhere that the stuff in the *Carolina Israelite* was one man's opinion.

But the opposition during 1943 and 1944 might have been fatal if Dr. Graham hadn't saved me. Dr. Frank P. Graham, at that time president of the University of North Carolina, sent me a letter clear out of the blue: "Dear Golden, I've just read your paper, and it is good, keep it up and come to see me."

And he didn't say, like most Southerners, "Come to see me sometime." He gave me a date, a place, and an hour. It was a Saturday afternoon and I went. And there in his home he had Jimmy Street, Noel Houston, and three or four professors, and I was photographed with them. When the Jews of Charlotte saw a picture of me with all those Gentiles, they figured I was kosher, and I was on my way.

Across the years I made certain with every issue that I would never become a stuck whistle. Between the "integration" and the "join the textile union" essays, I scattered dozens of little *meiselech* (tales) of the Jewish immigrants and the Lower East Side of New York, which the wives of Southern Senators and tycoons have been known to read to their husband after church on quiet Sunday afternoons. And from the toughest of all Southern conservatives came a letter that adorns my wall: "Dear Golden: Here is my three dollars for renewal. Half your paper stinks, but the other half gives us all lots of pleasure."

The Protestant wish

THE AVERAGE pay of the Protestant clergyman in the South is eight thousand dollars a year. The average pay of the rabbi in the South is twenty-two thousand dollars a year. Thus, a dream of every Protestant clergyman in the South is to continue to preach Christianity and to be paid by the Jews.

Converting the Gentiles

A REFORM rabbi in North Carolina told me that the Gentile bride of a young Jew applied to him for conversion to Judaism. This is far from uncommon these days.

The rabbi asked the young lady to come back three times and make the request on three separate occasions before he would consent to accept her. How all of these things are tied up with history. Thrice did Caesar refuse the crown, and thrice did Peter deny Jesus. Three is the magic number in all the folklore of mankind.

Contrary to general belief, there is nothing in Judaism that is against proselytizing.

But we would be doing the Christian a very great disservice. We would be asking him to surrender his "majority" status. Only a knave would ask a friend to do this, and only a fool would accept such a deal. Besides, he'd have to resign immediately from the City Club of Charlotte, and I haven't the heart to do this to him. It's like the old story of asking the black singer Pearl Bailey to sing "Eli Eli," and she says, "I haven't got enough trouble?"

The self-imposed silence

TELEVISION IS terrified and shocked at the prospect of censorship emanating from the government but for years it has gratefully listened to any censorship emanating from the advertising agencies or from as few as twenty anonymous postcards.

It is quite true the networks do handle on occasion controversy such as Medicare or racial integration. They are very nervous about such programs and God help them if the day after such a program has appeared some other controversy pokes its horned head above the surface. The hell with it, say the networks, we've already done our duty. The situation reminds me of the time I worked on a little weekly paper in North Carolina. I did all the makeup and there were weeks when at the last minute an advertisement would come into the office.

"Put it on the first page," the owner would say. "That isn't locked yet."

"I don't know about that," I'd say, "we have all our important stories there."

"We gave them lots of readin' matter last week, didn't we?" she'd say.

Once upon a time orators like Robert Ingersoll could make a cross-country tour, stopping in every town to challenge priest, minister, and rabbi to debate: "Resolved: there is no God." He filled halls with his opponents, there was lots of discussion, and a good deal of fun. It would be utterly impossible to hold such a discussion today. Not because everybody is a believer, but because everybody is scared to death.

The network commentators do not venture afresh into the fields of controversy.

Really, who made us cowards? Probably we ourselves. But if it had a start, it probably came with A. Mitchell Palmer, Attorney General in the Wilson Administration.

Up in New York, the legislature refused to seat five members who had been duly elected, because they were Socialists. Were we any better than the South American countries, which we scathingly called "Banana Republics"?

It is tragic when the network thinks it has gone far out with some controversial interview. Then the necessary preliminaries: the shaking-in-the-boots disclaimers; three Hail Marys; four Our Fathers; five Hear O Israels; facing Mecca at the same time.

This is precisely the extent of television's usefulness. It urges us to worship and believe in God—the God of our choice, that is.

262

What happens when we die?

WHAT HAPPENS when we die? Some people have no trouble with the idea of heaven. They not only accept it literally but can't wait to get there. A recent book by Ruth Montgomery, *The World Beyond*, gives us an eyewitness account by a famous medium, Arthur Ford, who died in 1971.

Before he discovered his psychic powers, Ford was an ordained Disciples of Christ minister.

Miss Montgomery reported Ford, who died of a heart attack, told her he couldn't have been more delighted with what he experienced when he passed over.

"The lightness, the heavenly elixir of being without the heavy flesh was beyond description," she said he reported from the other side. "The mind wills where we want to be and there we are without so much as a railroad ticket or walking a step."

How do people on that plane of existence influence somebody on earth? "The usual means," said Ford, according to Miss Montgomery, "is through the implantation of ideas into the subconscious mind, preferably when the other person is sleeping or meditating."

Some years ago I attended a dozen or so séances conducted by the most famous mediums in the country including such mediums as Margery, Mrs. M. E. Williams, and Frank Montsko. At these séances I also met some of the most famous people in history. I spoke with William James of Harvard and the Marquis de Lafayette, the French patriot who fought for America, and there were many others. But what concerned me about these séances and the whole business was that out of the millions of my ancestors who have died, not a single Yiddish-speaking fellow Galitizianer came through to speak to me.

The Passover

THE FEAST OF PASSOVER is probably the only religious holiday that is as old as recorded history. Some scholars believe it began as a festival in which the people performed rituals to keep their houses free of disease, sickness, and hunger. When the Hebrews left Egypt, Passover became an agricultural festival.

"And they baked unleavened cakes of the dough which they had brought out of Egypt, for it was not leavened, because they were thrust out of Egypt and could not tarry, neither had they prepared for themselves any provisions" (Exodus 12:39).

Unleavened bread was used regularly in the sacrificial ritual of the temple at Jerusalem. This ritual took place in the spring, the time of year when life is young and everyone wants to begin afresh, just as the Hebrews began afresh when they escaped from Pharoah. Thus, St. Paul says, "Clean out the old yeast that you may be fresh dough."

I remember how careful my mother was in "cleaning out the old yeast."

My sisters helped. They worked around the clock for the Passover holiday, which celebrates Jewish freedom.

If a little sister was four years old, she was not too young to help—she picked up crumbs or crusts of bread in the corners of the house, indeed in the pockets of all the garments in the household, and everybody kissed the little girl and held her up proudly when she found a few bread crumbs where no one else would have looked. And there was always some fun. The father would plant a few crumbs on a windowsill or in the corner of a room and lead the younger children on the search. You heard the little sister shout in ecstasy, "Here is some," and there were congratulations all around.

The well-to-do had complete sets of pots and pans and tableware used only on Passover. The poor cleaned and scoured everything, boiling each pot, plate, and utensil to remove every trace of what had gone before—and to prepare

264

for the unleavened bread of the "new grains" (matzoth) and the symbolic eating of the Paschal Lamb and the bitter herbs.

In the old days the Jews ate a lamb that had been sacrificed to God. Today a symbolic roasted shank bone rests on the center plate during the Seder Passover meal.

Every ritual at the Seder is symbolic of the history of our people. Next to the plate with the shank bone is the dish of salt water, beside it a few sprigs of parsley. Each of us dips the parsley into the salt water and tastes it. The parsley is green, for the new and happier life out of the tears; freedom out of slavery.

And halfway through the meal the youngest son opens the door and we say, "All who are hungry, let them come in and eat."

For the Jews, of course, Passover means the escape from bondage and slavery and the beginning of a history as a people. On Passover night, 1975, Jews everywhere in every nook and corner of this world, in battle, in camp, in the desert, on land and on sea will observe the Passover, and at the Seder they will read the Exodus story in a book called the Haggadah, which asks, "In every generation let each man look on himself as if he came forth out of Egypt."

This undiminished vitality the Jews have lent to Christianity and to Western civilization. The Plymouth Bay Colony expressly drew up its constitution on the same principle of Nehemiah after the Jews' return from the Babylonian exile. The Massachusetts Bay Colony also obeyed Moses in framing its laws.

And on the Liberty Bell in Philadelphia is the Passover prayer from Leviticus 25:10: "Proclaim liberty throughout all the land, unto all the inhabitants thereof."

We cannot fail to perceive that our foundations in laws, manners, and usages, as well as religion, are set deep in Jewish legislation and literature. This is particularly true of the English-speaking peoples.

There are no mysteries in the Jewish religion. Everything is

265

fact. The Lord God was the cornerstone fact and an ever-recurring historical fact. "I am the Lord thy God, who brought thee out of the land of Egypt, and out of the house of bondage," is the only one of the thousand passages that attest this. The Jews were never irrevocably wedded to religious forms and ceremonies. They have constantly changed them throughout all their history, from age to age, and according to their environment, in their dispersion throughout the world. But to their one great religious belief or fact they have remained true.

97155